A New Way to Learn

A New Way to Learn

Finding Calm, Ease, and Joy in Your Studies

Deena Kara Shaffer

BLOOMSBURY ACADEMIC
LONDON • NEW YORK • OXFORD • NEW DELHI • SYDNEY

BLOOMSBURY ACADEMIC
Bloomsbury Publishing Plc, 50 Bedford Square, London, WC1B 3DP, UK
Bloomsbury Publishing Inc, 1359 Broadway, New York, NY 10018, USA
Bloomsbury Publishing Ireland, 29 Earlsfort Terrace, Dublin 2, D02 AY28, Ireland

BLOOMSBURY, BLOOMSBURY ACADEMIC and the Diana logo are trademarks of Bloomsbury Publishing Plc

First published in Great Britain 2027

Cover design: Jade Barnett

A catalogue record for this book is available from the British Library.

ISBN:	PB:	978-1-350-57061-0
	ePDF:	978-1-350-57063-4
	eBook:	978-1-350-57062-7

Series: Bloomsbury Study Skills

Typeset by Integra Software Services Pvt. Ltd.
Printed and bound in Great Britain

For product safety related questions contact productsafety@bloomsbury.com.

Evelyn, Sasha and Andrew, you have taught me life's most beautiful lessons.

Contents

Acknowledgements xiv

WELCOME TO A NEW WAY TO LEARN 1

Why this book had to exist 1
What 'holistic' actually means (and why it matters) 2
Let's redefine success together 2
What you'll actually find in these pages 3
Your invitation 3
Making your way: how to use this book 4
Your book, your way 4
The learning experiment 5
How this book supports you 5

SECTION ONE: A NEW WAY TO PRIORITIZE 7

Breaking free from time management myths 7
A different conversation about time 8

1 HOW TO MANAGE YOUR TIME (WHEN THERE'S TOO MUCH TO DO) 10

The misrepresentation of time management 10
Time coherence 11
Take a moment: reflecting on your relationship with time 13
Dig deeper: beyond traditional time management 14
Understanding your time coherence 15
Student voices 16
A new way with time 17

2 HOW TO ALIGN YOUR TIME (WHEN THERE DOESN'T SEEM LIKE ENOUGH) 19

The five false priority systems 19
The problem with prioritization 20
Time alignment 21
The flow of academic sequencing 21
Notice your patterns: mapping your current alignment 22
Dig deeper: rethinking how we approach tasks 23

Try this today: the Flow Sequence Model 24
The weekly Flow State map 26
See it in action: meet Fatou 26
A new way with alignment 28

3 HOW TO CULTIVATE YOUR TIME (WHEN TO-DOS OVERWHELM) 29
An ecological approach to your attention 29
Habitats: creating environments for your attention 30
Rhythms: protecting your deep work seasons 31
Take a moment: discover your neuro needs 32
Try this today: energize your environments 33
Student voices 35
A new way with time ecology 36
Dig deeper: learning from focus experts 36

4 HOW TO HEAL TIME ANXIETY (WHEN MINUTES FEEL SCARCE) 38
Time anxiety 38
Take a moment: understanding your time anxiety 40
Try this today: the 'some is better than none' approach (aka the daily fit-in) 41
Fitting in the daily fit-in 42
Troubleshooting time obstacles 46
See it in action: meet Justin 46
A new way forward with time anxiety 48
Dig deeper: where does our time go? 50
Your time experiments: making it real 50

SECTION TWO: A NEW WAY TO STUDY 53
Breaking free from so-called 'study strategies' 53
A different conversation about learning 54

5 HOW TO REMEMBER WHAT YOU LEARN (SO YOU DON'T WASTE YOUR TIME) 55
The illusion of learning 55
Forgetting triggers 56
Take a moment: uncovering your memory challenges 57
Try this today: the Remember-Retrieve-Rest framework 57
Student voices 60
A new way with remembering 61
Dig deeper: what goes into lasting memory 62

6 WHAT GETS IN THE WAY (SO YOU CAN REMOVE THOSE DISTRACTIONS) 64
The false narrative of willpower 65
The three categories of study stumbling blocks 65
Your personal distraction profile 66
Notice your patterns: understanding your distractibility 66
Try this today: the clear-the-path framework 69
Student voices 71
A new way with distractions 72
Dig deeper: the science of attention and distraction 72

7 HOW TO WORK WITH OTHERS (SO YOU CAN SMOOTHLY ENGAGE IN GROUP WORK AND COLLABORATIVE PROJECTS) 75
No need to go it solo 75
Collective intelligence 76
The landscape of shared understanding 77
Take a moment: plotting your collaborative learning history 78
Try this today: building effective study groups 80
Student voices 82
A new way with collaborative learning 83
Dig deeper: the science behind collaborative learning 83

8 WHAT GOES INTO A TOP GRADE (SO YOU CAN RAISE THAT AVERAGE) 85
The universal success struggle 85
Building on balance 86
The five truths about top grades 86
Success seducers 87
The pendulation principle 87
Get strategic about stress 88
Notice your patterns: making sense of your relationship with 'success' 88
Try this today: the restore method for sustainable success 90
Fitting in time to RESTORE 91
Troubleshooting common obstacles 95
See it in action: meet Amara 96
A new way with sustainable excellence 97
Dig deeper: resources for sustainable academic success 99

9 WHAT EXAMS ARE REALLY FOR (SO IT DOESN'T FEEL POINTLESS) 101

The misperception of exams as pure evaluation 101
Try this today: the three-phase exam training method 102
The stress-to-strength protocol 103
The night-before game plan 104
The real purposes: your learning fitness centre 104
Take a moment: inquire into your relationship with exams 106
Troubleshooting when exams feel really hard 107
Student voices 107
A new way with exams 108
Dig deeper: the neuroscience of testing 109

SECTION THREE: A NEW WAY TO BE PRODUCTIVE 111

10 HOW TO START (WHEN YOU DON'T WANT TO) 113

The starting line isn't where you think it is 113
Tomorrow You, starting today 114
Befriending resistance 114
Multiple doorways in 115
Troubleshooting: when starting feels like climbing Everest 117
See it in action: meet Isaiah 118
The permission slip collection 120
Try this today: start with a getting started toolkit 121
A new way with starting 122
Dig deeper: the inner workings of task initiation 123

11 HOW TO FEEL MOTIVATED (WHEN YOU AREN'T FEELING IT ... AT ALL) 125

The five motivation mistakes 125
Motivation cultivation 127
Engagement as ecosystem 127
Notice your patterns: uncover your motivation topography 128
Try this today: motivation cultivation 132
The growth spiral 133
See it in action: meet Kwame 134
A new way with cultivation 136
Dig deeper: rethinking motivation 136

12 HOW TO FOCUS (WHEN IT FEELS IMPOSSIBLE) 138
The falsehood of perfect focus 138
Creating conditions for concentration 139
Take a moment: reflecting on your focus 140
Try this today: working with your wandering mind 141
Student voices 141
A new way with focus 143
Dig deeper: finding your own rhythm of attention 143

13 HOW TO DO WORK (WHEN IT ALL SEEMS SO HARD) 146
The hidden physics of stuck 147
Take a moment: mapping your stuckness 148
Try this today: the gentle momentum method 149
Student voices 152
A new way when work feels hard 153
Dig deeper: the science of starting (and continuing) 154

SECTION FOUR: A NEW WAY TO READ AND WRITE 157
Releasing yourself from the discipline dilemma 157
Stepping sideways 158

14 HOW TO WORK WITH CHALLENGING TEXTS (SO YOU DON'T GIVE UP READING) 159
When reading feels like wrestling 160
Take a moment: your reading resistance inventory 160
Try this today: the strategic reading toolkit 161
Student voices 164
A new way with reading 165
Dig deeper: reading strategically when texts are tough 165

15 HOW TO THINK CRITICALLY (SO YOU KNOW HOW TO REFLECT, ANALYSE AND READ BETWEEN THE LINES) 167
What critical thinking actually is (and isn't) 167
The four angles of critical thinking 168
Notice your patterns: your critical thinking courage 170
Try this today: practising criticality in context 170
Troubleshooting critical thinking challenges 175
A critical framework for critical thinking 175
Critical thinking as self-care 176

See it in action: meet Mariam 177
A new way with critical thinking 178
Dig deeper: thinking clearly and questioning narratives 179

16 WHAT TO DO WITH CITING (SO YOU DON'T PLAGIARIZE) 181
When citation feels like a trap 181
The real reasons we cite 182
The AI element (and elephant): a framework for ethical use 183
Notice your patterns: honest questions about citing 183
Try this today: your citation toolkit 184
Student voices 185
A new way with citation 185
Dig deeper: citing with integrity in the AI age 186

17 WHAT TO DO WITH A HARD ESSAY (TO GET IT HANDED IN ... WELL-CRAFTED ... AND ON TIME) 188
Procrastination reframe 188
The hidden cost of procrastination 189
Notice your patterns: your procrastination style 190
The science of wanting to work 191
Try this today: the start-small-build-momentum method 191
See it in action: meet Jamie and Alex 194
Troubleshooting: when ChatGPT feels like the only way out 195
A new way with hard essays 196
Dig deeper: breaking procrastination and finishing well 196

SECTION FIVE: A NEW WAY TO REACH YOUR GOALS 199
Moving beyond SMART 199
Where dreams meet daily life 200

18 HOW TO NAME YOUR AIMS (WHEN YOU'RE FULL OF AMBITIONS) 201
Where do these mixed messages come from? 201
The geography of ambition 202
Take a moment: tall poppies and other garden metaphors 202
Finding and honouring your heartfelt aims 204
Try this today: minimize minimizing 205
See it in action: Jordan's story 206
A new way with ambition 207
Dig deeper: naming your ambitions without shrinking 208

19 HOW TO MOVE TOWARDS YOUR INTENTIONS (WHEN YOUR LIFE IS FULL OF OTHER OBLIGATIONS) 210
The fairy tale of the fresh start 210
Notice your patterns: owning your obligations 211
Time isn't the only currency 212
The one small move method 212
The both/and schedule 213
Creating containers, not cages 213
Passion project partners 214
The practice of integration 215
Try this today: intention integration 215
Troubleshooting: when obligations and intentions clash 216
Student voices 216
A new way with taking action 217
Dig deeper: resources for living with complexity 217

20 HOW TO REMOVE OBSTACLES (WHEN YOU WANT TO ACCOMPLISH SOMETHING) 220
The obstacles we're actually talking about 220
Notice your patterns: observing your obstacles 221
The three-part framework for obstacle removal 221
Try this today: the obstacle audit 225
Student voices 226
A new way with obstacles 227
Dig deeper: understanding obstacles and resistance 228

21 HOW TO TAP INTO PURPOSE (WHEN YOU'RE BORED, LOSE MOMENTUM OR GET SIDETRACKED) 230
The distinction between motivation and purpose 230
When everything feels purposeless 231
Take a moment: unearthing the underpinnings of purpose 231
Try this today: paving your path to purpose 233
Troubleshooting: your purpose reminder toolkit 234
See it in action: meet Jamal 235
A new way with purpose 236
Dig deeper: purpose-building resources 236

Going Our Own Ways … 238

Index 241

Acknowledgements

To every student stepping into this new chapter – whether you're reading in a bustling campus library, a quiet corner of home or somewhere in between – every learning strategy comes from you.

To every lecturer, teacher and education decision-maker – I hope these teachings here bring more ease to your own.

To Collective Uplift – you teach me how to put presence into practice, listening so truly with the ears of the heart.

To Helen Caunce and the Bloomsbury UK team – you have taught me to keep wishing wildly.

To the Learning Specialists Association of Canada – for teaching me deep belonging.

To my Awakened Learning team – for the leap-of-faith-ness and alongside-ness you teach me.

To my mother and father, Anita and Ivan – I carry your lessons with me still, and always.

To Blaire, Anthony, Arianne, Agata and Vic – I learn from you the art of celebration.

To Sasha and Evelyn and to Andrew – you are my daily reminders that learning happens best when wrapped in tenderness, deep care and love.

May my sharing the *how* of learning – *and* how the how matters just as much as the what – make for a little more sweetness for a lot more students.

WELCOME TO A NEW WAY TO LEARN

You're exhausted.

Not just tired from last night's study session, but that bone-deep, soul-heavy exhaustion from trying to keep up with a system that seems designed to break you. You've been told to 'work smarter, not harder' (what does that even mean?). You've tried the colour-coded schedules, the productivity apps, those tomato timers. Yet here you are, probably when you should be studying, reading another study skills book, hoping – really hoping – this one might be different.

It is. I promise.

This book won't tell you to wake up at 5.00 am, optimize every minute or transform into some glossy Instagram-student version of yourself. Instead, I'm offering something that might feel radical: permission to be gloriously, messily, beautifully human whilst pursuing academic excellence.

Why this book had to exist

I've worked with thousands of students. First-generation, international and mature learners returning after decades away. Students managing chronic illness, students working three jobs, students caring for family members and students who thought they were 'broken' because traditional study methods made them want to cry.

You know what I discovered? Most study guides treat you like a robot needing better programming, as if you just found the right time management system or note-taking method, you'd suddenly transform into that mythical perfect student who colour-codes their notes for fun and never, ever procrastinates.

But you're not a machine, are you? You're a whole person trying to learn whilst also navigating relationships, money worries, family expectations, that part-time job that barely covers rent and the genuinely overwhelming question of who you're becoming. (And maybe also a global pandemic's aftermath, climate anxiety and social media that makes everyone else's success look effortless.)

This book meets you there – in your actual, complicated, non-Instagram, very-real life.

What 'holistic' actually means (and why it matters)

When I say 'holistic,' some of you might roll your eyes. I get it. How's 'holistic' going to help when you have three essays due and haven't slept properly in weeks?

But here's what I mean: you're not just a brain on legs, wandering from lecture to lecture. You're not a reading, writing, problem-solving machine. You're a whole person. Your mental health isn't separate from your ability to focus. Your financial stress isn't separate from your academic performance. Your cultural background, your family responsibilities, whether you ate breakfast, whether you feel like you belong here – it all matters.

Traditional study advice pretends none of this exists. It assumes you have unlimited time, perfect health, zero responsibilities, supportive family, stable housing and a brain that processes information exactly like everyone else's.

This book knows better.

Here, you'll find strategies that work whether you're studying at 2.00 am because that's when your house is finally quiet. Whether you're managing ADHD, autism, dyslexia, chronic illness or just a brain that works in ways distinct from what universities plan for. Whether you're the first in your family to attempt this whole university thing and you're secretly terrified of letting everyone down. Whether you're juggling studies with work, caregiving or just trying to keep yourself fed and functional.

Let's redefine success together

What if success included sleeping more than five hours most nights? What if it meant keeping those friendships that matter, even during exam season? What if – and stay with me here because this might sound wild – your university experience could include *actual* moments of joy? (It's possible.)

I'm not talking about lowering standards or accepting mediocrity. I'm talking about expanding what achievement means. Yes, marks matter (and yes, these strategies will help with those). But success might also look like:

- Finally understanding that concept that's been making you feel thick for weeks
- Completing an assignment without an all-night panic session
- Having the courage to visit office hours when you're lost

- Making it to most of your lectures even though getting out of bed feels impossible some days
- Eating a proper meal before your afternoon seminar
- Saying 'I need help' without shame

These aren't consolation prizes for those who can't achieve 'real' success. They're the foundation that makes everything else possible. A well-rested brain writes better essays. A properly fed student can actually focus. Someone who feels they belong contributes more confidently.

What you'll actually find in these pages

This book is organized into five sections, each building on the last, though honestly? Skip straight to whatever's on fire in your life right now. That's fine too.

Section One wrestles with time – not so much 'managing it' (which you'll find is impossible) but finding some kind of peace with it when everything feels urgent.

Section Two reveals how studying really works in your brain, not the myths you've been told since primary school.

Section Three is about the unglamorous reality of getting work done when motivation has completely abandoned you.

Section Four tackles academic reading and writing without losing your authentic voice (or your mind).

Section Five helps you hold on to your dreams whilst managing all those other obligations that won't politely step aside.

Throughout, you'll meet real students (names changed; struggles real). You'll find 'Try This Today' bits for when you need something right now, this minute. There'll be troubleshooting for when things go pear-shaped, because they will, because that's life, and that's okay.

Your invitation

This isn't about becoming a 'better' student according to some arbitrary standard set by people who've forgotten what it's like to be where you are. It's about finding ways of learning that don't require you to sacrifice everything that makes you human.

You can be ambitious without being miserable. You can achieve without burning out. You can struggle without being 'less than'. You can need support without being weak. You can define success in ways that include rest, friendship, creativity and dare I say it – happiness.

The pages ahead come from one simple belief I'll defend forever: learning shouldn't hurt this much. Education can be rigorous without being punishing. You can grow without grinding yourself down to nothing.

So take a breath. Put down the guilt about whatever you 'should' be doing right now. Give yourself permission to read this book however works for you – all at once, in bits, just the emergencies, whatever you need.

Your way of learning is valid. Your struggles don't make you broken. And your success – however you choose to define it – is absolutely possible.

Ready? (Or ready-*ish*?) (Or ready enough?) Let's begin this journey together.

Making your way: how to use this book

If you've picked up *A New Way to Learn*, chances are you're looking for something different. A fresh approach to your studies that feels less like a struggle and more like an uplift, and a clarification if it's all felt a little (or a lot) confusing up until now.

This book exists because that traditional 'work harder' message so often (*most* often) fails students. Not because you aren't working hard enough (you probably are), but because effective learning isn't about effort alone. It's about approach. It's about personalized systems that contribute to your own ease. It's about strategy.

The techniques shared here come from years of working alongside students just like you, discovering what actually works when conventional advice falls short.

Your book, your way

There's no 'correct' way to use this book. You might read it cover to cover, diving into each strategy in sequence. Or perhaps you'll spot a chapter title that speaks directly to a challenge you're facing right now. Please feel warmly welcomed and encouraged to start there. Both approaches work beautifully.

Think of these pages more as a conversation than a prescription. This book welcomes you exactly as you are. Whether you're studying engineering in Toronto, literature in London or medicine in Melbourne. Whether you're undeclared or already specializing. Whether you're in your first day of your first year, or on your sixth or seventh cycle through undergrad. Your background, learning experiences and current challenges all bring valuable context to how you'll engage with these ideas.

The learning experiment

Every strategy presented here is, at its heart, an invitation to experiment. Some will resonate immediately; others might feel uncomfortable at first or need adaptation for your specific context. This is completely normal and exactly as it should be.

Take what lands. Leave what doesn't. Adapt what's promising.

Integrate these approaches with strategies you've already developed, making your own personal mishmash. The key is maintaining a spirit of exploration; a willingness to try something new when your current approach isn't yielding the results you hope for.

Learning strategies aren't fixed formulas but flexible frameworks. What works brilliantly for calculus might need adjustment for linguistic analysis. What serves you well during a lighter term might need modification during more demanding periods. Likewise, what worked in the initial semester of your initial year may need tweaking as the years and complexity build. Too, your context, relationships and life will change – and so too can the strategies you turn to. *A New Way to Learn* acknowledges these realities and offers approaches versatile enough to adapt as your needs evolve.

How this book supports you

Throughout this book, you'll encounter several recurring elements designed to make these strategies come alive and feel doable.

Student voices

Each chapter features stories from actual learners; in some chapters you'll meet several, in others we learn about a single student's journey. Students who discovered how to work with their ADHD rather than against it, who transformed their stuckness with priorities into flowing productivity, who found ways to healthfully hold intense academic and part-time job commitments, and who left sleeplessness and unchecked stress behind for a true sense of flourishing. These aren't perfect success stories but heartfelt journeys with setbacks, breakthroughs and everything in between. You'll see how different students adapted these approaches to their unique circumstances, challenges and strengths.

Moments to reflect and consider

You'll regularly find invitations to stop and consider your own experience. These aren't tests or assessments; they're gentle prompts to help you notice patterns, identify what's already working and imagine new possibilities. Some might be quick thought experiments ('When did you last feel in flow with your learning?'). Others invite deeper exploration through journaling or mapping exercises. All are optional, all are judgement-free and all are designed to help you connect these ideas to your actual life.

Try this today

Because the gap between reading and doing can feel enormous, each chapter includes tiny takeaways to try immediately. Not next term, not when you 'have more time,' but literally today. The aim here is gentle, open-hearted, no-need-to-get-it-'right' experimentation.

Key insights

Quick this-is-the-main-point summations, inviting you to pay particularly close attention and not risk skimming over. (Look for the arrow – you can't miss them!)

Visual maps and models

For those who feel well-supported via visuals, you'll find plenty throughout. These aren't meant to be memorized but rather turned to as thinking tools – ways to see connections, understand processes and ultimately fashion your own mental models for how learning works.

Troubleshooting sections

Because we know that real life is messy, many chapters include, 'But what if …' sections addressing common obstacles. What if you *don't* have the suggested ten minutes? What if your roommate is loud? What if you've already tried everything? These sections acknowledge the very real constraints you face and offer adaptations, workarounds and alternative approaches.

Dig deeper

If you're keen to explore further, you'll find carefully chosen books, articles and talks that expand on each chapter's themes. Think of them like invitations for those moments when an idea or strategy really lands, and you want to unwrap it more fully.

SECTION ONE

A NEW WAY TO PRIORITIZE

Time.

We all have the same amount of it each day, yet for university students, it often feels like there's never quite enough. Perhaps you've heard one too many times that familiar refrain from well-meaning advisers, professors and, of course, parents: 'You just need to learn how to prioritize better!' As if prioritization were a simple skill you've somehow failed to master.

(It's not!)

In this section, we'll challenge that notion entirely. In truth, managing competing demands is genuinely complex, *especially* when everything feels simultaneously urgent *and* important. The pages ahead offer a fresh perspective on your relationship with time, without the guilt or oversimplification that often accompanies the usual advice.

Breaking free from time management myths

We'll begin by normalizing *why* everything feels pressing. That overwhelming sensation isn't a personal failing; it's a natural response to the post-secondary environment, where deadlines converge and expectations multiply.

From there, we'll explore approaches that move beyond endless to-do lists and impossible scheduling choreography. You'll discover practical strategies that respect your humanity rather than treating you like a productivity machine. These approaches recognize that effective prioritization isn't about squeezing more tasks into fewer hours but about making deliberate choices that align with your values and goals.

You'll learn how to:

- create protected spaces in your schedule
- honestly reconcile your commitments with the actual hours in your day
- address the emotional dimension of time pressure

Throughout, you'll find techniques for transforming existential worries into purposeful action and pursuing meaningful projects alongside your coursework.

A different conversation about time

When you think about time and university life, what words come to mind? Write a few here.

What emerged for you? Any themes or overlaps? Any *time*-related words come up, like 'rushed' or 'busy'? What about 'stressed'? Most time management advice assumes we all start from the same place: that we have the *same* twenty-four hours, the *same* energy reserves and the *same* responsibilities.

But we know that's not true, don't we?

Some of us are caring for family members. Some are navigating chronic illness or disability. Some are working multiple jobs. Some are learning in a second (or third) language. Our relationship with time is deeply personal and shaped by our circumstances.

So, let's try something different. Instead of me telling you how to manage your time, what if we explored together how you're already navigating it?

Think about yesterday. When did you feel most in flow with time? As if you had a sufficient amount of it? When did you feel most at odds with it? Jot down a memory or two.

What you won't find in these pages are rigid systems that ignore your reality or advice that assumes you can simply delegate your responsibilities. Instead, these chapters honour the actual constraints you face while opening up new possibilities for working within them.

Time may not be something we can truly 'manage' (I care so much about getting this message out that I did a whole TEDx Talk on it), but we *can* transform our relationship with it. This section offers a path toward that transformation, one that acknowledges your academic aspirations and the need for a sustainable, balanced approach to university life.

As you move through these pages – and please, do move through them in whatever way serves you best – know that these strategies are meant to be personalized. Take what resonates, adapt what's promising and weave these ideas together with approaches that already work for you.

Your way with time is uniquely yours. Let's get to know it together.

CHAPTER 1

HOW TO MANAGE YOUR TIME (WHEN THERE'S TOO MUCH TO DO)

It's Sunday evening. You open your course website and see, as if for the first time, that there are three assignments due this week, readings you haven't started despite best intentions, a group project meeting tomorrow and that part-time job you can't afford to quit.

Your stomach tightens. Your jaw clenches. Your what-if worries accelerate.

You reach for your phone to create yet another to-do list, determined that *this* time, *this* week, *this* term, you'll get organized and power through. (And while on your phone, you might even allow yourself a doom-scroll session to escape school dread.)

Fast-forward to Friday: you've completed some items but added twice as many new ones, and the most important, the most complex and the most demanding tasks remain untouched.

It is my heartfelt wish that you know that your struggle isn't about poor willpower or organizational skills.

What if the very *idea* of 'managing time' is what's been tripping you up all along?

The misrepresentation of time management

What most productivity experts won't tell you is that you cannot manage time.

There *are* clever acronyms that make disciplined planning seem just at your fingertips. There *are* apps that can help you rank and order tasks. And yes, there *are* ways of thinking about time that can help or hinder. But we need to get clear: we are not the boss of time.

We are, instead, in a *relationship* with time.

Time exists whether you acknowledge it or not. It moves at the same pace regardless of your to-do list, your calendar alerts or your deadlines. I know it might not feel that way – time can drag during the dullest lectures, or race by when you're running out of minutes to finish an essay. (Or feel entirely irrelevant in the early days of falling in love.) But minutes are moving along, and cannot be wrangled or whipped into shape.

What we call 'time management' might more accurately be called *task* management or project management. When we dig deeper, it could really be about managing our *attention* so we can focus on the work at hand. Or, going deeper still, it might be about time *integrity* – being honest about how we spend our minutes.

Whatever it is we're trying to do – generate ideas, work, maintain focus or wake up to how we treat time – getting through workloads and meeting deadlines is one of the hardest things to learn.

Yet there's no better time than while at university.

What I've discovered working with thousands of students is that time struggles aren't a character flaw. They're signals that we're working against our natural rhythms rather than with them. The systems we've inherited – rigid schedules, productivity hacks that assume we're all wired the same way, guilt-driven hustle culture – weren't designed for the beautiful diversity of human learning differences, life circumstances or the reality that we're whole people, not work machines.

The problem isn't you. The problem is trying to manage something that can't be managed. So, what if we tried something completely different?

Time coherence

Derived from Latin, coherence means things like 'to bring together,' 'sticking together' and even just 'with'. The root word 'cohere' is beautiful: 'holding' different parts together or – check this definition out – 'to be logically consistent'.

What does this have to do with time?

Of all the ways to describe time problems, *coherence* leaves me feeling most uplifted, hopeful and empowered.

And sometimes it's in a synonym that true understanding lands. (Other words for coherence include proportion, unity, correlation and harmony.)

Imagine a sense of proportion in your work tasks. A uniting of projects and personal pursuits. A correlation between your energy and the work that needs doing. Or, best yet, harmony between your mental, emotional and spiritual states, your academic responsibilities, your sense of purpose and the minutes you have available.

THAT'S why we're here!

If 'coherence' means things that stick together with logic and consistency, then *time coherence* means bringing together, in a compatible way, the key elements of our time and tasks:

- **Structure (the external):**
  Deadlines, calendar dates, scheduling mechanics – the actual availability of our minutes.
- **Energy (the embodied):**
  Physical capacity, natural rhythms, stamina – the availability of our capacity.
- **Focus (the cognitive):**
  Attention, concentration, mental engagement – the availability of our attention.
- **Meaning (the motivation):**
  Personal significance and relevance – the availability of our care.

Time coherence helps us make sense of how our priorities, pacing, presence and purpose come together in getting our work done.

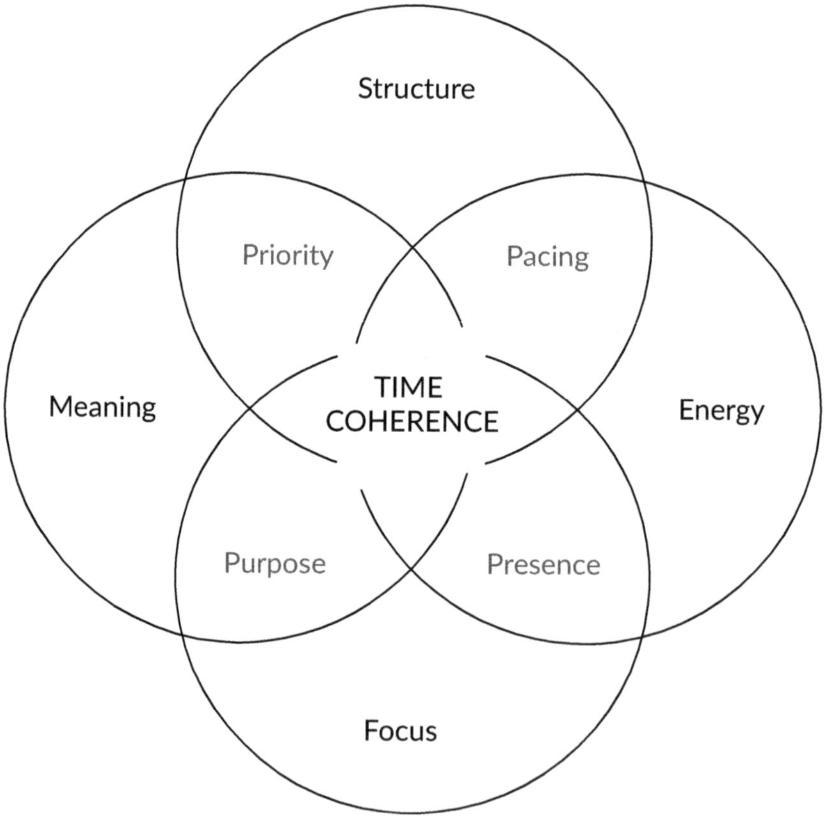

Figure 1.1 Time coherence model.

Time coherence is about alignment and integration – when your time choices truly reflect what you say matters to you. For first-year learners, this addresses that common disconnect where you might say you value your health or relationships but find yourself pulling all-nighters or cancelling plans.

Time coherence helps you consider, in a whole way, all that's on your plate and in your life. Coherence doesn't demand you become different – it welcomes you to become more yourself.

Take a moment: reflecting on your relationship with time

Your feelings about time – and your 'dance' with it – are intimate and deeply rooted.

Think back to when you were little: were you always on the go, darting between activities, shoes on and out the door before your parents could finish saying 'let's go to the park'? Or were you a lingerer with meals and crafting sessions that stretched on, the ability to focus for long crafting sessions and afternoons that seemed to extend ever longer?

When I think about my three daughters, they're each wound – each time-bound – so very (very!) differently. My stepdaughter has an exacting, deeply respectful, 'on it' relationship with time. My middle daughter has a languid tempo, and seems unable to hurry. My littlest is wired tightly, racing through everything, anxious to finish tasks well ahead of when they need to be done.

They're all bright, they're all respectful in their approach to work and they're all befriending time wildly differently.

I've come to think of it as akin to their pulse. It's an innate rate. And the key is not to deny their personal cadence, or to shame them about it, but to work *with* it.

Your relationship with time is integral to who you are. The goal here isn't to change it; it's to understand it, respect it and design your learning life around it.

To figure out your rhythm, consider:

When you feel 'behind' or overwhelmed, what words do you use to describe yourself?

- Notice the stories you tell yourself about your worth when time feels scarce. These internal narratives often reveal where shame has crept into your relationship with time.

How often do you say, "I don't have time for ... " versus "This isn't my priority right now"?

- The language we use shapes our experience. 'I don't have time' suggests victimhood, scarcity, powerlessness. 'This isn't my priority' acknowledges choice and agency.

Think of a recent achievement that required sustained effort. What made focusing on it possible?

- Understanding what conditions supported your success gives you data for creating those conditions again.

What time of day do you feel most alert? Most creative? When does your body crave movement versus stillness?

- These aren't luxuries to consider; they're essential data for designing a sustainable relationship with your academic work.

Dig deeper: beyond traditional time management

Sometimes seeing these ideas explored by others can help them click in new ways. Here are a few resources that expand on dancing with, relating to and *un*-managing your time.

Essential reading

Oliver Burkeman's *Four Thousand Weeks: Time Management for Mortals* (2021) challenges the entire productivity industry. He argues that trying to get everything done is not only impossible but misses the point entirely. Instead of optimizing our time, he suggests we learn to choose what matters and accept that we'll never do it all. This book is perfect for students who feel overwhelmed by endless advice about prioritization; it's practical and philosophical, offering encouragement to be human rather than a go-go-go, do-do-do machine.

Larissa Crawford's blog post on decolonizing time (2021) challenges dominant notions of time and urgency, exploring how colonial systems have imposed particular relationships with time that may not serve all learners. Her work invites us to question whose version of 'productivity' we've been taught to value and what alternatives might exist that feel more sustainable and humane.

TED Talks

Laura Vanderkam's 'How to gain control of your free time' (2016) explores how we actually have more time than we think; we just need to be more intentional about how we use it.

Dan Pink's 'The Puzzle of Motivation' (2009) counters traditional ideas about what drives us.

Understanding your time coherence

Before you can change your relationship with time, you need to understand what coherence looks like for you. This isn't about implementing a system yet, but rather developing awareness.

Try this: a simple daily check-in

Each day for the next week, ask yourself the following questions and either make note of them in a journal or notes app, or simply sit and contemplate for a moment:

1. **Structure**

   Did my schedule reflect reality today? Where did I underestimate or overestimate how long things would take? When did external demands conflict with what I actually had available?
2. **Energy**

   When did I feel most energized today? When did I feel depleted? What patterns am I noticing about my natural rhythms?
3. **Focus**

   When was I most present and engaged with my work? When was my mind elsewhere? What conditions seem to support my concentration?
4. **Meaning**

   Which tasks felt meaningful or connected to my larger goals? Which felt pointless or disconnected? What do I notice about my motivation patterns?

Don't try to *fix* anything; just notice. Being awake to and attuned to your natural rhythms, your peaks and valleys of energy, is the first step toward coherence.

Coherent breathing

This accessible technique can help you experience what coherence feels like in the body. It comes from research by the HeartMath Institute (McCraty and Shaffer 2015), which has found that specific breathing patterns can create *physiological* coherence, a state where your heart, breath and brain rhythms even out.

1. Breathe in for five counts, out for five counts (find your own comfortable pace; no counter or metronome needed).

2 Imagine breathing through your heart area.

3 As you breathe, bring to mind something you genuinely appreciate.

4 Continue for three to five minutes.

This technique can be helpful before starting a challenging task, when you feel overwhelmed or scattered, during transitions between different types of work or when you notice anxiousness about to-dos and tasks building.

Students often tell me that just a few minutes of this kind of breathing helps time feel more spacious and manageable. It's part of that coherence – bringing things together, including your energy, thinking and actions.

Student voices

Dinah: As a student with ADHD, Dinah struggled with traditional time management approaches that assumed consistent focus. 'I kept believing I just needed more willpower,' she shares. 'Everything changed when I stopped forcing myself into neurotypical productivity patterns and started working with my brain's natural rhythms.' Dinah now designs her schedule around twenty-minute focus blocks with movement breaks in between. 'I realized my brain isn't broken. Once I stopped fighting that, everything became more doable.'

Tariq: Working full-time while pursuing graduate studies left Tariq perpetually exhausted. 'I was trying to be productive every waking moment,' he recalls. Tariq discovered he was losing hours to decision fatigue, constantly reassessing which task deserved attention next. 'I learned that constantly choosing what to do next was draining me more than the actual work. Now I make those decisions once, first thing in the morning, and stick to them.'

Adam: As a first-generation university student working two part-time jobs, Adam felt constantly behind classmates who seemed to have endless time to study. Everything shifted when Adam started recognizing that his focused hours were often more productive than other people's distracted hours. 'I learned to work with intensity rather than duration. I might have less time but when I'm really present with it, I can accomplish a lot.'

→ **Key insight:** The goal isn't to do more. It's to understand how you relate to time so that you don't over-plan and under-produce, or under-plan and feel that scramble or walk around feeling as if your personal cadence is problematic.

A new way with time

So, what does it mean to have a new way with time? It starts with releasing the illusion that we can control it and, in its place, embrace the reality that all we can really do is *dance* with it.

This new way recognizes that your relationship with time is as unique as your fingerprint, honouring your natural rhythms instead of fighting them. It treats your attention as a precious resource to be stewarded, not a limitless supply to be depleted. It understands that coherence, not optimization, is the aim, like out-of-sync waves coming together, time coherence helps us move from that feeling of all-over-the-placeness to a smoother, more harmonious rhythm between the work waiting for you and your energy to do it.

When you welcome in this new way with time, something beautiful happens. The frantic urgency starts to settle. The shame-based productivity narratives lose their grip. You begin to trust your own rhythms and work with them instead of against them. Time starts to feel less like an enemy.

This is time coherence in action: when your structure, energy, focus and meaning coalesce to create not just productivity, but sustainability, satisfaction and a sense of wholeness that honours both your academic goals and your humanity.

In the next chapter, we'll explore how to align your time when there doesn't seem like enough – building on these insights about coherence to create better sequencing and flow.

References

Burkeman, O. (2021) *Four Thousand Weeks: Time Management for Mortals.* New York: Farrar, Straus and Giroux.

Crawford, L. (2021) 'Defining temporal de-colonization and why we say no to your urgency', *Future Ancestors Services.* Available at: https://www.futureancestors.ca/post/defining-temporal-de-colonization-and-why-we-say-no-to-your-urgency (accessed 1 October 2025).

McCraty, R. and Shaffer, F. (2015) 'Heart rate variability: New perspectives on physiological mechanisms, assessment of self-regulatory capacity, and health risk', *Global Advances in Health and Medicine,* 4(1), pp. 46–61.

Pink, D. (2009) 'The puzzle of motivation' [Video]. TED Conferences. Available at: https://www.ted.com/talks/dan_pink_the_puzzle_of_motivation (accessed 1 October 2025).

Shaffer, D.K. (2014) 'How to get from to-do to done' [Video]. TEDx Talks. Available at: https://www.youtube.com/watch?v=wZ2LVAXBpFU (accessed 1 October 2025).

Vanderkam, L. (2016) 'How to gain control of your free time' [Video]. TED Conferences. Available at: https://www.ted.com/talks/laura_vanderkam_how_to_gain_control_of_your_free_time (accessed 1 October 2025).

CHAPTER 2

HOW TO ALIGN YOUR TIME (WHEN THERE DOESN'T SEEM LIKE ENOUGH)

Hands up if you've been here before. You're surrounded by textbooks and sticky notes, laptop open, you've just spent two hours creating the most beautiful, colour-coded priority matrix you've ever made. Every assignment is categorized by urgency and importance, ranked from one to forty-seven, with due dates highlighted in increasingly alarming shades of red.

You. *Feel*. Productive.

Organized.

On top of things.

Then, you look at your 'urgent and important' quadrant and realize it contains fourteen items, all due by the end of the week. Your 'Important but not urgent' section is overflowing with readings it would've been wise to start earlier in the month. And somehow, despite all this careful categorization, you still have no idea what to *actually* do first.

You stare at the matrix. The matrix stares back. Next steps? Completely cloudy.

This is the prioritization trap – the illusion that sorting tasks into boxes will magically solve the problem of having too much to do.

But the entire premise of traditional prioritization doesn't match how learning really works. What if the problem isn't that you're bad at prioritizing, but that prioritization itself is the wrong goal?

The five false priority systems

Before we explore a better way, let's air out the (problematic – sorry!) approaches most students unknowingly use to 'choose' their priorities.

1 **Whatever hits first.**

Do you choose your priorities simply by responding to things as they happen? If so, your priorities are really choosing you.

2 **Easy button.**
When was the last time you heard yourself say, 'It's just easier to do this quick assignment first'? This isn't always wrong, but if you're saying it too often, you're probably avoiding the challenging work that would move you forward.

3 **Loudest voice wins.**
In most friend groups and families, it's not hard to identify who the squeaky wheels are. But it's worth considering whether their requests really require your immediate attention.

4 **Reluctant hero.**
'It doesn't look like anyone in our group is really going to start working on this project. I guess I'll do it.' These words should send up a bright red flag.

5 **Mood dependent.**
If you wait until you're 'inspired' to tackle your statistics homework, it probably isn't going to happen if stats aren't your favourite, even if the task truly is a high priority.

The problem with prioritization

Most productivity advice treats your to-do list like a military operation: identify what's urgent, rank everything by importance, tackle the high-priority items first and power through until victory is achieved.

But students don't live in neat quadrants. And university isn't a battle.

Most prioritization models assume you have genuine choices about what to do and when to do it. They assume you can 'just say no' to low-priority items, delegate what doesn't matter and focus solely on what's most important.

They assume you're the CEO of your own time.

But the reality for most students? You *can't* delegate your calculus homework. You *can't* say 'no' to the group project that's worth 30 per cent of your grade. You *can't* eliminate the part-time job that pays for your groceries. And you're not the CEO of your time – you're more like a project coordinator juggling multiple stakeholders, competing deadlines and limited resources.

What if instead of prioritizing, we focused on *aligning*?

Time alignment

Building on Chapter 1's Time Coherence approach of harmonizing structure, energy, focus and meaning, Time Alignment asks: *how do we sequence our tasks so they work with our natural rhythms, values and constraints rather than against them?*

Time Alignment isn't about choosing 'what matters most' (because honestly, most things on your list matter). It's about finding the most graceful way to move through your responsibilities so that each task supports rather than depletes your capacity for the next one.

Think of it like choreography (I know – back to a dance metaphor). In dance, the goal isn't to identify which movements are 'most important' and eliminate the rest. The goal is to *sequence* the movements so they flow naturally from one to the next, building momentum and creating something beautiful *and* sustainable.

Time Alignment recognizes three crucial truths about student life:

1. **Switching between different types of tasks is expensive.**
   Moving from writing an essay to studying for a maths exam to calling your mum, with phone checks and social scrolls throughout, requires your brain to completely change gears each time. The usual models of prioritization often ignore this cost, leading to days where you're technically productive but feel scattered and exhausted.
2. **Energy is dynamic.**
   Your capacity for creative work at 9.00 am might be completely different from your capacity at 9.00 pm. Your ability to focus after a difficult conversation is different from your ability to focus after a great workout. Time Alignment sequences tasks based on the energy they require – that you require – and the energy they generate.
3. **Meaning-making takes time.**
   The most important work – the kind that builds real understanding and lasting skills – often doesn't have urgent external deadlines. Most prioritization frameworks push this work aside in favour of whatever has the nearest deadline.

The flow of academic sequencing

What has most informed my understanding of productivity, far more than any book, has been watching my daughters navigate their homework.

My eldest approaches tasks like a chess player, thinking several moves ahead, arranging her work so that research for one project informs reading for another class.

My middle daughter sequences by mood and energy, doing creative work when she feels inspired and saving routine tasks for when her brain needs a break. My youngest batches similar activities together, knocking out all her maths before moving to writing, minimizing the cognitive cost of switching between different types of thinking.

They're all successful learners, but they've each discovered different ways to create flow in their academic work.

They've also figured out, through experimenting and finding their own unique way, that the order in which you approach tasks can be as important as the tasks themselves.

Academic sequencing pays attention to several factors that traditional prioritization ignores:

Cognitive load

- Some tasks require deep thinking; others are more routine. Sequencing allows you to cluster routine tasks together and protect uninterrupted time for complex work, or to create a balancing duet between a hard task with a mind-clearing organizational task.

Emotional energy

- Difficult conversations, challenging subjects or tasks that make anxiety bubble up require different emotional resources than work that feels engaging or straightforward.

Task type

- Your brain might be most creative in the morning but most analytical in the afternoon, or vice versa.

Social vs solitary

- Group projects require different energy from solo research.

Physical needs

- Some work requires you to be sedentary; other work allows for movement.

When you consider your needs, capacity and engagement, you're not just managing tasks; you're curating an experience that supports your whole self as a learner.

Notice your patterns: mapping your current alignment

Before we can improve your sequencing, we need to understand how you currently move through your days.

1 Consider tracking your **energy patterns** for three days.

Most productivity advice asks that you track where your minutes go, but I've always been resistant to this advice; it's hard not to feel like it's fundamentally shaming, as if every moment is supposed to be 'productive'. Here, the ask is that every couple of hours you lightly note: *What's my energy level right now? What kind of work would feel most doable? What's my emotional state?* Please resist the temptation to change anything. Just observe.

2. Pay attention to your **transition costs**.
   What exactly does *this* mean? It's the 'cost' of attention, energy, momentum and clarity of thought when you toggle between tasks. Notice, *when you switch between different types of tasks, how long does it take you to fully engage with the new activity? Which combinations feel jarring, and which feel natural?*
3. Turn your focus to your **momentum-builders**.
   Which tasks, when completed, make you feel energized and ready for more? Which ones leave you feeling drained? How might you use momentum-builders strategically?
4. Examine any **values conflicts**.
   Nothing zaps our energy quite like doing things we've said we actually *don't* want to be doing (nighttime doom-scrolling anyone?). With kind care, ask yourself: *when you feel guilty about spending time on something, what's usually happening? Are you choosing between two things you value?*
5. Take an inventory of your **honest constraints**.
   There will be immovables, and there will be things that come with some wiggle room. *What are the non-negotiable commitments in your schedule? Which deadlines are truly fixed, and which have more flexibility than you might think?*
6. Notice your **resistance patterns**.
   There are friction points all around us, like the academic work and part-time job schedule that are sometimes in tension. But there is also the *internal* tension we bring to our work. This impacts when we start our work and the energy we bring to it. *What types of tasks do you consistently avoid or postpone? What does your resistance teach you about your needs and preferences?*

The goal in engaging in this heartfelt reflection isn't to eliminate all friction – some resistance is normal, *helpful* even – and it's *never* to be hard on yourself. Instead, the goal is to understand your patterns in service of creating more ease.

Dig deeper: rethinking how we approach tasks

These resources explore different ways to think about sequencing, flow and working with your natural rhythms.

Essential reading

Cal Newport's *Slow Productivity* (2024) challenges the unsustainable pace of our current productivity culture, proposing a more humane alternative that emphasizes doing fewer big projects at once, working at a 'natural pace' and valuing quality over quantity. He cautions learners to resist pseudo-productivity and instead to focus on meaningful accomplishment through sustainable practices that honour both cognitive limits and the need for genuine rest.

TED Talks

Amy Cuddy's 'Your body language may shape who you are' (2012), one of the most watched and shared talks, shares how physical posture affects confidence and performance. Worth considering in the context of how we approach challenging tasks – bringing a statue-strong or slumped posture may influence the energy with which you move through your work.

Sean Achor's 'The happy secret to better work' (2012) poignantly demonstrates that happiness and positivity *fuel* better performance, not the other way around. It's not the A that leads to calm, ease and joy, but the opposite.

These resources share a common theme: sustainable productivity comes from understanding yourself and designing systems that work *with* your natural patterns rather than fighting them.

Try this today: the Flow Sequence Model

If making priority matrices leaves you cold, or in constant crisis mode, try this fresh approach to sequencing your tasks. The Flow Sequence Model organizes your work based on *energy flow* rather than urgency ranking.

The four flow states

Spark State high energy + creative focus

- Best for: Starting new projects, brainstorming, writing first drafts, problem-solving
- You feel: Alert, curious, ready to tackle challenges
- Timing: Often earlier in the day or after energizing activities

Deep State calm energy + sustained focus

- Best for: Research, reading complex material, detailed analysis, revision and editing
- You feel: Steady, focused, able to sustain attention
- Timing: When you won't be interrupted and have mental space

Flow State moderate energy + routine focus

- Best for: Completing assignments with clear steps, organizing notes, responding to emails
- You feel: Competent, efficient, in a rhythm
- Timing: When you need to feel productive but don't have peak energy

Rest State low energy + restorative focus

- Best for: Light reading, reviewing notes, planning tomorrow, gentle movement
- You feel: Tired but not depleted, needing renewal
- Timing: End of study sessions, between demanding tasks

Once you can identify these different energy waves in your own day-to-day, you can sequence them to align with your workload.

Feel out what it's like to start with Spark State. Why? Beginning your work session with something that energizes you creates momentum for everything that follows.

Consider it essential to protect Deep State time. This is your most valuable cognitive resource. Schedule it when you're least likely to be interrupted, sluggish or distracted.

Be strategic with your Flow State, as these tasks are perfect for building momentum when you're struggling to start. They're less open-ended, have clear benchmarks, milestones or inbuilt feedback. You know when these tasks start and end, and as such they can have that motivating, crossed-it-off-the-to-do-list vibe.

Your Rest State needs honouring, always. This isn't 'wasted' time, no matter what our pseudo-productivity-focused context might suggest. Rest is the foundation that makes all other states possible.

Okay, this is a huge one: aim to end with energy. I'll own that, as a person who basically uses up every last ounce of energy each day, this is a life project for me. But it's one I'm determined to stay dedicated to. Try to finish work sessions with something that leaves you feeling accomplished rather than depleted, with a little gas left in the tank.

The weekly Flow State map

As much as we like the sensation of crossing items off our lists, those running tallies of our daily to-dos aren't the be-all and end-all. Instead, try creating a weekly flow map:

1. List all your tasks for the week without ranking them.
2. Categorize each task by the Flow State it requires.
3. Having noticed your natural energy patterns throughout the week, match tasks to optimal energy states rather than to any available calendar block.
4. Sequence tasks within each day to create flow rather than friction.

Having an enumerated sequence like this can help with moment-to-moment decisions about 'What should I do now?' based on how you truly feel.

See it in action: meet Fatou

Fatou is a first-year arts student living in residence, trying to manage five courses plus her campus job at the library. When we first met, she was drowning in what she called a 'sequencing standstill'.

'I would make these elaborate lists ranking everything by importance,' Fatou tells me, 'But then I'd stare at them and feel completely overwhelmed. Everything felt urgent and important.' She was spending more time reorganizing her colour-coded priority matrices than actually doing the work.

Fatou's biggest struggle was that she treated every type of academic task the same way. Reading for English literature got the same energy allocation as solving calculus problems. Writing a reflection paper received the same time block as memorizing psychology terms. She was switching between completely different types of thinking each hour, leaving her mentally exhausted by noon.

The breakthrough

Everything changed when Fatou started paying attention to her natural energy patterns. She discovered that her most creative thinking happened mid-morning, around 10.00 am. Her brain was sharpest for analytical work right after lunch, when most of her peers felt a slump in energy. And she could focus on routine tasks like reading or note organization later in the afternoon when her energy was steady but not peak.

Instead of prioritizing by deadline urgency, Fatou began sequencing by energy alignment and then fiercely protecting those time windows.

Fatou's flow sequence discovery:

- **Spark State (10.00–11.30 am)**
  Essay brainstorming, creative writing assignments, starting new projects. 'This is when ideas just flow,' she says. 'I stopped forcing myself to do math during my most creative time.'
- **Deep State (1.00–3.00 pm)**
  Calculus problem sets, complex readings, detailed research. 'After lunch, my brain wants to dig into something challenging and stay with it.'
- **Flow State (3.30–5.00 pm)**
  Organizing notes, posting discussion board responses, reading assignments with clear structure. 'This is my rhythm time – I can just get things done without overthinking.'
- **Rest State (evening)**
  Time crafting, playing guitar and long walks with friends. In terms of work, at most, light reading or a little planning for tomorrow. 'I used to feel guilty about not doing "real work" in the evening, but now I see this as essential recuperation time.'

The results

Within three weeks, Fatou noticed dramatic changes. 'I stopped feeling as if I was constantly swimming upstream,' she reflects. 'Instead of fighting my brain's natural rhythms, I started working with them.'

Her grades improved because she was doing the right type of work when her brain was optimally ready for it. But more importantly, she stopped feeling scattered and exhausted. 'I actually have energy left at the end of the day now. I can hang out with friends without feeling guilty that I should be studying.'

Fatou also discovered that some tasks naturally flow into others. Her morning brainstorming sessions often generated ideas that enhanced her afternoon research. Reading in a calm evening state helped her process information that supported the following day's analytical work.

> → **Key insight:** 'I realized that the problem was never my willpower or my organizational skills,' Fatou says. 'The problem was that I was trying to force my brain to switch gears constantly instead of creating sequences that actually worked together.'

A new way with alignment

Traditional prioritization asks, 'What's most important?' But when there are many (many!) important tasks, it's really the *sequencing* that's tricky.

Time Alignment asks us to relate to time and tasks differently by zeroing in on how we're doing and how we're *feeling*. Time Alignment nudges us to pay attention and ask ourselves: *What order honours your energy? What sequence builds momentum? How can you arrange your responsibilities so that each one prepares you for the next instead of depleting you for it?*

This new way recognizes that you are not a machine that can be optimized for maximum output. You are a complex human being with varying energy levels, emotional needs, physical rhythms and multiple commitments that all deserve respect – and require heeding if you are to realistically accomplish your academic workload.

Alignment means your tasks work together instead of competing for your time and energy. It means your creative work energizes you for your analytical work, which prepares you for your routine tasks, which give you space to rest and restore so you can be creative again.

Most importantly, alignment means accepting that you have finite energy and designing your approach around that reality instead of pretending you can do everything at peak capacity all the time.

When you align your time, you stop feeling like you're constantly swimming upstream. Tasks begin to flow naturally from one to the next. You build momentum instead of constantly starting from zero. You end your days feeling accomplished rather than depleted.

In our next chapter, we'll explore how to create boundaries around your aligned tasks, giving your thoughtful sequencing the protected space it needs to flourish.

References

Achor, S. (2012) 'The happy secret to better work' [Video]. TED Conferences. Available at: https://www.ted.com/talks/shawn_achor_the_happy_secret_to_better_work

Cuddy, A. (2012) 'Your body language may shape who you are' [Video]. TED Conferences. Available at: https://www.ted.com/talks/amy_cuddy_your_body_language_may_shape_who_you_are

Newport, C. (2024) *Slow Productivity: The Lost Art of Accomplishment without Burnout.* New York: Portfolio.

CHAPTER 3

HOW TO CULTIVATE YOUR TIME (WHEN TO-DOS OVERWHELM)

Most students unknowingly approach their academic work like they're trying to grow a garden by throwing seeds in every direction. They scatter their attention across readings, assignments, studying and admin tasks, hoping something will take root. They're always busy tending to everything yet little seems to flourish.

The problem isn't the amount of effort (oh goodness, there's a lot of effort here!); it's the absence of intentional environments.

Our brains need natural habitats to function effectively. Different environments nourish different types of thinking, evoke different energies and support (or block) our movement between different kinds of work. Depending on the work environments we create, curate or find ourselves in, we might exist in a state of continuous *partial* attention – always *somewhat* engaged with everything but never *fully* present to anything. This is exhausting, and ultimately ineffective.

The solution isn't another scheduling app; it's creating a time ecology.

An ecological approach to your attention

Nope, this is definitely *not* going to be a biology lesson. But we *are* going to explore habitats and ecologies – not of salamanders or beavers, not of marshes or wetlands (um, you can tell I'm a Canadian author, *eh*?), but rather an ecosystemic view of *you* and how you go about your work.

Time ecology is about creating purposeful environments where different types of learning can naturally flourish. Think of it as tending different gardens for your attention – designing spaces where specific kinds of thinking can take root and grow.

There are two ecological principles that, when used together, can transform your relationship with those overwhelming to-do lists: creating habitats and honouring rhythms.

Habitats are specific environments for different categories of work. Each habitat has natural thresholds: what belongs in it, what doesn't, how long you tend it and what you expect to grow there.

Rhythms are the natural cycles of focused attention: protected seasons where you commit to tending one habitat without letting concerns from others intrude.

Together, habitats and rhythms create what folks in learning science and cognitive psychology fields like to think of as 'cognitive architecture': structures that support deep work, reduce decision fatigue and help you feel more accomplished with less stress.

Habitats: creating environments for your attention

Creating habitats is based on the simple truth that different types of work require different types of attention, thinking and energy. Reading is not the same as writing. Studying via practice questions is different from analysing arguments. Creative brainstorming is different from responding to a discussion post.

When you try to do all these different types of work in the same literal location, without clear thresholds between them, you might be creating 'task interference,' where the leftover thoughts from one activity interfere with your ability to fully engage with the next.

Academic habitats

Consider creating separate physical spaces for different types of academic work. You might have a 'Reading Habitat' (for consuming information), a 'Writing Habitat' (for producing original work), an 'Analysis Habitat' (for thinking through complex problems), a 'Practice Habitat' (for retrieval practice and memorizing key facts) and an 'Admin Habitat' (for the university tasks that don't fit elsewhere).

Or

Subject habitats

Keep different courses in separate environments. When you're in your 'Biology Habitat', you're only thinking about biology. That way, your psych, stats and anthropology homework exist in different ecosystems and will be less likely to intrude on your focus.

Or

Energy habitats

Match your habitats to your energy states from Chapter 2's Flow Sequence Model. Create a 'High-Energy Habitat,' like a loud-print, groovy-music café, for your most challenging generative work, a 'Moderate-Energy Habitat' for routine assignments and a 'Low-Energy Habitat' full of muted tones and natural light for tasks that don't require peak cognitive function.

The key to making habitats successful is respecting the *thresholds*. When you're in the Writing Habitat, you don't check email. When you're in the Biology Habitat, you don't think about your English essay. When you're in the Low-Energy Habitat, you don't attempt high-cognitive-load tasks.

Rhythms: protecting your deep work seasons

Whilst *habitats* organize the types of work you do, *rhythms* protect the time you need to do it well. Natural rhythms create protected, uninterrupted seasons where you can build momentum and achieve flow states.

As Newport argues in *Deep Work* (2016), our ability to focus deeply on cognitively demanding tasks is becoming increasingly rare and increasingly valuable. Most students have trained themselves to work in continuous distraction, never allowing themselves to reach true focus.

- **Duration matters**
  Effective rhythms need to be long enough for your brain to settle into focused work. It takes an average of twenty-three minutes to fully focus after a distraction (Mark 2022). Some researchers say that we do best with fifty-seven minutes of work before a brief break. But what's most important is how you live and experience time. Consider your natural work rhythms, which for some might be a thirty-five-minute sprint, an hour and a half deeper dive or three hours to really immerse. And note that these might change depending on the challenge level of the work, your familiarity with the task and, above all, your capacity.
- **Thresholds matter**
  During a focused rhythm, you don't check your DMs, respond to texts, or browse social media. You don't switch to other assignments or let your mind wander to other concerns.
- **Surroundings matter**
  Honouring rhythms often requires tending to your physical environment. This might mean going to the library, putting your phone in another room or finding a space where you won't be interrupted.

- **Preparation matters**
  Before entering a work rhythm, you need to know exactly what you're going to work on. The rhythm itself isn't for deciding what to do; it's for *doing* it.
- **Recovery matters**
  After a deep work rhythm, your brain needs genuine recovery time. This isn't time for 'productive' activities; it's time for rest, movement or activities that restore your cognitive resources.

Take a moment: discover your neuro needs

Before designing effective habitats and rhythms, let's explore your current relationship with focused work. This isn't about finding 'deficits' – it's about understanding *your* unique neuro-patterns as a starting point for creating supportive structures.

For many learners, perhaps especially those with ADHD, autism or other neurodivergent traits, maintaining focus and managing time can feel especially challenging. Universities often assume one 'standard' way of working, but brains work differently. What feels like personal failure might more likely be a mismatch between your brain's natural patterns and the environment's expectations.

Over the next few days, get curious about your attention patterns:

- **Track your focus flow.**
  How often do you switch between different types of tasks? When you sit down to work, how long does it take to settle into focus? When interrupted, how long before you're back in the flow? (If you have ADHD, you might notice either intensified difficulty focusing or periods of hyperfocus where hours disappear).
- **Notice your natural groupings.**
  What types of work feel similar or naturally paired? Which combinations flow smoothly, and which feel jarring? Some students find switching between reading and writing feels natural, whilst others need to batch similar tasks together.
- **Observe your starting patterns.**
  What makes beginning feel harder? Do you avoid starting because you don't know when you'll stop? Do large time blocks feel overwhelming? For autistic students, the need for clear instructions, endpoints and structure might be strong.
- **Identify your distraction pulls.**
  What draws you away from work? Internal pulls (racing thoughts, anxiety, sudden curiosity about unrelated topics) or external ones (notifications, flatmates, competing responsibilities)? Understanding your specific disruption patterns helps you design better defences.

- **Recognize your flow conditions.**
  When do you lose track of time in the best way? What conditions support your deepest thinking? This might be completely different from what works for your friends – and that's perfectly fine.

This exploration isn't about *fixing*. It's about wayfinding approaches that sync *with* your wiring and ways of being, rather than working against them.

Try this today: energize your environments

There are key considerations for implementing time ecology in your academic life.

Design your academic habitats

Start by identifying distinct approaches for different types of academic work – even if you're working from the same corner of your bedroom, kitchen table or that one spot in the library that's usually free.

The reality? Not everyone has access to multiple workspaces. You might be studying in a shared flat with paper-thin walls, at your parents' kitchen table between meals or in the only quiet corner you can find on campus. That's okay. 'Habitats' can be as much about mindset shifts and small environmental tweaks as physical locations.

For students who have access to multiple spaces.

- **Info Intake Habitat**: Readings, research, watching lecture recordings
  Best for: When you have good focus but don't need to produce original ideas
  Environment: Comfortable reading space, minimal distractions
- **Creative Challenge Habitat**: Writing, brainstorming, problem-solving, connecting ideas
  Best for: When your mind feels fresh and creative
  Environment: Inspiring space, access to resources
- **Deep Thinking Habitat**: Problem sets, detailed analysis, logical reasoning
  Best for: When you feel mentally sharp and systematic
  Environment: Quiet, organized space with minimal visual distractions
- **Steady Stream Habitat**: Lighter tasks, school and life admin
  Best for: When your energy is moderate but steady
  Environment: Efficient workspace, good organization systems
- **Integration Habitat**: Connecting ideas across subjects, preparing for exams
  Best for: When there's an exam on the horizon
  Environment: Clean space to spread out materials

For students working from one space.

Transform your single workspace through small shifts:

- **Change one thing** to signal different work modes: face a different direction, change your laptop background, use different coloured pens, adjust lighting if possible, or even just clear everything except what you need for that specific task.
- **Use sensory cues**: Different lo-fi, ambient or classical playlists for different work types (or silence versus sound), a specific mug for deep work sessions or putting on a particular jumper that means 'writing time'.
- **Time as habitat**: If you can't change where, change *when*. Maybe mornings are your 'creative challenge' time whilst afternoons become 'steady stream' time.
- **Portable habitats**: Headphones can create a 'quiet' space in chaos. A clipboard can turn any surface into a workspace. Even changing which browser you use for different tasks can create mental separation. Get creative and welcome some scrappy DIY bootstrapping workarounds.

Do take heart; learners have succeeded whilst studying on night buses, in 24-hour cafés when home was too loud, at laundrettes whilst washing clothes and yes, from their beds when that was the only private space available. Your habitat doesn't need to be Instagram-worthy to be effective.

Plant these approaches into your calendar, naming both work type and whatever small environmental shift you can manage. Aim for efficient, attentive time windows with ample, feel-good breaks – even if you're just standing up and stretching in the same room.

Design your threshold rituals

Inertia can take over such that it's a challenge to pack up and move to a different physical space. Create personal rituals to support crossing thresholds between habitats.

- **Entry Rituals**
  Clear your workspace, set an intention, put away distracting items, review what you plan to accomplish to ensure you've not unintentionally piled on too much.
- **Transition Rituals**
  Close out previous work completely, take a brief break, move to a different location, reset your environment.

- **Exit Rituals**
  Capture unfinished thoughts, tidy your final workspace, acknowledge what you accomplished, plan next steps and spaces.

Working-to-habitat will support you best if you:

- Stick to your specific intended work type within each habitat
- Ensure clear start and stop times to move to a different location
- Communicate clearly about your focused sessions
- Incorporate *digital* thresholds, like browser lock-downs, to minimize distractions

Student voices

Leila: As a commuter student juggling classes and family responsibilities, Leila felt as if she was always working but never accomplishing enough. 'I would sit down to study and immediately feel overwhelmed by everything I needed to do. I'd end up switching between subjects every fifteen minutes and feeling scattered all day.' Leila started creating subject habitats, dedicating specific spaces to each course. 'Knowing I had "my place" at the student centre where I'd only go to work on bio and a library carrel on my fave library floor made everything feel clearer and more manageable.'

Rashid: Rashid struggled with 'fake productivity', being busy all day but accomplishing little he felt of substance. 'I was constantly doing school-related activities, but I was never doing any single thing deeply enough to really understand it.' He found an off-campus café where he'd tackle his most challenging coursework. 'By week three, I was getting more done at that café than I used to accomplish in entire days.'

Zara: A perfectionist who avoided starting assignments because she felt that she needed to finish them in one session, Zara would 'avoid starting essays because I thought I needed a whole day to do them properly'. In trying out this ecosystemic approach and tying task-to-place, Zara embraced smaller, contained work sessions in specific locations. 'Now I have a research nook, a drafting nook and an essay-revision nook in my dorm building. My writing quality is way better because when I sit down to work, I *really* work.'

→ **Key insight:** These students learned that time ecology isn't about restrictions; it's about ensuring environments where their best work could naturally emerge.

A new way with time ecology

Commonplace productivity advice treats time like a resource to be mined. Something to extract maximum value from through force and discipline. But time ecology reveals a gentler truth: when we invite the right conditions, our best work emerges naturally.

If you think about it, a garden doesn't grow faster when you pull on the plants. A river doesn't flow better when you try to push the water. Natural systems thrive when we understand their needs and create supportive environments.

When you practise time ecology through habitats and rhythms, you're not forcing yourself to be productive; you're creating environments where your best thinking, problem-solving and connection-making can occur. You're tending spaces where your attention can go deep, where your creativity can unfold, where your learning can take root and grow.

This ecological approach recognizes that your brain needs different environments for different types of work. And thresholds create a kind of protective boundary. When you know your deep work time is protected and contained, with rituals into, through and out of it, you can relax into the work.

But remember, healthy ecologies are responsive and adaptive, not rigidly architected or arbitrary. They serve your growth and learning, not some external idea of how you 'should' work. They adapt when life demands it but return to their natural patterns when stability is possible.

When you embrace time ecology, whether it's through habitats, rhythms or a unique approach that you cultivate yourself, overwhelm begins to dissipate. Not because you have less to do, but because you've created sustainable environments for doing it. Your work becomes more effective because your attention has the right conditions. Your rest becomes more restorative because it's genuinely separate from your work.

In our next chapter, we'll explore how to heal the time anxiety that often underlies our struggles with overwhelm, learning to transform scarcity fears into purposeful action whilst honouring both your academic obligations and your deepest aspirations.

Dig deeper: learning from focus experts

Essential reading

Cal Newport's *Deep Work* (2016) is an impactful guide to creating boundaries around your most important, if not most precious, cognitive work. He shares how the ability to focus deeply is becoming both rarer and more valuable and provides practical how-tos for protecting your attention from constant distractions.

TED Talks

Conor Neill's TEDx talk, 'The discipline of finishing' (2013), explores why starting projects is easy but finishing requires different skills and structures.

Tim Ferriss's talk, 'Why you should define your fears instead of your goals' (2017), demonstrates how clear parameters can reduce anxiety and improve decision-making.

References

Ferriss, T. (2017) 'Why you should define your fears instead of your goals' [Video]. TED Conferences. Available at: https://www.ted.com/talks/tim_ferriss_why_you_should_define_your_fears_instead_of_your_goals (accessed 1 October 2025).

Mark, G. (2022) *Multitasking in the Digital Age*. New Haven: Yale University Press.

Neill, C. (2013) 'The discipline of finishing' [Video]. TEDx Conferences. Available at: https://www.youtube.com/watch?v=zXCiv4sc5eY (accessed 1 October 2025).

Newport, C. (2016) *Deep Work: Rules for Focused Success in a Distracted World*. New York: Grand Central Publishing.

CHAPTER 4

HOW TO HEAL TIME ANXIETY (WHEN MINUTES FEEL SCARCE)

How do you feel about time?

I'm not asking whether you're usually late or early to appointments. I'm not asking if you're timely with handing in assignments. And I'm not really asking whether your days feel long or short.

Rather, what I'm curious about here is what sensations come up when you're confronted with the word 'time'. What mood comes over you when you think about your task list, and what you most long to do with your time. Most of all, what does 'time well spent' bring up for you.

If, in reflecting on time, worry comes up for you – an ever-present whisper that it's all going by so quickly, or a louder anxiety that there's never enough time for all that you long to do – this chapter is dedicated to you.

'Time anxiety' is real, and both honouring and tending to it can be a key part of a more healthful approach to study skills and academic excellence. After all, alongside all your to-dos – the local pressures of the day, *these* lectures to attend, *those* projects to move along – there are also larger, sweeping and more existential worries about life feeling short, ambitions feeling big, and how on earth to reconcile all this while being a student.

Time anxiety

Doesn't it seem as though we're always in an awkward tango with time? Sometimes, it's us barely making it to class. Sometimes we're lit up with alertness, getting through reams of tasks, efficiently on it. Sometimes we're behind, sluggish in our research or dragging … our … heels on a group project. Sometimes we're in relax mode, off the clock entirely. At other times, we're trying to do two or more to-dos at once, making slow, disjointed, taxing progress.

In my own office hours, you'll find a first-year stating, 'I feel like I'm always running, but I'm not actually getting anywhere'. A third-year telling me, 'I love what I'm studying, but I keep thinking about all the things I'm *not* doing. It's as if I'm missing my own life'. And there's the grad-bound student who admits, 'I thought I'd have more time to figure out who I am by now, but I feel more scattered than ever'.

I regularly hear wonderings like, 'Does anyone else feel as though they're wasting their college years by only studying?' or 'How do you balance wanting good grades with actually having a life?' or 'I feel guilty every time I do something fun because I could be studying'.

This is just to reassure you that you're not alone in feeling this tug-of-war between obligation and aspiration.

These conversations are happening everywhere because this struggle is real and widespread. The beautiful thing is that more and more students are pushing back against the idea that college should be all work and no meaningful personal pursuits.

By 'time anxiety', I'm not referring to chronophobia, the literal, clinical fear of time's passage. Rather, it's about the more common tension caused by a nagging sense that we've let too much time slip by, that it's moving quickly, that there's a lot to get done and above all that we want to spend more of our time meaningfully.

Put together, these feelings can make it very hard to start. To be sure, we've got a lot of obligatory academic tasks – papers to write and tests to study for. We feel the pressure of tasks and projects, performances and portfolios, presentations and examinations – all pinned against time.

But underneath, we're also aware of a kind of *preciousness* about time. An awareness that we don't get our already spent minutes back; that time moves in one direction only. That there are 'sliding doors' decisions to make that open up life paths ... and close off others.

I'm not trying to be morbid, not in the slightest. I actually find this *life-affirming*! It's just that our mortality is with us, always.

There's so much we want to do with our finite minutes!

While time's preciousness is a deep truth, it's also worth naming that we're living in what some call 'productivity culture' – a social environment where being busy is seen as virtuous, where every moment comes with the expectation that it be 'optimized', where rest is often perceived as needing to be *earned* rather than held as necessary. This pressure often reflects dominant Western, colonial approaches to time that demand we do more, faster and better, which may not align with many other ways of understanding our relationship with time and work.

Just know, your time anxiety isn't a personal failing – it's a reasonable response to cultural assumptions that may not serve your well-being or honour your own relationship with time.

Take a moment: understanding your time anxiety

Not everyone experiences time anxiety, but if you've ever felt that nagging sense that there aren't enough minutes, that time is slipping away from what you long to do, or that it's 'too late' to begin what matters to you, this exercise can help you understand what's happening.

First, begin by mapping your relationship with time.

Start by identifying what you're longing for versus what's actually filling your days. This gap is often where time anxiety lives.

- **Your shelved dreams:** What activities or projects do you keep thinking about but have convinced yourself you 'can't' pursue right now? Maybe it's learning guitar, starting a podcast, getting back into art, training for a 5K, learning another language or diving into photography.
- **Your current reality:** What (honestly) fills your time instead? Scrolling? Work shifts? Assignments? Lying in bed *worrying about* assignments?
- **The feeling between them:** When you compare these two lists, what emotion surfaces? Frustration? Grief? Resignation? This feeling IS your time anxiety.

Next, notice when and how worry shows up.

Time anxiety has patterns. Catching these patterns helps you prepare for and work with them.

- **Physical signals:** That tight chest when looking at your calendar? The stomach knot when thinking about everything you 'should' be doing? These body signals often appear before conscious worry.
- **Trigger moments:**
  - Is it worst in the evening when the day feels 'wasted'?
  - When seeing others' achievements on social media?
  - Sunday nights thinking about the week ahead?
  - During assignment deadlines when passions feel impossibly distant?
  - **Your anxiety's voice:** When time worry hits, what does your inner monologue sound like? 'I'm wasting my youth?' 'Everyone else manages to do more?' 'It's too late to start?'

Finally, connect the dots.

Here's what these pieces tell you:

- The gap between your dreams and daily reality shows you what's creating the anxiety

- Your trigger patterns reveal when you need strategies most
- Your body signals become early warning systems
- Your inner voice reveals what specific fear needs addressing

For example, if you dream of learning guitar but spend evenings scrolling instead and feel most anxious at night with thoughts of 'another day wasted', your time anxiety is specifically about the gap between intention and action. The strategy? Start with ten minutes of practice before your evening scroll, addressing the gap directly.

This isn't about judging yourself. It's about understanding your specific version of time anxiety so you can work with it rather than against it. Some students feel it intensely, others not at all. Both are normal. What matters is knowing your own pattern.

Try this today: the 'some is better than none' approach (aka the daily fit-in)

How often have you said to yourself, 'Oh, I'd so love to do [insert favoured activities XYZ] but I have too much studying to do'? (I hear students say this all the time!)

Here's the big pitch: start.

How? If you want to create ten pieces for your fashion line, one hundred videos or eight songs, but don't start with thirty (or five) minutes of sewing today, one film session, or picking up your guitar to practise, know that tomorrow there will be the same desire ... but fewer minutes.

It's also true that today's *quality* of time – that sense of meaning, significance and purpose – will feel diminished, because our minutes were entirely directed to our have-tos instead of any of our heartfelt want-tos.

The daily fit-in method

Step 1: List your meaningful stuff

What are one to three things you genuinely want to do but feel you 'don't have time for'?

- Creative projects → Writing, art, music
- Physical activities → Sports, dance, martial arts, hiking
- Learning pursuits → Languages, skills, hobbies
- Community involvement → Volunteering, activism

Step 2: Start ridiculously small

For each thing you want to do, figure out the tiniest possible daily bit.

- Want to write a book? → fifty words per day
- Want to learn guitar? → ten minutes of practise
- Want to create art? → one sketch or one photo
- Want to stay fit? → twenty-minute walk or short workout

Step 3: Fit it into what you're already doing

Instead of waiting for 'enough time', squeeze tiny actions into your day.

- At transition times → Between classes, before dinner, after study sessions
- As a bookending strategy → Start or end study periods with meaningful activities
- As a reward system → Complete the least appealing academic task, then enjoy your passion project

What actually works

Academic Work + Passion Stuff + Rest = A Life That Actually Works

This isn't about perfect time management but making sure that some part of each day connects to what makes you feel alive and like yourself.

Fitting in the daily fit-in

Let's walk through this together. Take your time with each step; there's no rush.

1 **Notice the anxiety.**
What does time anxiety feel like in your body? Where do you hold the tension? What thoughts race through your mind?

2 **Identify what you're longing for.**
Beneath the anxiety, what are you really hoping for from your life? What untapped potential or heartfelt pursuit can you sense?

3 **Start tiny today.**
What's one small thing – the smallest step – that you could try today that moves you toward what you're longing for? (Remember, tiny means *tiiiiiny*; five minutes counts!)

4 See what happens.

After trying your tiny step, what did you notice? Any surprises? Any impact on your outlook, mindset or even the quality of your academic work when you permitted yourself time and space to tend to your life projects and ambitions?

5 Keep track.

How will you keep track of your feelings and growth? Notes on your phone? A journal? Where can you reflect on pursuing your passions and on the ripples for your schoolwork? Where can you identify whether you're spending enough time, too much time or if things get out of balance?

6 **Adjust as you go.**
Based on what you noticed, what small adjustment might you make tomorrow?

7 **Celebrate the small wins.**
What's worth celebrating from this week, no matter how small? (Starting counts, noticing counts and being kind to yourself as you figure things out counts.)

Consider this your personal map. Return to it whenever time anxiety creeps in. Each journey through these questions teaches you something new about yourself and the life you're designing for yourself.

Troubleshooting time obstacles

'But I don't have even ten minutes!'

If you truly can't find ten minutes, can you find three minutes? one minute? Sometimes we need to start so small it feels almost silly. One minute of guitar practice. One sentence written. One photo taken. The point isn't the amount; it's the connection to what matters to you.

'It doesn't feel like enough.'

This is where the grief lives, isn't it? The gap between how much you *want* to do and how much time you *truly* have. This feeling is valid and real. And also, *some* really is better than *none*. That tiniest bit of progress on your project – that micro-connection to your heart's passion – can shift your entire day.

'I feel guilty doing anything fun when I have so much school work.'

This guilt is productivity culture talking. Your worth isn't determined by how much academic work you complete. You're a whole human being with varied interests and needs. Taking fifteen minutes for something you love doesn't make you lazy or irresponsible – it makes you human.

'What if I start and then can't keep it up?'

Then ... you start again. There's no perfect streak requirement here. This isn't about becoming someone who does their passion project every single day without fail. It's about creating more opportunities for meaning and joy in your life. Some days you'll do it, some days you won't. Both are okay.

There will, of course, be days when all of this feels impossible. When you have three papers due and two exams coming up and the last thing you want to think about is squeezing in time for your passion project. That's exactly when this approach matters most.

On those overwhelming days, make your 'some' even smaller. Instead of fifteen minutes of writing, write one sentence. Instead of twenty minutes of exercise, do ten jumping jacks. Instead of practising a whole song, play one chord.

The point isn't the amount of time or the level of achievement. The point is maintaining that thread of connection to what makes you feel like yourself, even in the midst of high intensity academics.

See it in action: meet Justin

Meet Justin, a first-year university student exploring general arts and sciences, still discovering which academic path feels right. They entered university as a strong student with marks above average, though they're finding that their current grades have shifted to a solid but slightly lower range as they navigate new academic expectations. This learner brings unique ways of thinking and processing information, including diagnoses of ADHD and a learning disability, which shape how they engage with their studies.

Justin and I worked together for three years, from about halfway through their high school journey through their transition into higher education. Perhaps it was the profound challenges with attention, or that he was in many ways a polymath – so good at so many things – but Justin really struggled to get through any academic work they felt was 'boring'. (And they found *lots* of work boring.)

Outside their school commitments, they had three core passions: music making, playing sports and engineering-related games, toys and puzzles. They longed to spend their day (ideally only) on these.

When we met, Justin was at an elite, IB-focused, high expectation private secondary school. Their family had big dreams for them and even bigger expectations. But every evening, as they sat down to get through their homework, they struggled. Oh! Did they struggle! Justin struggled to start, to sustain focus and find the energy to produce and to complete work tasks.

All the while, they were longing to spend their time on what mattered most to them: composing new songs, playing basketball and fiddling creatively with K'nex-style sets.

The breakthrough

We tried many ADHD-supporting strategies and core learning skill strategies. They were ... okay. But not wholly transformative. What wound up being most impactful was zeroing in on the loudest worry for Justin – that with schoolwork filling up their days, evenings and weekends, they would never get to do what they really wanted to do.

They were looking ahead to the years that would unfold, seeing them as being entirely full of obligatory courses and programmes – life seemed dreary, a little unfair even. It's no wonder their underlying anxiety was growing – when would they (*finally*) be able to pursue what they wanted?

So, we started.

Did I get any initial pushback? You bet I did – most commonly in the form of 'I don't have time', 'I have too many assessments to do', 'If I'm going to do what I want, I need more time', as well as 'But I want to do all *three*, not just *one* of my passions!'

The daily fit-in in action

- **Sports first (30–40 minutes).**

Shooting hoops in the local park between classes and evening work. This helped them shake off the school day, use up extra ADHD energy and see daily progress.

- **Hardest academic task next.**

  We bookended the most unappealing work with their favourite activities. The reward was worth – and fuel for – the difficult work getting done.

- **Music making as a reward.**

  After other work tasks were completed, they ended with composing or playing music.

- **Building blocks for winding down.**

  Fun but challenging construction activities became their mind-clearing, pre-sleep routine.

The results

What Justin was most amazed by was that giving themselves encouragement to engage in their most beloved activities each day meant they were chipping away at their big hopes AND becoming more efficient in their much less beloved work tasks. The work didn't feel like it was eclipsing their whole life ... *because* they made space in their life for what they most longed for.

Their minutes felt more balanced, less anxious and full of meaning.

→ **Key insight:** By honouring both academic obligations and personal passions daily, Justin discovered that time anxiety diminished and academic performance actually improved. The meaningful activities energized the required work and knowing that every day they'd be able to engage, if even a little, in their biggest passions made the academic tasks feel more manageable.

A new way forward with time anxiety

We can get really stuck when we have big hopes and big dreams, maybe *especially* when we have wild ambitions. Sometimes the breadth of our hopes and the vision for our future lives are so big it actually stops us from starting. All the while, we're super aware of days going by *without* having started on what we so long for.

Time anxiety is real. That stuckness between wanting and starting, between passion and procrastination.

My hope is that your biggest takeaway is feeling not just permission but the warmest welcome to start – today! – to work towards your biggest dreams. Your passions, your entrepreneurial ideas, your beloved hobbies, these aren't at odds with academic work or academic excellence. In fact, having a *full* life that lets you be the *fullest* version of who you are and pursue what matters most to you makes that academic excellence more likely.

When you allow yourself to spend even tiny amounts of time on what you truly care about, everything shifts.

First, your academic work often becomes easier, not harder. Why? Because you're no longer trying to get all your meaning and fulfilment from assignments that were never designed to provide those things.

Second, you stop feeling resentful about your academic work. When you know you've got fifteen minutes of guitar practice waiting for you after you finish your reading, that reading becomes more doable.

Third, you start to see possibilities everywhere. When you're actively engaged in the things that matter to you, even in small ways, you begin to notice connections, opportunities and ideas that were always there.

Students tell me about unexpected benefits:

- 'I'm sleeping better because I'm not lying awake thinking about all the things I'm not doing.'
- 'I feel more like myself, even knee-deep in a stressful semester.'
- 'My friends are noticing that I seem happier.'
- 'I'm more focused during study time because I know I've got something to look forward to.'
- 'I'm actually enjoying my classes more because I'm not asking them to be everything.'

No longer does the life of a student have to be just work-work-work. Instead it can be work *and* passion projects in mutually motivating balance. That's the medicine for time anxiety, and a true recipe for a more successful semester ahead.

And wouldn't you know, the very habits you build now, the ways you learn to integrate meaning into busy times, the skills you develop in honouring both your obligations and your aspirations – these will serve you for the rest of your life.

The professional world is full of people who never learned how to do this, who spend their whole careers feeling like they're waiting for their 'real' life to begin. *You* have the opportunity to start differently, and *practise* differently, to prioritize meaning in your daily minutes.

The question isn't whether you have time for what matters to you. The question is, *what small step can you take today to honour both your responsibilities and your dreams?*

What would it feel like to end today knowing you'd made progress, however tiny, on something that fills you with life?

Your time anxiety is trying to tell you something important – that you want your life to matter, that you have things you care about, that you're aware of the gift of time you've been given. Listen to it. Respect it. And then, gently and persistently, start.

Dig deeper: where does our time go?

Essential reading

Cal Newport's *Digital Minimalism* (2019) talks about something he calls 'high-quality leisure', activities that are demanding, skill-building and socially valuable. What I love about his work is how he challenges the idea of downtime as mindless or passive. Instead, he suggests that our free time should involve activities that require effort and skill, that contribute to something meaningful, and that often involve other people. This connects beautifully to time anxiety because so often what we're really craving isn't more time but more meaningful time. Newport's work shows that when people engage in high-quality leisure activities – learning instruments, woodworking, volunteering, playing sports – they actually feel like they have more time, not less.

TED Talks

Tim Urban's 'Inside the mind of a master procrastinator' (2016). If you haven't seen this TED Talk – viewed by over 73 million people – it's worth a watch. Urban's hand-drawn illustrations of a procrastination monkey and panic monster capture something elemental about our relationship with time and productivity. Most compelling to me is what lies silent between the monkey and the monster – between the desire to play and the pressure to produce – namely, the yearning for time well spent.

Your time experiments: making it real

Let's make this practical and personal. The strategies in this section matter most when they connect to your actual life.

What landed for you?

Look back through these chapters. What made you think 'Oh, THAT'S why that happens' or 'I need to try that'? Don't write what you think you should have noticed – write what caught your attention.

Your personal time discovery

Based on what you've read, what's your main time challenge?

- The coherence challenge (your energy, calendar and meaning are working against each other)
- The habitat issue (no boundaries between different types of work)
- The anxiety spiral (that nagging sense there's never enough time for what matters)
- Something else entirely: ____________

Your smallest possible experiment

If you could shift just ONE thing about how you relate to time this week – something so small it would be silly not to try – what would it be?

Not an overhaul. Not a new system. Just one tiny shift.

Maybe it's:

- Trying coherent breathing before your next lecture
- Putting your phone in another room for one study session
- Doing your passion project for literally five minutes tomorrow
- Naming your energy state before choosing what to work on
- Something even smaller: ____________

Your accountability moment

Who could you tell about this experiment? (Even if it's just your diary or your cat.) When will you try it? What would make it more likely to happen?

After a week, come back to this page:

Did you try it? What happened? What did you learn about yourself? Take some time to jot your insights.

The point is *never* perfection. It's not about becoming a time management influencer. It's about finding one small way to make time feel less like an enemy and more like ... well, if not quite a friend, maybe at least a neutral acquaintance you can work with.

References

Newport, C. (2019) *Digital Minimalism: Choosing a Focused Life in a Noisy World*. New York: Portfolio/Penguin.

Urban, T. (2016) 'Inside the mind of a master procrastinator', *TED2016* [Video]. Available at: https://www.ted.com/talks/tim_urban_inside_the_mind_of_a_master_procrastinator (accessed 1 October 2025).

SECTION TWO

A NEW WAY TO STUDY

Studying.

It's what university students spend countless hours doing, yet most of us were never actually taught how to do it effectively. Perhaps you've been told by well-meaning advisers, professors and parents, 'You just need to study harder!' As if the solution were simply more hours hunched over textbooks, more late nights, more caffeine-fuelled cram sessions.

(It's not).

In this section, we'll challenge that entire approach. The truth is, most students – and most teachers and most parents – were never taught evidence-based study strategies. The result? Generation after generation recreating the same inefficient habits, like rewriting notes, retyping lecture slides and re-reading the same material over and over ... and over, all in the hope that something, *anything*, will stick.

Breaking free from so-called 'study strategies'

In this section, we'll begin by acknowledging why so many typical study skill-building methods feel so natural; they truly do seem as though learning and remembering are happening. Mostly because they keep us busy. That sense of 'doing something' isn't wrong; it's just not an effective path to genuine understanding and retention.

From there, we'll explore approaches that move us beyond busy work and marathon study sessions. You'll discover strategies rooted in how memory and comprehension function – techniques that can genuinely transform your confidence and exam performance while leaving you feeling more rested and whole.

These methods respect both your intelligence and your time. They recognize that effective studying isn't about working harder or longer but about working in ways that align with how your brain naturally processes and retains information.

A different conversation about learning

In the chapters ahead, you'll learn how to transform passive review into active engagement that creates lasting memory. You'll pick up how to work with distractions rather than against them, creating sustainable focus. You'll figure out how to harness the power of collaborative learning for deeper understanding. You'll discover how to achieve academic excellence without sacrificing your well-being. And you'll be introduced to reframing exams as learning opportunities rather than threats.

When you reflect upon your study habits to date, what have they been like?

Tedious?

Scattered?

Successful on some types of timed assessments, but less so on others?

Mentally scan prior quizzes, tests, midterms, oral exams, critiques, finals. How has studying gone for you in the past?

Throughout the chapters in this section, you'll find techniques for moving beyond the anxiety-inducing cycle of 'Am I studying enough?' toward purposeful, confident preparation that honours who you are as a whole person.

What you *won't* find here are rigid systems that ignore your learning needs, or advice that assumes you have unlimited time and energy. Instead, these chapters meet you in your actual life – with all its complexity, commitments and challenges – while offering practical alternatives to the study habits that may be leaving you exhausted from effort, yet underprepared.

Let's begin this journey toward studying that actually works – for your brain, for your life and for your future.

CHAPTER 5

HOW TO REMEMBER WHAT YOU LEARN (SO YOU DON'T WASTE YOUR TIME)

It's 9.00 pm. You've spent the last four hours 'studying' for tomorrow's exam. Your textbook is covered in highlighter – pages and pages of yellow, pink and blue. Your notebook sits beside you, filled with carefully rewritten notes from class, now colour-coded and organized into neat categories.

You close the textbook and try to recall what you've just spent so much time reviewing. Your mind goes blank. Panic creeps in. You flip back through the highlighted passages, and they look familiar, sure, but when you try to explain the concepts to yourself, the words feel slippery, as if they're just out of reach.

So, you start over. Re-reading the same highlighted sections. Re-reviewing your beautifully rewritten notes. Telling yourself that this time – *this* time – the info will get into your brain and stay there.

If this sounds like you, you might be caught in the most common study bait-and-switch: confusing recognition with recall, familiarity with understanding and busy work with (sorry!) real and sturdy learning.

Most students spend the majority of their study time on activities that create virtually no lasting memory. They're working hard, feeling productive and getting nowhere.

The illusion of learning

What you're experiencing isn't laziness or an indication of having a 'bad memory'. Rather, it's the predictable result of study methods that *feel* like learning but aren't. When you re-read highlighted text, your brain recognizes the information and tricks you into thinking you know it. When you rewrite notes, the act of writing feels productive, but it doesn't strengthen what's actually needed for recall.

These methods persist because they're comfortable.

What do I mean?

Re-reading doesn't require much mental effort.

Highlighting comes with a sense of purpose.

Rewriting notes creates beautiful, organized materials that make you feel prepared.

But here's what's really happening: you're engaged in what folks in my field call 'pseudo-studying' – activities that look and feel like learning but don't create the memory consolidation you need for exams, essays or real-world application.

Building on the time coherence, alignment and boundaries you learned in Section One, this chapter will show you how to transform those well-structured study sessions into sessions that build real, lasting memory.

Forgetting triggers

You'll often hear learners say, or say yourself, 'I forgot how to do that' or 'I couldn't remember that term (or concept or formula)' after a tricky test. Put this way, it might seem like 'forgetting' is just one thing; like not remembering comes in one shade.

But there are actually a few different ways that memory struggles can make themselves known.

For example, there's interference forgetting, which is when similar concepts get confused with each other. You can imagine – or perhaps you've lived this yourself – just how common this is in subjects like psychology, biology or history where many terms and theories overlap.

There's also context-dependent forgetting, which is when you can remember information in one setting, like your dorm room while studying, but not another, as when you're writing in the exam room itself.

You might've experienced what's called retrieval failure. That's when the information is 'in there' but you can't access it when you need it. I think of this as having no bridge between what you do indeed know but what isn't prompted by the test question alone.

And there's decay forgetting, when information simply fades because it wasn't reinforced enough.

To figure out *your* personal memory-forgetting experience, after each study session, consider what methods you used – re-reading, highlighting, note-taking, flashcards, teaching others, study groups. This isn't about judging your current methods or throwing them all out the window – it's about developing awareness of what genuinely works for your brain versus what just *feels* productive.

Take a moment: uncovering your memory challenges

Before diving into new strategies, let's better understand your current relationship with remembering and forgetting.

There are guaranteed things you truly do remember well – maybe song lyrics or sports stats or book characters – and there are no doubt things that you naturally struggle to remember.

In the academic sphere, there are contexts and types of material that help things stick, just as there are certain texts, teachers and types of information that seem to leave your brain soon after being introduced.

Think back to your most recent exam or major assignment. As you review that experience, consider:

- What you studied versus what you remembered.

  How much of your study time was spent on activities like re-reading, highlighting or reviewing notes? When you sat down to take the exam, how much of that material came back easily?
- Your confidence patterns.

  Have you ever felt completely prepared for an exam, only to sit down and realize you couldn't recall information that seemed so familiar during your study sessions?
- Your study-to-retention ratio.

  How many hours of studying does it typically take before you feel confident that you'll remember something a week later? A month later?
- Your studying durability.

  How quickly do you forget material after an exam? Can you still explain concepts the day after you walked out of the exam, or has it all vanished?

Try this today: the Remember-Retrieve-Rest framework

Based on what genuinely supports memory and taking a holistic approach that prioritizes your well-being, here's a practical system for studying that keeps you well and builds lasting memories.

Stage 1: Remember (building memory anchors)

The goal isn't to memorize isolated facts but to create meaningful connections that your brain can easily retrieve.

Personal connections

Link new information to things you already know well. If you're learning about mitosis, connect it to something familiar – perhaps the process reminds you of how your family divides up household chores, or how your friend group splits into smaller groups at parties.

Place connections

For sequences or lists, mentally place items in familiar locations. Walk through your childhood home and place historical events in different rooms or use your daily route to campus to remember the steps in a biological process.

Word connections

Create memory devices using words and phrases from your own life. Instead of generic acronyms, use names of friends, inside jokes or memorable experiences.

Visual connections

Turn abstract concepts into mental images. Make them vivid, unusual or emotionally meaningful. The more your visualization departs from ordinary experience, the more memorable it becomes.

Start with one approach – whichever feels most natural – and give it a consistent try for your next test.

Stage 2: Retrieve (strengthening recall pathways)

This is the door through which most students don't know to enter; instead, most stop at recognition without ever (knowing to) practise retrieval.

Practice questions first

Before you feel 'ready', take practice tests or attempt end-of-chapter questions. Getting answers wrong is part of the learning process, not a sign of failure. With AI tools available, you can easily generate practice exams for any topic.

Create your own questions

As you read or review notes, constantly ask yourself, 'What would a good exam question about this material look like?' Then answer your own questions without looking back.

Question yourself, explain to others

Find someone who doesn't know the material and teach it to them. If you can't find a willing audience, explain concepts out loud to yourself, a pet or even a potted plant.

Question by flashcard, strategically

Focus on concepts you get wrong, not the ones you get right. Use spaced repetition, reviewing cards at increasing intervals (one day, three days, one week, two weeks).

Question your memory, artistically

For subjects with diagrams, processes or visual components, practise drawing or diagramming from memory, then check your accuracy.

Stage 3: Rest (allowing consolidation)

Memory consolidation happens during downtime, not during study time.

Space your sessions

Instead of six-hour study marathons, use thirty-, forty-five- or ninety-minute sessions spread across multiple days. The gaps between sessions are when your brain strengthens the memories.

Sleep strategically

Protect those seven to nine hours! At all costs! Budging for nothing and no one! For an exam you're particularly nervous about, you may wish to *lightly, briefly, gingerly* review challenging material before sleep as your brain continues processing and strengthening memories during rest. Don't push, don't ruminate, but do consider a light scan of the hardest formulas and concepts before lights out.

Take real breaks

Between intense study sessions, do something completely different. Take a walk, exercise or engage in a hobby. This isn't time wasted; this is when consolidation happens.

Interleave subjects

Rather than studying one subject for hours, switch between different topics. Just as material isn't presented linearly on a test, consider moving between different themes, chapters or sections as you study. This prevents 'interference' and helps your brain distinguish between similar concepts.

Remember-Retrieve-Rest implementation strategy

If you've got a quiz coming up, aim to start studying seven–ten days prior. This allows for lots of space, rest and consolidation.

- Day 1: Take a practice test to identify what's sticking and what isn't
- Day 2: Try out your preferred Remember technique
- Day 3: Rest day!
- Day 4: First retrieval practice session
- Day 5: Rest day!
- Day 6: Second retrieval practice session
- Day 7: Rest day!
- Day 8: Third retrieval practice session
- Day 9: Rest day!
- Day 10: Final retrieval practice before assessment

Each session should be shorter but more mentally challenging than how you've usually been going about your study sessions. And any frustration you might feel over forgetting is a *great* sign – that stretch, that wrestle, well, that means you're genuinely studying!

And here's the biggest pro tip: you don't need an assigned quiz, test or exam date to start. This can become a regular post-lecture rhythm so that you're always studying – a little at a time, never rushed and using the most efficient strategies.

Student voices

Simone: A second-year physics student, Simone was spending six or so hours a day 'studying' but barely passing her exams. 'I would read the same chapters over and over, highlighting everything that seemed important, which was basically everything.' When Simone switched to the Remember-Retrieve-Rest framework, she saw immediate changes. 'Instead of re-reading, I started making flashcards after my first read-through, then testing myself constantly. I felt, strangely, a lot calmer and more rested going into exams because I wasn't spending as much time with the material. My grades went from C+ to A-! More importantly, I actually remember stuff from previous semesters now.'

Yuki: Yuki, a history major, struggled with keeping track of dates, names and cause–effect relationships across different time periods. 'Everything just blurred together. I'd study the French Revolution and somehow mix it up with information about the American Revolution.' Yuki began placing historical events throughout their apartment. 'The French Revolution lived in my kitchen – I put the storming of the Bastille by my coffee maker because it was about breaking barriers to get what you need.' It might seem unconventional, but Yuki's exam scores improved dramatically, and he stopped confusing historical periods.

Sarah: Psychology student Sarah felt overwhelmed by the volume of terms, theories and research findings. 'I would make these beautiful study guides with every single detail colour-coded and organized, but when exam time came, I'd blank out completely.' Sarah learned to prioritize retrieval practice over beautiful notes. 'I started creating practice tests for myself after every class. Instead of perfect study guides, I had chaotic, only-made-sense-to-me documents full of questions I'd written and answered repeatedly. It felt chaotic compared to my old system, but I was actually learning instead of just organizing.'

→ **Key insight:** Learning that lasts happens not through endless re-reading or marathon study sessions, but through the challenging work of pulling information from memory (even when you get it wrong), combined with strategic rest periods that allow your brain to consolidate and strengthen those memories. The gaps between study sessions – the rest – are when real learning happens, not during the cramming.

A new way with remembering

Traditional studying treats your brain like a storage device: put information in, hope it stays there, panic when it doesn't. But remembering material for an exam isn't about storage; it's about retrieval. Every time you successfully recall information, you strengthen the pathways that make future recall easier.

This new way recognizes that forgetting is useful. When you struggle to remember something and then succeed, you create stronger memories than if recall had been effortless. The agitation you feel when you can't immediately remember something isn't a sign that you're failing; it's a sign that real learning is happening.

This approach respects the reality that memory takes time. You can't cram lasting memories into existence the night before an exam. But when you work with your brain's natural processes – building meaningful connections, practising retrieval and allowing time for consolidation – you create understanding that lasts far beyond any single test.

Instead of *hoping* information will stick, you develop reliable methods for making it stick. Instead of feeling anxious about forgetting, you gain confidence in your ability to learn and retain. Instead of studying harder, you study smarter.

The goal isn't perfect memory; it's reliable memory. Memory you can count on not just for the next exam, but for the deeper understanding that makes your education meaningful and your learning sustainable.

Dig deeper: what goes into lasting memory

Understanding how memory actually works can transform your entire approach to studying. Here are key resources that reveal why traditional study methods fail and what works instead:

Essential reading

In *Make It Stick: The Science of Successful Learning* (2014), Cognitive scientists Peter C. Brown, Henry L. Roediger III and Mark A. McDaniel, illuminate why most conventional study habits fail. The authors present research showing that the most effective learning strategies often feel harder in the moment, while the most popular strategies – like re-reading – provide minimal long-term benefit.

Key research

- The Testing Effect

  Retrieving information from memory – even when you get it wrong – strengthens memory far more than re-exposure to the same information. This explains why practice tests are more effective than reviewing notes (Roediger and Karpicke 2006).

- The Spacing Effect

  Spreading out study sessions over time, with gaps in between, creates much stronger memories than massed practice, otherwise known as cramming. The brain needs time to consolidate information (Cepeda et al. 2006).

- The Generation Effect

  Information you generate yourself – by answering questions, creating examples or explaining concepts – is remembered far better than information you simply review (Slamecka and Graf 1978).

If you're curious about the learning science underneath the most effective study strategies, check out this research. It lays bare why traditional study methods fail, which is to say that all those handed-down techniques prioritize immediate familiarity over long-term retention, comfort over challenge and passive consumption over active retrieval.

References

Brown, P.C., Roediger, H.L. and McDaniel, M.A. (2014) *Make It Stick: The Science of Successful Learning*. Cambridge, MA: Harvard University Press.

Cepeda, N.J., Pashler, H., Vul, E., Wixted, J.T. and Rohrer, D. (2006) 'Distributed practice in verbal recall tasks: A review and quantitative synthesis', *Psychological Review*, 113(3), pp. 354–380.

Roediger, H.L. and Karpicke, J.D. (2006) 'Test-enhanced learning: Taking memory tests improves long-term retention', *Psychological Science*, 17(3), pp. 249–255.

Slamecka, N.J. and Graf, P. (1978) 'The generation effect: Delineation of a phenomenon', *Journal of Experimental Psychology: Human Learning and Memory*, 4(6), pp. 592–604.

CHAPTER 6

WHAT GETS IN THE WAY (SO YOU CAN REMOVE THOSE DISTRACTIONS)

It's Tuesday night, 9.47 pm. You've been meaning to start studying for your exam since Sunday. Maybe even last week, if you're being honest. Your textbook sits on your desk, bookmarked to Chapter 7, exactly where you left it after your last attempt to study.

You sit down with genuine determination. It's going to be different ... starting now! You open the book, get your sticky notes out and settle in for an intended solid two hours of focused studying.

Ping!

A text from your friend about weekend plans. You glance at it quickly – 'just to make sure it's not urgent' – and somehow find yourself scrolling through Instagram.

Twenty minutes later, you snap back to awareness. 'Okay, focus time! For real now!'

You read the first paragraph of Chapter 7. Your stomach rumbles. When did you last eat? You realize you're quite hungry, and you can't concentrate when you're hungry, so you should probably grab a snack first.

In the kitchen, you run into your flatmate who's stressed about their chemistry assignment. You spend fifteen minutes helping them figure out molecular structures because you're a good friend. Back to your room. Chapter 7, paragraph 1. Again.

Your phone buzzes with a notification. It's now 10.43 pm.

You feel a familiar knot of anxiety in your stomach. The exam is in two days. You haven't finished the reading, let alone started reviewing. You flip frantically through the remaining chapters, highlighting randomly, hoping something will stick.

By 11.30 pm, you're exhausted, stressed and barely more prepared than when you started. You promise yourself you'll wake up early tomorrow to study properly.

If this is you (and it's most of us, truly), please, please, please know: you're not lazy, you're not unfocused and you're not lacking willpower.

You're experiencing an entirely predictable result of trying to study without addressing the obstacles that make focused learning nearly impossible in our hyper-connected, attention-fragmenting world.

The false narrative of willpower

Most productivity advice erroneously assumes that the main barrier to studying is not trying hard enough; a combination of lacklustre motivation and poor time management. 'Be more disciplined!' 'Set better goals!'

Discipline, goal-setting and motivation aren't the problem, though. Most students *want* to do well. They *want* to learn. They *want* to feel prepared for exams. The problem is that our modern environment has been engineered to capture and shatter our attention in ways that make sustained focus incredibly difficult.

Your phone has been intentionally programmed to be irresistible. Social media platforms employ variable reward schedules – the same psychological principles that make gambling addictive – to keep you scrolling. Your brain, evolved for a much simpler world, simply isn't equipped to resist these alluring modern attention snares without deliberate strategies.

Building on the time coherence, alignment and memory strategies from previous chapters, this chapter addresses the elephant in the room: what happens when you know what to do but can't seem to do it? How do you create the conditions for deep learning when everything around you is designed to distract?

The three categories of study stumbling blocks

Most barriers to focused studying fall into three interconnected categories:

- **Environmental friction**
  Your physical and digital environment isn't set up to support sustained attention. This includes obvious things like phone notifications and noisy spaces, but also subtler factors like poor lighting, uncomfortable seating or cluttered visual fields that tax your cognitive resources.
- **Internal friction**
  Your mind and body aren't in a state conducive to learning. This might be physical (hunger, fatigue, restlessness) or emotional (anxiety, overwhelm, boredom, loneliness). This internal static isn't something you can willpower your way through – it needs to be addressed directly.
- **Purpose friction**
  Your personally meaningful reasons for doing the work might have taken a holiday, or the connection between your current studying and your larger goals feels abstract or distant. When studying feels pointless or disconnected from what you care about, your brain naturally seeks more engaging alternatives.

Your personal distraction profile

Everyone has a unique constellation of distractions. Some people are primarily derailed by digital temptations. Others struggle more with internal restlessness or environmental pulls. Some find their focus crumbles when they're emotionally dysregulated, while others can study through almost anything except physical discomfort.

Understanding your profile helps you prepare targeted solutions rather than trying to address every possible distraction – which is impossible and exhausting.

Notice your patterns: understanding your distractibility

Before you can address distractions, the key is to understand your personal patterns. Distractions aren't random; they follow predictable pathways unique to each person's habits, environment and emotional needs.

Charting your distraction triggers

For the next few days, become a detective of your own attention. When you sit down to study and find yourself doing something else instead, take a pause, notice and reflectively make note of what gets you off track.

Notice what pulled you away.

Was it a notification, a wandering thought, a physical discomfort or an emotional state? Was it something external (noise, interruption) or internal (boredom, anxiety, hunger)?

Notice when you are most distractible.

Are there particular times of day when your focus feels more fragile? Do distractions hit harder when you're tired, stressed or dealing with other life pressures?

Notice what you are frequently taken off course from.

Is it a specific class or subject, a recurring academic task like reading or problem-solving or a type of assignment that continually finds you disengaged?

Notice what the distraction provides.

Distractions often meet legitimate needs – social connection, mental stimulation, emotional regulation or physical comfort. Understanding what your distractions do for you helps you find better ways to meet those needs.

Notice how you feel afterward.

Guilty? Frustrated? Relieved? Satisfied? These emotions provide important information about whether the distraction served a helpful purpose or just derailed your goals.

Try this today: the clear-the-path framework

Based on attention research and real student experiences, let's try a stepping sideways, utterly different, systematic approach to removing obstacles that derail your studying.

Phase 1: Environmental supports

Create physical and digital environments that support rather than undermine your focus.

Digital boundaries

Put your phone in another room, not just face-down on your desk. Use website blockers, aeroplane mode and even consider turning your phone off during study sessions. At a minimum, turn off all non-essential notifications. Create a separate user account on your computer for studying, without access to social media or entertainment sites. Your environment should make focused behavior easier and distracted behavior harder. Don't rely on willpower to resist a phone within arm's reach.

Physical setup

Choose a study location that signals 'work mode' to your brain. This might be a specific chair, a library cubicle or even just facing a different direction at your desk. Ensure good lighting, comfortable temperature and minimal visual distractions.

In-between routines

Create a brief routine that helps your brain shift into study mode. This might be making a cup of tea, doing five minutes of breathing exercises or writing down your study intention. These kinds of mini-routines for in-between moments help bridge the gap between 'regular life' and 'focused work'.

Phase 2: Internal preparation

Address the internal conditions that interfere with sustained attention.

Physical check-in

Before you sit down to study, honestly assess: *Am I hungry? Thirsty? Tired? Do I need to move my body?* Addressing basic physical needs prevents them from becoming distractions later.

Emotional check-in

Notice your emotional state without judgement: *Am I feeling anxious? Stressed? Bored? Lonely?* These feelings won't disappear through willpower but acknowledging them helps you decide how best to proceed.

Energy check-in

Align your study tasks with your current energy level. If you're feeling sharp and alert, tackle challenging new material. If you're tired but not completely depleted, review familiar content or do practice problems.

Cognitive load check-in

Before starting, clarify exactly what you want to accomplish in this study session. Vague goals ('study sociology') create cognitive load as you constantly decide what to do next. Specific goals ('complete practice problems 1–15 in Chapter 6') free up mental energy for actual learning.

Phase 3: Sustainable focus systems

Build study sessions that work with your brain's natural rhythms.

The 45–15 Method

Study in forty-five-minute focused blocks followed by fifteen-minute complete breaks. This respects your brain's natural attention span and prevents the fatigue that leads to seeking out distractions for relief.

Active breaks

During breaks, do something that genuinely restores your mental energy. Move your body, step outside, have a genuine conversation. Avoid activities that provide stimulation without restoration, like sitting in the same place, or bouncing around social media.

Productive procrastination

When you notice yourself avoiding a particular task, ask, 'What am I procrastinating on, and what am I procrastinating with?' Sometimes productive procrastination – doing a different study task when you can't face the main one – is better than abandoning studying altogether.

The two-minute rule

When you notice yourself getting distracted, commit to just two ... more ... minutes of focused work before allowing the distraction. Often, this brief recommitment is enough to regain momentum and strengthens our stick-to-itiveness capacity.

Attention anchors

Develop simple techniques for returning your attention when it wanders. This might be taking three deep breaths, reading the last paragraph out loud or writing one sentence summarizing what you just studied.

Phase 4: Purpose (re)connection

Strengthen the connection between your studying and what you genuinely care about.

Personal relevance

Before each study session, spend one minute identifying how this material connects to something you care about. *How might it be useful in your life? How does it relate to your goals or interests?*

Learning for its own sake

Sometimes the connection is simply the joy of understanding something new. Give yourself the 'yes' you need to be curious about the material rather than just trying to get through it.

Future self-visualization

Regularly remind yourself of who you're becoming through your education and how your current studying serves that larger vision.

Student voices

Cameron: A third-year engineering student, Cameron, felt constantly derailed by his phone during study sessions. 'I would put it face-down and promise not to look, but I'd still reach for it automatically every few minutes.' Cameron tried the environmental architecture approach, literally putting his phone in his car during study sessions. 'The first few days were weird – I kept reaching for it and feeling anxious when it wasn't there. But after a week, something shifted. My brain stopped expecting the phone to be available, and I could actually concentrate for longer than five minutes.'

Priya: Priya struggled with what she called 'fake studying' – sitting at her desk with books open but absorbing nothing. 'I would spend hours "studying" but feel like nothing was going in.' When Priya started paying attention to her internal state before studying, she realized she was trying to study when anxious about other life issues. 'I learned that if I'm really worried about something, I need to address that first – either by problem-solving or just acknowledging the worry – before I can focus on studying.'

MD: MD discovered that his biggest distraction wasn't digital; it was his own restless energy. 'I'm someone who needs to move. Trying to sit still for hours was torture.'

MD redesigned his study approach around movement. 'I pace while reading, do flashcards while walking and take frequent standing and jumping-jack breaks. Some people thought it was weird, but my focus improved dramatically when I stopped fighting my need to move.'

→ **Key insight:** Real, lasting learning happens through actively pulling information from memory, even imperfectly, rather than passive re-reading. Strategic rest, ongoing movement and reconnecting to purpose between sessions are essential for memory consolidation. It's the gaps between studying, not the cramming marathons, where your brain solidifies and strengthens what you've learned.

A new way with distractions

Traditional advice treats distractions like character flaws to be overcome through discipline and willpower. But distractions aren't moral failings; they're predictable responses to environmental and internal conditions that don't support sustained focus.

This new way recognizes that your brain is doing exactly what it evolved to do: scan for stimulation, seek social connection, avoid discomfort and conserve energy for important tasks. The problem isn't your brain, and it most certainly isn't *you*; it's a mismatch between your environment and your goals.

When you understand that distractions serve purposes – like managing emotions, meeting needs and providing stimulation – you can address those underlying needs more effectively rather than just trying to suppress the symptoms.

As always, some idealized, 'perfect' focus isn't the goal; *sustainable* focus is. Some days your attention will be scattered, and that's human. The aim is to create conditions where focused learning is much more likely.

The obstacles that get in the way of learning aren't roadblocks; think of them as information. They tell you what needs attention, what needs adjustment and what needs care. When you learn to clear the path skilfully, studying becomes not just more effective, but more enjoyable and sustainable.

Dig deeper: the science of attention and distraction

Understanding how attention works – and why it's so easily hijacked – can help you design more effective strategies for protecting your focus.

Essential reading

Johann Hari's *Stolen Focus* (2022) investigates why we can't pay attention anymore, revealing how technology companies deliberately engineer addiction into their products. His exploration of 'surveillance capitalism' shows how our attention has become a commodity to be harvested and sold.

Key research

- The Fantasy of Multitasking

  What we call multitasking is actually rapid task-switching, and each switch carries a cognitive cost. Research by Sophie Leroy (2009) demonstrates that when you switch from Task A to Task B, part of your attention remains stuck on Task A, reducing your cognitive capacity for Task B.

- The Neuroscience of Willpower

  Roy Baumeister and others show that willpower operates like a muscle – it can be strengthened with practice, but it also gets fatigued with use (Baumeister et al. 1998). This explains why trying to resist distractions through sheer force of will becomes harder throughout the day.

- The Default Mode Network

  Marcus Raichle's research on the brain's default mode network reveals that our minds naturally wander when not actively focused on a task (Raichle et al. 2001). This isn't a character flaw; it's how brains work. The key is learning to work *with* this tendency rather than fighting it.

- The State of Flow

  Mihaly Csikszentmihalyi's (1990) research on flow states shows that deep focus is most achievable when tasks are appropriately challenging (not too easy, not too hard) and when we have clear goals and immediate feedback.

References

Baumeister, R.F., Bratslavsky, E., Muraven, M. and Tice, D.M. (1998) 'Ego depletion: Is the active self a limited resource?', *Journal of Personality and Social Psychology*, 74(5), pp. 1252–1265.

Csikszentmihalyi, M. (1990) *Flow: The Psychology of Optimal Experience*. New York: Harper & Row.

Hari, J. (2022) *Stolen Focus: Why You Can't Pay Attention – and How to Think Deeply Again*. New York: Crown.

Leroy, S. (2009) 'Why is it so hard to do my work? The challenge of attention residue when switching between work tasks', *Organizational Behavior and Human Decision Processes*, 109(2), pp. 168–181.

Raichle, M.E., MacLeod, A.M., Snyder, A.Z., Powers, W.J., Gusnard, D.A. and Shulman, G.L. (2001) 'A default mode of brain function', *Proceedings of the National Academy of Sciences*, 98(2), pp. 676–682.

CHAPTER 7

HOW TO WORK WITH OTHERS (SO YOU CAN SMOOTHLY ENGAGE IN GROUP WORK AND COLLABORATIVE PROJECTS)

Imagine walking into one of your classes on Monday morning and hearing this announcement: 'Next week's exam will be conducted in groups of four. You'll solve problems together, discuss concepts aloud and submit one set of answers that represents your collective understanding.'

How does that land for you? Relief that you won't face those intimidating equations alone? Anxiety about being grouped with people who might slow you down? Excitement about the possibility of deeper learning through discussion?

Now imagine this: your instructor continues, 'Research shows that students who prepare for individual exams in study groups not only perform better on tests but retain information longer, develop stronger critical thinking skills and report feeling more connected to their learning community.'

What if the secret to academic success wasn't found in isolated study sessions, but in the transformative work of learning alongside others?

No need to go it solo

University learning has traditionally been framed as a solitary pursuit – you against the textbook, you against the assignment, you against the clock and you against your peers to be the highest grade-earner in a course. But this narrative misses something essential: humans are social learners. We've always learned best in community – through conversation, through the productive tension of different perspectives encountering each other.

Yet most students approach group work and collaborative learning with a mixture of dread and resignation. Why? Because we've been taught to see others as competition rather than collaborators, as threats to our individual success rather than partners in collective understanding or perhaps most commonly in this go-go-go time, as impediments to our efficiency.

This chapter invites you to reimagine what it means to learn with others – not just when it's required for an assignment, but as a fundamental strategy for deeper, more joyful and more effective studying.

Collective intelligence

Building on traditional ideas about study groups as mere review sessions, Collective Intelligence asks: *what if we approached group studying not as individuals comparing notes, but as a living system where each person's understanding becomes a resource that amplifies everyone else's learning?*

Collective Intelligence isn't about dividing up the workload, although that can happen. It's about recognizing that when learners genuinely collaborate, they create something more powerful than the sum of their individual efforts – a shared mind that can hold complexity, catch blind spots and generate insights none of them could reach alone.

Think of it like a jazz ensemble. Each musician brings their own instrument and expertise, but the magic happens in the interplay – how the bass line supports the melody, how the drums create space for improvization, how listening becomes as important as playing. The music that emerges couldn't exist without each unique contribution *and* the responsive collaboration between them.

Collective Intelligence recognizes three crucial truths about group learning:

1. **Understanding is multi-dimensional.**
   The way you grasp a concept through visual mapping might unlock something for someone who's been stuck in verbal processing. Your confusion with one aspect might reveal a gap in everyone's understanding that no one else noticed. Each person's learning style, cultural lens and life experience becomes a different doorway into the material.
2. **Teaching solidifies learning.**
   When you explain something to your study group – especially when they ask questions in response that you hadn't considered – you're not just helping them. You're discovering the edges of your own understanding, filling in gaps you didn't know existed and creating memory pathways that are far stronger than solo review could build.
3. **Vulnerability accelerates growth.**
   Most students (most humans!) hide their confusion, pretending to understand until they're alone with the material. In a Collective Intelligence approach,

confusion becomes a gift to the group; your 'I don't get this part' opens space for everyone to admit what they're struggling with, leading to breakthrough moments that wouldn't happen if everyone stayed safely silent.

The landscape of shared understanding

What's most transformed my understanding of group learning, beyond any research study, is witnessing students discover their collective power.

I've watched a study group where one student's question about a minor detail unlocked the entire concept for everyone else. I've seen learners who thought they were 'bad at science' become the ones who could translate complex formulas into everyday analogies that made everything click. I've observed groups develop their own languages – inside jokes that were sophisticated mnemonics, silly drawings that captured essential concepts, shared metaphors that made abstract ideas concrete.

They weren't just studying together; they were building a collective brain, a shared intelligence that belonged to all of them and none of them simultaneously.

Collective Intelligence attends to several elements that traditional study groups often miss:

- **Cognitive diversity**
  Different ways of thinking aren't obstacles to overcome but resources to leverage. The detail-oriented processor, the big-picture thinker, the practical applicator, the theoretical wonderer: each lens and viewpoint and way of communicating reveal something essential.
- **Emotional reciprocity**
  Supporting someone through their statistics anxiety while they help you navigate essay structure creates bonds that make learning feel less isolating and more sustainable.
- **Cultural wealth**
  The examples, stories and frameworks each person brings from their own background enrich everyone's understanding and make knowledge more three-dimensional.
- **Mistake celebration**
  Errors become teaching moments for the whole group, removing any hidden shame and turning confusion into collective clarity.
- **Energy exchange**
  When one person is depleted, others can carry the momentum; when someone has an insight burst, that energy lifts everyone.

When you engage in Collective Intelligence, you're not just managing study time, nor is it just a case of hyper-efficient material consolidation; you're participating in a living system of mutual support where everyone's learning – including struggles – becomes a resource for collective growth.

Take a moment: plotting your collaborative learning history

Before we dive into creating effective study groups and collaborative approaches, let's explore your current relationship with learning alongside others. Take time to consider the *what* and *why* of your feelings about working with others.

- What's your group work history?

  Think back through your educational experiences with group work and collaborative learning. *What patterns do you notice about the joys and frustrations you feel in working with others? What are your preferences, strengths and irritations?*

- What have your go-to study strategies been in terms of interacting with others?

  Do you typically study alone, or do you seek out others to work with, and why? When you do study with others, is it mostly social or have you found it a helpful way for test prep? What interests or discourages you from collaborative study approaches? There's no right answer (here, or anywhere in this book). It's about coming to know and name what helps and what hinders, so that you can make ever more intentional choices about when and how to engage others in your academic work.

- How do you communicate when under pressure?

  Making plans with others involves deadlines, differing opinions and the stress of shared responsibility. All of this occurs under the umbrella of a nearing midterm or final. *How do you typically communicate when you're feeling pressure? Do you become more directive, more withdrawn, more accommodating? What happens to your communication style when you disagree with someone or when you feel your standards aren't being met?* Understanding your stress communication patterns helps you prepare for the inevitable moments of tension in collaborative work and gives you language to share with others about how you function under pressure.

Try this today: building effective study groups

The difference between study groups that flourish and those that flounder often comes down to intentional design. Here are frameworks for creating collaborative learning experiences that support everyone's success.

The study group foundation model

Purpose clarity

Begin every study group relationship by getting explicit about why you're coming together. Are you processing readings? Working through problem sets? Reviewing for exams? Different purposes require different structures and approaches.

Relationship investment

Start with connection rather than content. Share your learning goals, study preferences, stress patterns and what you hope to contribute and receive from the group. This foundation of knowing each other makes everything else more effective.

Structure and tempo

Effective study groups have predictable structures. This might include rotating facilitation, consistent start and end times, agreed-upon preparation expectations and clear protocols for how you'll engage with material together.

Assessment and adaptation

Build in regular check-ins about how the group is functioning. What's working well? What could be adjusted? These conversations prevent small frustrations from becoming group-ending conflicts.

The collaborative study session flow

Rather than just 'studying together', try this structure for active collaborative learning:

- **Check-In (10 minutes)**

  Share what you've prepared, what you're struggling with and what you're hoping to accomplish. Beginning as humans makes study sessions more productive.

- **Individual processing (15–20 minutes)**

  Even in collaborative learning, individual thinking time is essential. Work quietly on readings, problems or review materials while sharing the same space.

- **Collective engagement (30–45 minutes)**

  This is where the magic happens. Share insights, ask each other questions, explain concepts to each other, work through problems together, debate different interpretations.

- **Integration and next steps (10 minutes)**

  What did you learn from working together that you wouldn't have discovered alone? What will you continue exploring individually? What preparation will support your next group session?

The study partnership approach

Not ready, not interested or not available for a full group? Study *partnerships* can be incredibly effective and less complex to coordinate.

- **The teaching partnership**

  Take turns explaining concepts to each other. Research shows that teaching others is one of the most effective ways to strengthen your own understanding.

- **The question partnership**

  Come prepared with questions about the material and spend your time together working through each other's confusion rather than reviewing what you already understand.

- **The accountability partnership**

  Focus on supporting each other's study habits and goals rather than engaging directly with academic content.

- **The different strengths partnership**

  Partner with someone whose academic strengths complement yours – perhaps you're strong in analysis and they excel at synthesis.

Navigating common collaborative learning challenges

- **Different paces**

  Some people need more time to process, others think quickly out loud. Create structures that honour both – quiet thinking time before discussion or rotating between explanation and processing moments.

- **Different preparation levels**

  Rather than excluding less-prepared members, use these differences productively. Those who are caught up benefit from explaining concepts, while those behind can ask questions that deepen everyone's understanding.

- **Scheduling conflicts**

  Instead of insisting everyone always meets, consider flexible formats: core group sessions, smaller subset meetings, asynchronous shared documents and rotating participation.

- **Personality conflicts**

  Focus on shared academic goals rather than personal compatibility. You don't need to be friends to learn effectively together, but you do need mutual respect and clear communication.

Student voices

Maria: Maria dreaded her organic chemistry course until she reluctantly joined a study group after failing her first exam. 'I was convinced I was too behind to contribute anything', she says. 'But explaining basic concepts to newer students actually helped me understand them more deeply.' Maria's group developed a teaching rotation where each member became the expert on different reaction mechanisms. 'By the end of the semester, I wasn't just passing – I was actually excited about chemistry. And I had a study community that carried me through the rest of my pre-med courses.'

David: As an international student, David initially struggled to participate in class discussions and group projects. 'In my home country, we weren't expected to challenge professors or share opinions,' he explains. David's study group became a safe space to practise academic conversation. 'We realized we each had different strengths – I was strong in making connections between ideas, Cici was excellent at synthesis and Blake was strong in mathematical reasoning. Instead of trying to be the same, we learned to be complementary.'

Nadia: Nadia struggled with procrastination and isolation in her online degree programme. 'Everything felt optional and disconnected.' She started a virtual study group with classmates from across the country. 'We'd have cameras on while we worked on assignments, take breaks together and hold each other accountable for reading deadlines. Having people who knew what I was working on and cared whether I showed up completely changed my relationship with school.'

→ **Key insight:** True collaborative learning happens when individual learners stretch out of their comfort zone and into study groups, and when they in turn move beyond comparing notes to create a shared intelligence system, where each person's unique understanding, confusion and perspective become a resource that amplifies *everyone's* learning – making the group collectively smarter than any individual could be alone.

A new way with collaborative learning

Working with others in academic contexts isn't just about improving your grades. It's about recognizing that learning is fundamentally social, that your understanding deepens when tested and refined through interaction with others and that the challenges of collaborative work are opportunities to develop skills you'll use throughout your life.

In our increasingly connected world, the ability to learn alongside people who are different from you, to navigate disagreement constructively and to contribute your unique strengths to collective goals isn't just helpful; it's essential.

The invitation is simple: instead of seeing others as obstacles to your academic success, begin to see them as partners in the adventure of learning. Instead of protecting your knowledge, practise sharing it generously. Instead of avoiding the challenges of working across difference, lean into them as opportunities for growth.

When you do, you'll discover that learning with others isn't a compromise of your individual academic journey – it's an expansion of what becomes possible when we study, grow and succeed together.

Dig deeper: the science behind collaborative learning

Essential reading

The Art of Gathering (2018) by Priya Parker is written for professional facilitators, but the principles for creating purposeful gatherings translate well to study groups. She offers concrete strategies for establishing group norms and creating spaces where everyone can contribute meaningfully.

James Surowiecki's *The Wisdom of Crowds* (2004) explores collective intelligence. He shows how groups can make remarkably smart decisions under the right conditions. This helps explain why diverse study groups often outperform individual learners.

Podcast

The Cult of Pedagogy by Jennifer Gonzalez – 'Making Cooperative Learning Work Better' (3 February 2020) – Gonzalez explores why traditional group work often fails and shares research-backed strategies for structuring collaborative learning that ensures meaningful participation from all members. She provides practical frameworks for accountability and role distribution that prevent common pitfalls.

TED Talk

Harvard Business School professor Linda Hill's 'How to manage for collective creativity' (2014) explores how organizations like Pixar foster innovation through 'creative abrasion' – the productive collision of diverse perspectives. Her insights about managing different viewpoints apply directly to study groups navigating complex material together.

References

Gonzalez, J. (2020) 'Making cooperative learning work better', *Cult of Pedagogy*, 3 February. Available at: https://www.cultofpedagogy.com/making-cooperative-learning-work-better/

Hill, L. (2014) 'How to manage for collective creativity' [Video]. TED Conferences. Available at: https://www.ted.com/talks/linda_hill_how_to_manage_for_collective_creativity (accessed 1 October 2025).

Parker, P. (2018) *The Art of Gathering: How We meet and Why It Matters*. New York: Riverhead Books.

Surowiecki, J. (2004) *The Wisdom of Crowds: Why the Many Are Smarter than the Few*. New York: Doubleday.

CHAPTER 8

WHAT GOES INTO A TOP GRADE (SO YOU CAN RAISE THAT AVERAGE)

'Doing well.'

When you read that, what does that mean to you?

I'm not asking about your grade or whether you made the dean's List. I'm not asking if your parents are proud or if you got into your programme of choice. I'm not asking whether you study for three hours or thirteen.

Rather, I want you to contemplate what feelings arise when you think about academic success. What sensations come up when your marks come in? What does it mean to you when someone says, 'You'd do better if you just worked a little harder'? Most of all, what would 'true success' feel like in your body, not just on your transcript?

If you feel a tightness in your chest, a weight on your shoulders or a nagging sense that you're never doing quite enough, this chapter is for you.

The universal success struggle

Every semester, I watch the same pattern unfold. Students arrive at my office, exhausted and frustrated, saying some version of, 'I'm studying harder than ever, but my grades aren't improving'. They've tried *everything* – longer hours, more highlighters, endless flashcards, pulling all-nighters before exams. They're doing what they've been told: working ... harder.

But 'work harder' is perhaps the most useless advice in the academic world. It's like telling someone who's lost to 'just find their way'. What does 'harder' even mean? More hours? More intensity? More *suffering*?

I see students interpreting 'work harder' as 'sacrifice more', like the second-year student who hasn't seen friends in weeks because they're 'too busy studying'. There's the fourth-year who's developed chronic headaches from lack of sleep but pushes through because 'that's what it takes'. And there's the master's student who tells me, with a strange mix of pride and despair, 'I haven't taken a real break in months'.

What troubles me most is how we've normalized this suffering. As if exhaustion were a badge of honour. As if depleting ourselves were the price of admission to academic success.

Building on balance

You've now learned how to manage time without losing yourself, how to align your energy with your tasks and how to heal time anxiety by honouring what matters to you. Yet even with all these strategies in place, there's often a lingering question: but how do I *actually* go about improving my grades?

This chapter reveals what truly drives academic performance – and it's *not* about studying until your eyes blur or memorizing until your brain hurts – it's about understanding the hidden curriculum of academic success; the variables that truly matter but rarely get discussed in study skills workshops.

The five truths about top grades

1. **Rest is not optional.**
   Your brain consolidates learning during sleep. Not during another hour of reviewing. Not during that fifth cup of coffee. During actual, restorative sleep. Students who sleep seven to nine hours consistently outperform those who 'power through' on four to five hours, even when the sleep-deprived group studies twice as many hours (Walker 2017).
2. **Stress blocks learning.**
   When you're in chronic stress, your brain literally cannot form new memories effectively. The stress hormone cortisol interferes with the hippocampus, your brain's memory centre. So that panicked, jaw-clenched studying? It's not just unpleasant – it's counterproductive.
3. **Connection enhances performance.**
   Students who feel they belong – in their programme, in their classes, in their study groups – consistently perform better than isolated students, regardless of prior academic preparation. Belonging isn't a nice-to-have; it's a biological need that directly impacts cognitive function.
4. **Movement makes you smarter.**
   Regular physical activity improves executive function, memory and processing speed. A twenty-minute walk can boost performance on cognitive tasks more than an extra twenty minutes of studying.

5 **Pendulation powers learning.**
Your brain needs oscillation between focus and diffusion, effort and ease, engagement and rest. Just like muscles grow during recovery, not just during exercise, your brain integrates learning during downtime.

Success seducers

For the next week, notice which of these beliefs creep up in your academic life:

'If I'm not stressed, I'm not working hard enough'

- 'Taking breaks is wasting time'
- 'Sleep is for after exams'
- 'Asking for help means I'm not smart enough'
- 'Good students don't need downtime'
- 'If I'm enjoying myself, I must not be learning'

These seductive, wildly untrue stories are so pervasive in academic culture that we rarely question them.

But what if everything you've been told about academic success ... is the opposite?

The pendulation principle

At the heart of sustainable academic success is what trauma therapist Peter Levine calls 'pendulation'. Think of it as the natural rhythm between activation and settling, effort and ease, expansion and contraction (Levine 1997).

Your nervous system isn't designed for constant activation. We're not meant to be stuck in a loop of go-go-go, push-push-push, all the time. We're designed to *oscillate*. When we override this natural rhythm – pushing through exhaustion, ignoring our need for rest – we don't become more productive. We become less capable.

Think about how a muscle grows. Not during the workout, but during recovery. Your brain works the same way. The studying creates neural activation; the rest allows for integration and consolidation.

So, when you take that walk after studying, you're not 'wasting time'; you're allowing your brain to integrate what you've learned. When you sleep instead of pulling an all-nighter, you're literally allowing your brain to convert short-term memories into long-term learning.

Get strategic about stress

Pang's (2016) research reveals head-spinning and heart-healing insights about peak performers that we can directly apply to academic work.

Morning routines matter

- They protected mornings for their most important cognitive work
- They didn't start with email or reactive tasks
- They worked in focused blocks, not scattered fragments

Walks are work

- Darwin took several walks daily and credited them with his best insights
- Walking meetings were common among innovative thinkers
- Movement literally helps your brain process information

Naps are needed

- A twenty-minute nap can restore cognitive function better than caffeine
- Many peak performers had regular nap schedules
- Rest during the day improves nighttime sleep quality

Hobbies help

- Having interests outside your field improves performance within it
- Creative hobbies enhance problem-solving abilities
- Play stimulates brain regions involved in innovation

Boundaries build success

- Clear stop times prevent diminishing returns
- Protecting downtime improves next-day performance
- Saying no to overcommitment enables saying yes to excellence

Notice your patterns: making sense of your relationship with 'success'

Before we explore new strategies, let's uncover what conditions genuinely help you thrive academically. And I don't mean what you think *should* work, but what actually does.

Mapping your success conditions

Bring to mind two contrasting academic experiences:

Experience A: A time when you performed well (however *you* personally define that, like a good mark, understanding something complex or completing something you're proud of).

- What were the circumstances? Were you sleeping regularly? Eating properly? Studying with others or alone?
- How did you feel during the work itself? Energized or depleted? Calm or anxious?
- What made this possible?

Experience B: A time when you worked incredibly hard but results disappointed you.

- What was different about your circumstances?
- How did the effort feel in your body? Sustainable or overwhelmed and frantic?
- What got in the way?

Now, compare them: What patterns emerge? Maybe you perform better with regular sleep (obvious but so so so often ignored). Maybe you need study partners for accountability. Maybe cramming creates an illusion of productivity but doesn't lead to actual learning. These patterns are goldmines of self-knowledge.

Inherited beliefs versus lived experience

Quick check: What messages about academic success did you absorb growing up?

- 'You have to sacrifice everything for good marks'
- 'Smart people don't need to work so hard'
- 'If you're not stressed, you're not trying'

Now the crucial question: Does your actual experience support these beliefs? Often what we've been told about success doesn't match what actually works for our specific brain and life.

Your body's wisdom

Your body often knows you're on the right track before your mind does:

- When genuinely learning (not just memorizing), how does your body feel? Energized? Settled? Alert?
- When you're forcing yourself through ineffective study methods, what physical signals appear? Tension? Exhaustion? That heavy, dragging feeling?

These sensations are data. They're telling you what actually supports your learning versus what just looks productive.

Why does all this self-inquiry and reflection matter? Well, the point is definitely *not* to judge your current approaches, but rather to identify what genuinely helps YOU succeed. Not your flatmate who seems to thrive on all-nighters. Not that person you sit near in lecture who highlights everything and somehow remembers it all. You.

Once you know your actual success conditions – like sleep mattering more than you admitted, needing movement breaks every hour, remembering better by teaching others – you can stop forcing yourself through strategies that don't serve you and start creating your own conditions for success.

Try this today: the restore method for sustainable success

Feel out the RESTORE approach for academic achievement that honours your humanity.

R – Rest Intentionally

- Schedule sleep as you would schedule classes (fixed, non-negotiable and unskippable)
- Take ten-minute breaks every forty-five to sixty minutes of studying
- Have one full day off per week

E – Engage Your Body

- Move for twenty to thirty minutes daily (walk, dance, stretch or be active in any way that feels good)
- Study in different positions, heights and locations
- Use movement to transition between subjects

S – Seek Connection

- Study around others, like in the library, at least once per week
- Visit office hours even when you don't have specific questions
- Join a study group or create one

T – Trust the Process

- Focus on understanding, not memorizing, by implementing learning strategies, even if they're very different from prior study habits

- Celebrate small improvements
- Remember that learning isn't linear

O – Oscillate Naturally

- Alternate between focused and diffuse work
- Switch between challenging and easier tasks
- Honour your natural energy rhythms and fluctuations

R – Reflect Regularly

- Weekly self-check-ins about what's working
- Adjust strategies based on outcomes and experiences
- Notice patterns in when you learn best

E – Embrace Enjoyment

- Find what interests you in each subject
- Make learning pleasurable when possible
- Remember that engagement enhances retention

What actually works

Sustainable Practice + Strategic Rest + Social Connection = Actual Academic Success

This isn't about lowering your standards; it's about raising your understanding of what truly goes into performance.

Fitting in time to RESTORE

Let's create your personal success map, slowly and contemplatively.

1 **Assess your current state.**
How are you really doing right now? Not just academically, but as a whole person? What does your body need? Your mind? Your spirit?

2 **Identify your restoration needs.**

What kind of rest do you most need? Physical? Mental? Social? Creative? When did you last feel truly restored?

3 Choose one RESTORE element.

Which element feels most resonant or appealing right now? What's one tiny way you could honour it today?

4 Design your experiment.

How could you test this approach for one week? What would you track? How would you know if it's working?

5 **Find your allies.**

Who in your life would support you in working more sustainably? Who models the kind of balance you want?

6 **Notice the resistance.**

What voices (internal or external) tell you this won't work? What are they protecting? What would you like to say back?

7 **Celebrate the shift.**
What small change have you already made just by considering these ideas? How can you honour this new awareness?

This is your restoration roadmap. Return to it whenever academic culture tries to convince you that suffering equals success.

Troubleshooting common obstacles

'But my programme is genuinely demanding – I can't work less!'

Fair point. Some programmes have intense workloads. But even within demanding programmes, students who build in rest and recovery consistently outperform those who don't. Can you find twenty minutes for a walk? Can you protect seven hours of sleep? Start tiny.

'I feel guilty when I'm not studying.'

This guilt is academic culture talking, not wisdom. Would you feel guilty for putting petrol in your car? For charging your phone? Rest is not a luxury – it's maintenance.

'My parents/partner/culture expects me to work constantly.'

This is real and challenging. Sometimes we need to educate those around us about what drives performance. Share the research. Show them your improved results when you work sustainably.

'I've tried resting but I just feel more anxious.'

> If you've been in chronic stress, rest can initially feel uncomfortable. Your nervous system might interpret stillness as danger. Start with 'active rest' – gentle movement, creative activities, social connection.

'What about competitive programmes where everyone works constantly?'

> Even in the most competitive environments, the students who ultimately excel are those who work sustainably. They might not advertise their rest practices but do pay attention – top performers usually have strong self-care routines.

See it in action: meet Amara

Amara arrived at university as what everyone around her called a 'perfect student'. Straight As through secondary school, captain of the debate team, volunteer tutor, scholarship recipient. She was used to success coming from outworking everyone around her.

First year went exactly as she expected. She studied constantly, rarely slept more than five hours and maintained a 3.9 GPA. She was exhausted but thought that was the price of excellence.

Second year started the same way. But by October, something shifted. She was studying more than ever but retaining less. Her grades started slipping. She'd read the same page five times and remember little. During exams, her mind would go blank.

'I just need to work harder', she told me during our first meeting, exhaustion in her eyes, hands jittery from caffeine.

The breakthrough

When I suggested she might need more rest, not more work, Amara actually laughed. But then she got a C on an exam – her first ... ever. For someone who'd built her identity on academic achievement, it was devastating. It was also the wake-up call she needed.

We started with tiny changes:

- One twenty-minute walk daily
- Stopping work by 11.00 pm
- One meal per day without textbooks
- Joining a study group

Implementing RESTORE

The first week was torture for Amara. She felt constantly guilty and worried that her grades would slip further. But by week two, something interesting happened: she noticed she understood material faster during her shortened study sessions. Her focus was sharper. Her recall was better.

We added:

- Seven hours of sleep as a minimum
- Saturday mornings off
- Regular meetings with professors
- Exercise three times a week

The results

By the end of that semester, Amara's GPA was back up to 3.8. But more importantly, she was enjoying learning again. 'I used to memorize everything through brute force,' she told me. 'Now, I actually understand it. And I have a life outside the library.'

What struck Amara most was discovering that her best academic performance came during weeks she was most balanced. When she had volleyball tournaments – forcing her to study less – she often did better on exams.

Amara still struggles with old patterns sometimes, especially during finals. But now she has evidence that sustainable practices lead to better outcomes.

'I wish someone had told me in first year that rest isn't the enemy of success,' she reflected recently. 'It's the foundation of it.'

She graduated with distinction, got into her top choice graduate programme and now mentors younger students. Her new motto? 'Rest is revolutionary.'

→ **Key insight:** Academic burnout isn't solved by working harder; it's healed by working rhythmically, *humanely*. Amara's story reveals that sustainable excellence comes not from grinding through exhaustion but from treating rest, movement and connection as essential ingredients of success, not luxuries that compromise it.

A new way with sustainable excellence

We can get stuck when we equate academic success with personal suffering. Sometimes the pressure to achieve is so intense it prevents us from achieving.

Meanwhile, we're exhausting ourselves in pursuit of grades that feel increasingly out of reach despite our ever-increasing efforts.

My hope is that your biggest takeaway is the heartfelt invitation to succeed differently – starting today – and to do so by working towards your academic goals while honouring your humanity. Your well-being, your need for rest, your desire for connection – these aren't obstacles to academic excellence. They're the very foundations that make genuine excellence possible.

What happens when you implement these changes?

First, your studying becomes more effective, not less. A rested brain actually *retains* information. A calm nervous system can access what you've learned during exams.

Second, you stop resenting your academic work. When you know you've protected time for lunch with friends, your evening study session becomes more focused.

Third, you start seeing possibilities everywhere. When you're not exhausted, you notice connections between ideas. You have energy for insights. You remember why you chose your field.

Students report unexpected benefits:

- Understanding concepts instead of just memorizing them
- Anxiety during exams almost disappearing
- Looking forward to classes again
- Sleeping through the night for the first time in years
- Better relationships because they're not always stressed
- No longer getting sick every exam period
- Energy for extracurriculars and volunteer work
- Creativity returning

There will be moments when choosing rest over one more hour of studying feels impossible. When everyone around you is pulling all-nighters and you're going to bed at 11.00 pm. When your inner critic screams that you're not doing enough.

That's exactly when this approach matters most.

On overwhelming days, make your rest even more deliberate. Instead of skipping your walk, make it shorter but still take it. Instead of cancelling dinner with friends, set a timer and enjoy even thirty minutes of connection. Instead of abandoning all self-care, choose just one small act of kindness towards yourself.

The culture won't change overnight. Your peers might not understand. Your family might worry. But your grades will tell a different story. Your well-being will tell a different story. Your ability to sustain this pace through your entire degree – and beyond – will tell the *real* story.

This isn't about lowering standards or caring less about achievement. It's about understanding what achievement truly requires: a brain that functions well, a body that's resourced, a spirit that remembers why you're here.

You're not just learning course material. You're learning how to be a human who does challenging cognitive work sustainably. And that might be the most important lesson of all.

Remember, students getting top grades aren't necessarily the ones studying longest or suffering most. They're often the ones who've figured out how to work with their brains; who've learned that rest is productive, connection is powerful and joy isn't the enemy of achievement.

Your academic success doesn't require sacrificing your well-being. In fact, it requires prioritizing it.

Dig deeper: resources for sustainable academic success

Essential reading

Alex Soojung-Kim Pang, a Silicon Valley consultant turned rest researcher, makes a revolutionary argument in *Rest: Why You Get More Done When You Work Less* (2016): rest isn't the absence of work; it's work's partner. He documents the daily routines of incredibly productive people throughout history – Darwin, Dickens, Angelou and contemporary Nobel Prize winners – and the pattern is striking. Each worked intensely for about four to five focused hours a day, then spent the rest of their time walking, napping, pursuing hobbies or socializing. Our 'non-work' hours aren't empty; Pang explains that this is when we're integrating, connecting and creating. Pang introduces the concept of 'deliberate rest,' not just collapsing in exhaustion but actively engaging in restorative activities that complement intense cognitive work.

Tricia Hersey's *Rest Is Resistance: A Manifesto* (2022), along with her accompanying Instagram and podcast appearances. Founder of the Nap Ministry, Hersey reframes rest as a form of resistance against capitalism and white supremacy. She makes crystal clear that rest doesn't have to be 'earned,' and how crucial it is – physiologically, psychically and politically – that we lay our work and our bodies down.

References

Hersey, T. (2022) *Rest Is Resistance: A Manifesto.* New York: Little, Brown Spark.

Levine, P.A. (1997) *Waking the Tiger: Healing Trauma.* Berkeley, CA: North Atlantic Books.

Pang, A.S.K. (2016) *Rest: Why You Get More Done When You Work Less.* New York: Basic Books.

Walker, M. (2017) *Why We Sleep: Unlocking the Power of Sleep and Dreams.* New York: Scribner.

CHAPTER 9

WHAT EXAMS ARE REALLY FOR (SO IT DOESN'T FEEL POINTLESS)

It's the night before your exam. Your desk is a landscape of highlighted notes, empty mugs of tea and crumpled attempts at mind maps. Your roommate peeks in to check on you and you respond with what can only be described as a feral growl.

'Why do we even *HAVE* exams?' you mutter, staring at your notes as if they've personally betrayed you. 'What's the *POINT* of memorizing all this just to forget it next week?'

Your brain feels like an overstuffed filing cabinet, papers spilling everywhere. You're simultaneously exhausted and wired, wondering if any of this matters, if exams are just an elaborate hazing ritual designed by academics who've forgotten what it's like to be a student.

Perhaps you recognize this scenario?

That frustration you're feeling isn't because exams are meaningless. It's because no one has ever explained what they're for. We've been so focused on surviving exams that we've forgotten to ask why they exist in the first place.

It might not feel true yet, but exams truly aren't about torture, gatekeeping or proving your worth as a human being. What if they're actually doing something quite remarkable for your brain – something that no amount of passive reading or lecture-attending can accomplish?

The misperception of exams as pure evaluation

Ooh, let's go ahead and bust the biggest misperception about timed assessments right from the get-go: exams *aren't* just about measuring what you know. If that were true, we could just figure out a way to scan your brain and call it a day.

Most students (and honestly, many educators) treat exams like a one-way transaction: you studied → you perform → you get judged. End of story. But this misses what cognitive science has been showing us for decades: the act of being examined actually changes your brain in powerful ways.

Traditional thinking gets a few things wrong about exams.

Misperception 1: 'Exams just test what you already know.'

Reality: The act of retrieving information during an exam strengthens those neural pathways, making the knowledge more permanent and accessible. Testing memory by way of exams enhances learning and reduces forgetting more than other study opportunities do (Roediger and Karpicke 2006).

Misperception 2: 'Exam stress is always harmful.'

Reality: When learners are taught to reframe challenges as opportunities and channel stressful energy into things they can control, their perceived stress levels are significantly lower (Hughes et al. 2011; NCFE 2023). Some stress can enhance memory consolidation (Strack and Esteves 2015).

Misperception 3: 'Exams only measure memorization.'

Reality: Well-designed exams require synthesis, application and critical thinking – skills that become stronger through the exam process itself.

Misperception 4: 'Cramming proves exams are pointless.'

Reality: While cramming can lead to better outcomes on test day, students who space their learning tend to retain much more in the weeks, months and years after. The spacing effect shows that distributed learning leads to superior long-term retention (Yoquinto and Sarma 2020).

What do these realities come together to reveal? Exams are less like judgement day and more like going to the gym for your brain. And just like physical exercise, understanding *why* you're doing it changes everything.

Try this today: the three-phase exam training method

Phase 1: Pre-Exam training programme

Instead of languaging your experience as 'studying for the test', try phrasing it as, 'designing your training programme'.

- Build connection circuits between topics (your Strength Training Zone)
- Practise performance reps by explaining concepts aloud (your Cross-Training Circuit)
- Log your weekly gains (your Performance Tracking)
- Identify your peak training times (your Personal Training Lab)

Phase 2: Exam day as game day performance

Reframe the exam experience itself.

- Before entering, say to yourself: 'This is my chance to test my training and build stronger mental muscle'.
- When stuck, say to yourself: 'My brain is doing heavy lifting; it's building new strength right now'.
- After difficult questions, say to yourself: 'I've just identified which muscles need more work'.

Phase 3: Post-exam recovery and growth

Don't forget, the training continues after you hand in your exam.

- Celebrate the mental workout you just completed (active recovery)
- Note which areas showed real strength (successful training)
- Identify muscles that need more work (training opportunities)
- Reflect on your pacing and endurance (performance insights)

The stress-to-strength protocol

Even with this refreshed, purpose-rich mindset, exam anxiety will still rise. When it does, give this athletic reframe a try.

1. **Notice the sensation.**
   'I'm feeling my pre-game nerves. It's a sign of readiness. Of activation. Of feeling ready to go.'
2. **Reframe the meaning.**
   'This stress response is my body's pre-performance warm-up. My increased heart rate is pumping more oxygen to my brain, exactly like before a race' (NCFE 2023).
3. **Channel the energy.**
   'Like an athlete, I'll focus on what I *can* control.'

- Your breathing (like a runner before the starting signal);
- Your self-talk ('I've trained for this');
- Your game plan (start with warm-up questions that build momentum).

4 **Trust your training.**
Remember that taking the exam is like completing the workout – you're getting ever stronger, regardless of this specific exam's time or score.

The night-before game plan

Let's revisit the scenario from the beginning of this chapter, seeing it with our new mindset.

> It's the night before your exam. Your desk is a landscape of highlighted notes, empty mugs of tea and crumpled attempts at mind maps. But now you think: 'Tomorrow isn't judgement day, it's *game* day. My brain is ready to show what all this training has built. The exam will test my current fitness level and show me where to focus my next training cycle. Even the pre-game nerves I'm feeling are priming my brain for peak performance.'

It might not feel true yet, but exams truly aren't about torture, gatekeeping or proving your worth as a human being. They're inviting your brain to do something remarkable – something that no amount of passive reading or lecture-attending can accomplish.

I'd love to know: how does that feel? Any different? Any more purposeful, or less daunting, at all?

The real purposes: your learning fitness centre

After years of working with students and diving deep into learning science, I've come to see that there is worth to exams. Think of these purposes as different training zones in your personal learning fitness centre – each one strengthening essential muscles for your growth.

The memory strength training zone

Exams help move scattered knowledge into lasting knowledge.

To build lasting strength

Memory consolidation is like progressive overload in weight training – converting temporary effort into long-lasting strength. Think of new experiences as beginning to lift with light weights; then, through repeated practice over time, you establish robust muscle memory. Exams are your heavy lifting days, transforming lectures and lessons into lasting intellectual muscle and body memory.

To identify weak points and gains

Like a fitness assessment that shows which muscles need work, exams reveal where your understanding is strong and where it needs targeted training. This isn't about adjudication; it's about aligning a personalized workout plan.

To build retrieval endurance

Every time you pull information from memory during an exam, you're doing mental reps. It's like building muscle memory – the more you practise these movements, the more automatic and powerful they become.

The cross-training circuit

Exams help you develop skills for life's varied challenges.

To train under pressure

Exams are like interval training for your brain – short bursts of intense focus that prepare you for job interviews, presentations and high-stakes meetings. Many of us experience that heart-racing stress response in challenging situations (Harvard Stress & Development Lab 2024). Exams help us build stamina to channel that adrenaline productively.

To prepare for professional marathons

Many careers require certification exams – far from sprints, these are like long runs against time. University exams are marathon-training, helping you build endurance, develop pacing strategies and gain confidence for these future challenges.

To strengthen critical thinking muscles

Exams push you beyond simple recall to complex synthesis – like moving from isolated exercises to compound movements. When you're connecting ideas under time pressure, you're doing the mental equivalent of burpees – challenging but incredibly effective for overall fitness.

The performance tracking studio

Exams help you measure your gains.

To record your progress

Exams create measurable benchmarks in your learning journey – like taking progress photos or tracking your jogging times. They're not just about grades; they're about seeing your intellectual fitness improve bit by bit over time.

To encourage deep training over quick fixes

Good exams reward true fitness over shortcuts. They test your functional strength – *can you actually use what you've learned?* – rather than just your ability to temporarily cram information.

To help coaches improve the programme

Your exam performance provides crucial feedback to educators – like telling your trainer which exercises work and which don't. When many students struggle with the same concept, it signals where the training needs adjustment.

The personal training lab

Exams help you discover your own, optimal training regimen.

To develop your training schedule

Preparing for exams reveals your natural training style. Are you a consistent daily trainer or an intensive boot-camp person? Do you perform best with morning or evening sessions? This self-knowledge becomes your personalized fitness philosophy for academic work … as well as in your professional pursuits and beyond.

Take a moment: inquire into your relationship with exams

Bring to mind an exam that went surprisingly well. Not necessarily your highest grade, but one where you felt genuinely prepared and capable. *What made that experience different?*

Next, think of an exam that felt particularly stressful or difficult. Looking back, try to identify what was really happening for you. *Was it the exam content or context itself, or something else – fear of judgement, time pressure, uncertainty about expectations?*

Now, let's try a thought experiment. *If exams were genuinely about learning rather than judgement, how might you approach them differently?*

These reflections matter because how we think about exams shapes how we experience them.

Troubleshooting when exams feel really hard

Even with these new mindsets and tools, exams can be genuinely difficult. If you have test anxiety, learning differences or life circumstances that make traditional exams challenging, know that your struggles are valid. Understanding the purpose of exams doesn't erase these challenges.

But here's what it might do: it might help you advocate for accommodations that preserve the learning benefits while addressing your needs. It might help you work with support services to find approaches that work for your unique brain. At a minimum, it might simply help you feel less alone in the struggle, knowing that the difficulty isn't pointless.

Please remember, you're not being tested on who you are as a person. You're engaging in a learning process that happens to involve assessment. Your worth isn't determined by your exam performance, but your learning *can* be enhanced by engaging with exams as the complex learning tools they are.

Student voices

Indira: Indira is a second-year engineering student who *used* to experience severe exam anxiety – but no longer! 'I always saw exams as these huge threats. It felt like my entire future depended on each test,' she shares. 'When I learned about memory consolidation and retrieval practice, everything shifted. Now I think of exams as "memory workouts". I still feel nervous, but it's more like pre-game energy than debilitating fear.' Indira started using the Three-Phase Approach: 'During revision, I'd tell myself, "I'm not cramming, I'm strengthening neural pathways." It helped! My exam performance improved, but more importantly, I actually remember what I learned last term.'

Alexander: First-year psychology student, Alexander, struggled with the transition from secondary school. 'In sixth form, I could memorize everything the night before. At uni, that stopped working.' Alexander discovered that understanding the purpose of exams changed his entire approach. 'When I learned that spaced practice leads to better long-term retention than massing, I started studying differently. Little bits throughout the term built strength and confidence, slowly but surely.' The result? 'My first-year exams felt manageable instead of overwhelming. I wasn't just surviving them; I was using them to lock in my learning.'

Adaeze: A third-year literature student who reframed her relationship with exam stress, Adaeze explains how she 'used to think feeling anxious meant I wasn't prepared enough. But learning that moderate stress can *improve* memory consolidation changed everything. Now when I feel that pre-exam energy, I think "my brain is priming itself to remember this."' Her favourite discovery, she shared, was that 'exams actually help my creative connections. When I'm writing an essay under time pressure, I make links between texts I never noticed before. The constraint forces innovation.'

→ **Key insight:** When students understand the science behind exams – that they're memory consolidation events, not judgement days – everything shifts. Indira's 'memory workouts', Alexander's distributed practice, and Adaeze's reframing of stress as brain priming all reveal the same truth: exams become less threatening and more effective when you understand they're leading to stronger learning, not just a measurement of it.

A new way with exams

So, what *are* exams really for?

They're not arbitrary hurdles or outdated traditions. They're sophisticated learning events that:

- Transform temporary knowledge into lasting understanding
- Build essential life skills through practised pressure
- Create visible milestones in your growth as a learner
- Reveal your unique learning rhythms

What's crucial is that exams are *for* you. Not for ranking, not for gatekeeping, but for deepening and strengthening your learning in ways that no other academic activity quite achieves.

This doesn't mean exams are perfect. They can be improved, made more inclusive, designed more thoughtfully. But understanding their true purpose transforms them from obstacles into opportunities.

As you close this chapter and face your next exam season, you have a choice. You can continue seeing exams as necessary evils, surviving them through sheer willpower and caffeine. Or you can step into a new understanding:

Exams are memory consolidation events. They're skill-building. They're progress. They're like labs or studios where you learn the tempo, pacing, needs and beauty of your own mind.

When you sit down to your next exam, you're not just being tested on a course's content; you're actively building your brain. Every question you answer, whether correctly or incorrectly, strengthens your comprehension. Every connection you make under pressure becomes more permanent. Every moment of productive stress primes your memory for long-term storage.

The real revolution isn't in making exams easier or eliminating them entirely. It's in understanding what they're actually doing for your learning and working with that process instead of against it.

Dig deeper: the neuroscience of testing

Essential reading

Logan Fiorella and Richard E. Mayer illuminate why testing enhances rather than merely measures learning in *Learning as a Generative Activity* (2015). Through comprehensive analysis of eight learning strategies, they reveal that the cognitive work required during exams - generating answers under pressure - creates deeper, more lasting understanding than any passive review method could achieve.

Key research

- Desirable Difficulties
    - Challenges that feel hard in the moment, like exam pressure, actually enhance long-term learning by forcing your brain to work harder at encoding and retrieval (Bjork and Bjork 2011).
- Memory Consolidation
    - More than a century of research has established the fact that sleep benefits the retention of memory (Rasch and Born 2013), and exam preparation creates natural coherence and consolidation periods where your brain integrates new learning during rest.

Additional resources:

James E. Zull's *The Art of Changing the Brain* (2002) explains how testing creates physical changes in brain structure, literally rewiring your neural networks through active retrieval.

Dr Saundra Yancy McGuire's *Teach Students How to Learn* (2015) revolutionizes how we think about learning and assessment, showing students how to become active architects of their own understanding.

References

Bjork, E.L. and Bjork, R.A. (2011) 'Making things hard on yourself, but in a good way: Creating desirable difficulties to enhance learning'. *Psychology and the Real World: Essays Illustrating Fundamental Contributions to Society*. New York: Worth Publishers, pp. 56–64.

Fiorella, L. and Mayer, R.E. (2015) *Learning as a Generative Activity: Eight Learning Strategies that Promote Understanding*. Cambridge: Cambridge University Press.

Harvard Stress & Development Lab (2024) 'Positive reframing and examining the evidence'. Available at: https://sdlab.fas.harvard.edu/cognitive-reappraisal/positive-reframing-and-examining-evidence (accessed 15 September 2025).

Hughes, J.S., Gourley, M.K., Madson, L. and Blanc, K.L. (2011) 'Stress and coping activity: Reframing negative thoughts', *Teaching of Psychology*, 38(1), pp. 36–39.

McGuire, S.Y. (2015) *Teach Students How to Learn: Strategies You Can Incorporate into any Course to Improve Student Metacognition, Study Skills, and Motivation*. Sterling, VA: Stylus Publishing.

NCFE (2023) 'How educators can help learners turn exam stress into academic success'. Available at: https://www.ncfe.org.uk/exam-stress-to-academic-success/ (accessed 15 September 2025).

Rasch, B. and Born, J. (2013) 'About sleep's role in memory', *Physiological Reviews*, 93(2), pp. 681–766.

Roediger, H.L. III and Karpicke, J.D. (2006) 'The power of testing memory', *Perspectives on Psychological Science*, 1(3), pp. 181–210.

Strack, J. and Esteves, F. (2015) 'Exams? Why worry? Interpreting anxiety as facilitative and stress appraisals', *Anxiety, Stress, & Coping*, 28(2), pp. 205–214.

Yoquinto, L. and Sarma, S. (2020) 'Cramming may help for next-day exams. But for long-term memory, spacing out study is what works', *The Washington Post*, 30 November.

Zull, J.E. (2002) *The Art of Changing the Brain: Enriching the Practice of Teaching by Exploring the Biology of Learning*. Sterling, VA: Stylus Publishing.

SECTION THREE

A NEW WAY TO BE PRODUCTIVE

Assignments. Projects. Exams.

Nobody warns students that sometimes the hardest part of university isn't understanding new, complex theories or mastering difficult concepts. Sometimes the hardest part is simply … starting (yet another) new academic task. Or focusing for more than three minutes. *Or* doing any work at all when your brain feels like it's buffering on 2 per cent battery and your motivation has apparently moved out without leaving a forwarding address.

This section is about the unglamorous, everyday struggles that don't make it into university brochures. The moments when you sit at your desk, know exactly what you need to do, have all the tools to do it and yet find yourself reorganizing your bookshelf, researching the history of staplers or staring at a blank document as if it's written in a language from another dimension.

Here's what I won't do: pretend these struggles mean you're lazy or don't belong here. I won't offer you 'productivity hacks' that treat you like a malfunctioning robot that just needs better programming. I won't shame you for being human in a system that often demands you be superhuman.

Here's what I *will* do: explore why starting, focusing and working can feel so impossibly difficult sometimes. I'll unpack the hidden physics of being stuck – how overwhelm, perfectionism and exhaustion tangle up with our work until even simple tasks feel mountainous. Most importantly, I'll share gentle, practical ways to work with your humanity instead of against it.

Because truthfully, every successful student you see has days when they can't start, can't focus, can't make themselves do the work. The difference isn't that they've conquered these challenges; it's that they've learned to navigate them with compassion and creativity.

In these chapters, you'll meet students who've found their own ways through the maze of academic demands. Learners who discovered that 'starting' begins long before you actually start writing. Learners who learned that motivation isn't something you have or don't have, it's something you cultivate. Learners who realized that focus isn't about perfect attention but about gently returning when your mind wanders.

This isn't about becoming a productivity machine – (quite the opposite!) – it's about finding sustainable, human ways to engage with your work even when – *especially* when – everything feels hard. It's about shrinking overwhelming tasks until they're approachable, creating conditions where focus can flourish and building bridges between where you are (stuck, overwhelmed, possibly still in yesterday's clothes) and where you need to be.

Your struggles with starting, focusing and working aren't failures. They're information about what you need. They're invitations to develop kinder, cleverer approaches. They're proof that you're a whole human being trying to learn and grow in challenging circumstances.

So, deep breath, wherever you are in your relationship with academic work – whether you're reading this instead of starting that essay, taking a break from a focus session or trying to figure out how to climb out of an overwhelm pit – you're in the right place. These chapters are for the real you, not the idealized student you think you should be.

Ready to explore a more compassionate, more human, more doable way forward?

CHAPTER 10

HOW TO START (WHEN YOU DON'T WANT TO)

You know this already. You've felt it in your bones when you stare at a blank document, when the textbook sits unopened on your desk, when the assignment instructions feel like they're written in another language entirely. That heavy feeling? That's not laziness. That's not weakness. That's human.

Task initiation – the fancy term for 'getting started' – is genuinely one of the most challenging aspects of academic work (Pychyl 2013). If starting feels impossible sometimes, you're not broken. Your brain is doing exactly what brains do when faced with uncertainty, complexity or tasks that feel overwhelming (Steel 2007).

The starting line isn't where you think it is

Let me tell you about Marissa, a first-year student and Awakened Learning client. In her contact form when she initially reached out (timestamp 11.30 pm), she shared, 'I've been trying to start a lab report for six hours. I've reorganized my desk twice, made three cups of tea, and watched approximately forty-seven TikToks about productivity. Why can't I just START?'

In our work together, here's what Marissa discovered: she *had* started. Every time she thought about the lab report, every time she opened the document (even to immediately close it), every time she wondered how to begin, these were all part of starting. We've been taught that starting means diving straight into productive action, but that's like expecting yourself to run a marathon without stretching first (Boice 1990).

When we face a task we don't want to do, our brains often interpret it as a threat. Not a sabre-toothed-tiger threat, but a threat nonetheless. The unknown project, the complex reading, the intimidating assignment – they all activate the same systems that once kept our ancestors safe.

Understanding this helps us work with our brains instead of against them. When starting feels impossible, your brain might be saying: 'This feels unsafe because I don't know how to do it perfectly', or 'This feels too big to handle', or simply 'I need more information before I can proceed'.

Tomorrow You, starting today

Newsflash: Tomorrow You is not a superhero. Tomorrow You is just Today You with one more day of experience. Stop waiting for Tomorrow You to have magical starting powers that Today You lacks. (You don't lack anything!)

We can spend weeks telling ourselves that we'll start a particular project 'tomorrow, when we feel ready'. But we can remind ourselves,

> 'Dear Tomorrow me, I'm starting badly today so I don't have to be perfect tomorrow. You're welcome.' Write this on a Post-it note and place it on your laptop or desk.

Starting isn't binary; it's not a switch that flips from 'not started' to 'working productively'. It's more like a dimmer switch, gradually brightening. Celebrate every increase in light (Amabile and Kramer 2011).

Consider this personal manifesto (and invite personalization, refining it as you wish):

> *I am allowed to start imperfectly.*
>
> *I am allowed to start small.*
>
> *I am allowed to start in the middle.*
>
> *I am allowed to start scared.*
>
> *I am allowed to start uncertain.*
>
> *I am allowed to start badly.*
>
> *Starting imperfectly is infinitely better than not starting at all.*

You opened the document? *That's* starting.

You read the assignment instructions? *That's* starting.

You thought about it in the shower? *That's* starting.

You vented to a friend about it? *That's* starting.

You're reading this chapter? *That's* preparation to start.

And, like any skill, starting gets easier with practice.

Befriending resistance

It might surprise you to hear that resistance to starting isn't your enemy. It's information. When the mood of 'I don't want to' comes to visit, try asking it questions (Sirois and Pychyl 2013).

- What part feels hardest?
- What am I afraid might happen?
- What do I need to know before I can begin?
- What would make this feel 5 per cent easier?

One student told me about a 'Resistance Journal' they kept in which they'd write letters to their procrastination: 'Dear Resistance, I see you're visiting again about this essay on the Industrial Revolution. What's scaring you today?' This practice helped them identify patterns; their resistance was usually strongest when they didn't understand the assignment requirements clearly. Another student, in 'interviewing' their resistance, came to see that it wasn't the *whole* project that gave them pause; it was writing the first sentences of essays – which is often the case for learners, that there's one aspect in particular that feels harder, and thus more dreaded, than the rest. Get to know it!

Multiple doorways in

The beauty of task initiation is that there's no one 'right' way to start. Think of beginning a task like entering a building. Sure, there's a front door, but there are also side entrances, back doors, windows you could climb through (metaphorically speaking), and sometimes even secret passages.

The tiny door

A breakthrough can come just by crafting the title page. That's it. Name, course code, date. How so? Well, something magical can happen when we do that. Once the document exists with something in it, writing one sentence didn't feel so monumental. That made it easier to write a second sentence. The tiny door led them inside (Fogg 2020).

Challenge: Choose the absolute smallest piece of your task. Not the introduction; think *smaller*.

- Create and name the document
- Write your name at the top
- Copy and paste the assignment instructions
- Find one source (just one!)
- Write the worst possible first sentence (you'll fix it later)

The side quest door

Another way in is to start with a 'side quest' first. Instead of diving into an essay, spend 10 minutes creating a playlist that *felt* like the essay topic. Choosing songs, for example, for a post-writing walk break – songs that match the vibe of, for instance, constitutional amendments – might sound silly, but it gets our brain thinking about whatever topic we're writing about without the pressure of 'real' work. It's not about positive thinking our way in (Oettingen 2014), but about setting the tone.

Challenge: Choose the most tangential, creative, or goofy way to start.

- Make a mood board for your project
- Text a friend one interesting fact about your topic
- Draw a terrible diagram of your main idea
- Find or curate the perfect study spot for this specific task
- Choose a special pen or font just for this project

The Messy Middle Door

Shhhh, it's a little-known secret, but you don't have to start at the beginning. If you can't write your introduction (yet), don't. Start, instead, by brain-dumping everything you know about, say coral bleaching right in the *midpoint* of your document. No structure, no sentences even, just ideas scattered like puzzle pieces. Starting in the centre removes the pressure of 'getting it right' right off the top (Lamott 1994).

Challenge: Begin with a middle-starting strategy.

- Write the part you're most excited about first
- Start with examples instead of explanations
- Begin with what you already know
- Create a conversation with yourself about the topic
- Skip the interior ... and begin with the conclusion first (wild, but it works!)

The body double door

Sometimes we need company to cross the threshold. Students often discover that it's easier to start just about any assignment with a study buddy – whether sitting side-by-side at the library or in a dorm room together, or on a video call with cameras on, audio off, working in parallel. The co-regulating effect of shared presence with another person attempting their own mountain can make yours feel more climbable (hooks 1994).

Challenge: Find your body double.

- Virtual study rooms with friends
- Library study spaces (strangers count!)
- YouTube 'study with me' videos
- Asking someone to sit nearby while you work
- Productivity apps with virtual co-working spaces

The timer door

Try 'the ten-minute lie' by telling yourself, 'I only have to work on this for ten minutes, then I can stop'. Setting a timer can make starting feel less like committing to the full work session. Interestingly, learners rarely stop at ten minutes; just knowing you *could* stop can make all the difference. Devote those ten minutes to a single academic task (Fiore, 2007).

Challenge: Experiment with three different time variations this week.

- The five-minute sprint (even shorter!)
- The lo-fi YouTube timer (ambient beats combined with a countdown)
- The deadline timer (work until your next meal)
- The song timer (work for exactly three songs)
- The random timer (set a timer without looking for anywhere between seven to twenty-three minutes)

Troubleshooting: when starting feels like climbing Everest

Some days, every strategy will feel impossible. On those days, I want you to remember that you're not done for. What you might be, however, is *depleted*. Sometimes, when starting feels impossible, it's because you need:

- Rest (real rest, not scrolling rest)
- Food (brains need fuel)
- Movement (even a two-minute dance break)
- Connection (text someone who makes you smile)
- Permission to do it imperfectly (micro progress beats no progress)

Spend time creating a starting ritual – like a series of small actions that signal your intention to the brain that it's time to begin (Gollwitzer and Sheeran 2006):

1. Make a specific beverage (like chai or matcha).
2. Light a candle or turn on a specific lamp.
3. Put on your 'focusing glasses' (a metaphor, not an actual prescription).
4. Write the date at the top of your document.
5. Set your preferred timer.
6. Begin.

Let this ritual become the doorway when you've exhausted every other way in.

See it in action: meet Isaiah

Isaiah was a third-year psychology student who hadn't opened his statistics textbook in six weeks. 'Every time I look at it, my brain just ... leaves,' he told me during our first session. 'I've reorganized my entire room three times. I've colour-coded all my other notes. I've even started learning Portuguese on Duolingo. Anything but stats.'

The assignment that had him stuck at starting? A data analysis project worth 30 per cent of his grade, due in ten days.

The breakthrough

Together, we discovered Isaiah's resistance pattern: he was a perfectionist who couldn't start unless he understood everything completely. Statistics felt like a foreign language, and his brain interpreted 'I don't understand this perfectly' as 'I can't start at all'.

His starting attempts looked like this:

- Open textbook to Chapter 1 (he needed Chapter 8)
- Decide he should review everything first
- Feel overwhelmed by how much he didn't remember
- Close textbook
- Promise to try again 'when his mind was fresher'

Isaiah's starting toolkit in practice

Isaiah needed the Messy Middle Door. Instead of starting with understanding, we started with doing. He opened a document and typed, 'Things I sort of maybe know about t-tests'. Then, 'Things that confuse me about t-tests'. Then, 'Questions I'm embarrassed to ask about t-tests'.

No structure. No correctness. Just brain-dumping his confusion onto the page.

'This doesn't feel like real work,' Isaiah said after fifteen minutes of typing.

'Good,' I replied. 'Real work is what's been stopping you for six weeks.'

After three days of 'fake work' (his term), Isaiah had accidentally created a twelve-page document of questions, half-remembered concepts and copied formulas he didn't understand. On day four, he took this mess to office hours.

'My professor was thrilled,' Isaiah reported back, amazed. 'She said my questions showed I was thinking deeply about the material. She didn't care that I was confused – she cared that I'd started engaging.'

With his professor's guidance, Isaiah turned his 'confusion document' into an outline. The outline became a rough draft. The rough draft became a submitted project that earned him a B+.

The results

Isaiah graduated last year and is now in graduate school. He sent me this message recently:

> I still use the Messy Middle Door for everything. Thesis proposal? Started by writing 'Things that interest me about memory.' Grant application? Began with 'Why I think this research matters (maybe?).' I've learned that starting 'badly' isn't just okay; it's often the only way I can start at all. My adviser calls it 'productive confusion', but I still call it the Messy Middle Door. It's saved my academic career.

His three rules for starting:

1 Confusion is information, not failure.
2 Writing badly about something beats thinking perfectly about nothing.
3 Tomorrow You will thank Today You for any start.

Isaiah's story reminds us that the 'right' way to start is the way that gets you started. Even if that means beginning with a document titled 'Things I Don't Understand About This Assignment (A Very Long List)'.

→ **Key insight:** The 'right' way to start is whatever gets you started, even if that means beginning with a document confessing everything you don't understand. Isaiah's breakthrough came not from conquering his confusion but from documenting it, transforming 'I don't understand this perfectly' from a barrier into a doorway and discovering that productive confusion is often more valuable than perfect preparation.

The permission slip collection

Consider this as your official compilation of permission slips, available whenever you need.

- ✓ Permission to start badly
- ✓ Permission to start in the middle
- ✓ Permission to start for just five minutes
- ✓ Permission to start with the easy part
- ✓ Permission to start by complaining about starting
- ✓ Permission to start messily
- ✓ Permission to start over if needed
- ✓ Permission to celebrate tiny beginnings

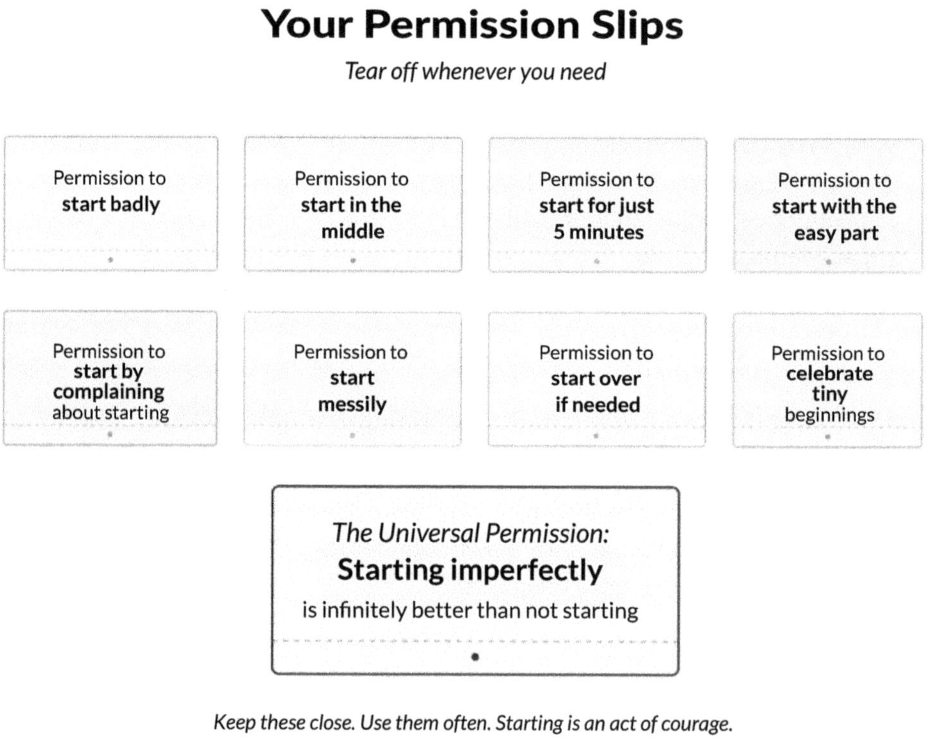

Figure 10.1

Try this today: start with a getting started toolkit

Different tasks need different doorways. Build your personal starting toolkit by experimenting with these approaches.

For Reading Tasks:

- Start by reading just the headings
- Begin with the conclusion
- Read one paragraph and summarize it to your pet/plant/wall
- Start by looking at all the pictures/graphs first

For Writing Tasks:

- Start with bullet points, not sentences
- Begin by writing what you don't want to say
- Start with, 'The thing I'm trying to figure out is … '
- Write to a specific person (dear Grandma, let me tell you about mitosis …)

For Problem Sets:

- Start with the easiest problem
- Begin by writing out what you know
- Start by finding a similar example
- Do the first problem badly on purpose

For Creative Projects:

- Start with the worst possible version
- Begin by collecting inspiration
- Start with materials play (scraps, arranging, sensory exploration)
- Make a terrible rough draft to improve later

Remember, every expert was once a disaster at starting. Every beautiful final product began with someone staring at a blank page, feeling exactly how you feel when you can't begin. The difference isn't that they wanted to start, it's that they kept trying to find their doorway in (Duckworth and Gross 2014).

Your doorway exists. It might be tiny, it might be weird, it might be different from everyone else's. But it's there, waiting for you to find it.

And when you do start – however messily, however incompletely, however reluctantly – you join the ranks of every human who has ever chosen to begin despite not wanting to. That's not just productivity. That's courage.

So, what's the smallest possible way you could start something right now?

A new way with starting

What if, all along, we've been overcomplicating starting? Making the already tough task of starting *even* tougher?

The old way tells us that we should be motivated when we start, that we should wait until we feel like it, that we should know exactly what we're doing before we begin. (But this old way makes starting feel like a test we keep failing.)

But you're learning a *new way*.

In this new way, starting is imperfect ... and that's perfect. Starting happens in tiny increments that barely feel like starting at all. Starting can happen in a third of the way through, at the end or somewhere completely unexpected. Starting is not a single moment but a series of small choices – the when, where, how (Webb and Sheeran 2007) of engaging with your work – however imperfectly.

In this new way:

- Resistance is a conversation partner, not an enemy
- 'Not wanting to' is a valid feeling that doesn't have to stop you
- Every tiny movement toward your task counts
- You don't need to feel ready to be ready enough
- Starting badly is a victory, not a failure

This new way with starting isn't about conquering your reluctance or pushing through resistance. It's about working with your whole human self – the part that's scared, the part that's uncertain, the part that would rather do literally anything else – and starting anyway, gently, with compassion for how hard this is (Brown 2018).

Your relationship with starting is uniquely yours. The strategies in this chapter aren't rules – they're invitations to experiment. Mix them, match them, modify them, make them yours. The goal isn't to start when your feelings, determination, clarity of thought and physical environment all align perfectly. The goal is to start, period.

And wouldn't you know, every time you practise starting when you don't want to, you're building evidence for your brain that you *can* do difficult things. Not because they necessarily come easy, but because you become someone who starts anyway.

Dig deeper: the inner workings of task initiation

Essential reading

Steven Pressfield's *The War of Art* (2002) names the force that stops us from starting: Resistance. He personifies it as a universal force that rises whenever we attempt creative or meaningful work. While Pressfield writes for artists, his insights apply perfectly to academic work – that feeling of dread before opening a textbook, the sudden urgent need to clean when an essay is due. His approach of 'turning pro' (showing up regardless of feelings) offers a practical philosophy for consistent starting.

Anne Lamott's *Bird by Bird* (1994), though focused on writing, contains the most compassionate and practical advice about starting any daunting task. Her concept of 'shitty first drafts' gives permission to begin badly, while her father's advice to her brother – 'bird by bird, buddy, just take it bird by bird' – when facing an overwhelming school project on birds has become legendary wisdom for breaking that immobilized state through tiny actions.

TED Talk

Mel Robbins's 'How to stop screwing yourself over' (2011) introduces the '5 Second Rule' – counting backwards from five to one and then physically moving to start a task before your brain can talk you out of it. Her explanation of how our brains are wired to stop us from doing anything uncomfortable, new or different provides crucial context for why starting feels so hard, while her simple countdown technique has resonated with millions seeking relief for their brain's resistance to beginning.

References

Amabile, T. and Kramer, S. (2011) *The Progress Principle: Using Small Wins to Ignite Joy, Engagement, and Creativity at Work*. Boston: Harvard Business Review Press.

Boice, R. (1990) *Professors as Writers: A Self-Help Guide to Productive Writing*. Stillwater, OK: New Forums Press.

Brown, B. (2018) *Dare to Lead: Brave Work. Tough Conversations. Whole Hearts*. New York: Random House

Duckworth, A.L. and Gross, J.J. (2014) 'Self-control and grit: Related but separate determinants of success', *Current Directions in Psychological Science*, 23(5), pp. 319–325. Available at: https://doi.org/10.1177/0963721414541462 (accessed 1 October 2025).

Fiore, N. (2007) *The Now Habit: A Strategic Program for Overcoming Procrastination and Enjoying Guilt-Free Play*. New York: Tarcher/Penguin.

Fogg, B.J. (2020) *Tiny Habits: The Small Changes That Change Everything*. Boston: Houghton Mifflin Harcourt.

Gollwitzer, P.M. and Sheeran, P. (2006) 'Implementation intentions and goal achievement: A meta-analysis of effects and processes', *Advances in Experimental Social Psychology*, 38, pp. 69–119.

hooks, b. (1994) *Teaching to Transgress: Education as the Practice of Freedom*. New York: Routledge.

Lamott, A. (1994) *Bird by Bird: Some Instructions on Writing and Life*. New York: Anchor Books.

Oettingen, G. (2014) *Rethinking Positive Thinking: Inside the New Science of Motivation*. New York: Current.

Pressfield, S. (2002) *The War of Art: Break through the Blocks and Win Your Inner Creative Battles*. New York: Black Irish Entertainment.

Pychyl, T.A. (2013) *Solving the Procrastination Puzzle: A Concise Guide to Strategies for Change*. New York: TarcherPerigee.

Robbins, M. (2011) 'How to stop screwing yourself over', TEDxSF. Available at: https://www.ted.com/talks/mel_robbins_how_to_stop_screwing_yourself_over (accessed 15 September 2025).

Sirois, F. and Pychyl, T. (2013) 'Procrastination and the priority of short-term mood regulation: Consequences for future self', *Social and Personality Psychology Compass*, 7(2), pp. 115–127.

Steel, P. (2007) 'The nature of procrastination: A meta-analytic and theoretical review of quintessential self-regulatory failure', *Psychological Bulletin*, 133(1), pp. 65–94.

Webb, T.L. and Sheeran, P. (2007) 'How do implementation intentions promote goal attainment? A test of component processes', *Journal of Experimental Social Psychology*, 43(2), pp. 295–302. Available at: https://doi.org/10.1016/j.jesp.2006.02.001 (accessed 1 October 2025).

CHAPTER 11

HOW TO FEEL MOTIVATED (WHEN YOU AREN'T FEELING IT ... AT ALL)

You're sitting at your desk, laptop open to a blank document. The assignment that's due tomorrow morning stares back at you, cursor blinking like a judgemental metronome. You've tried everything. Changed locations three times. Made two cups of chai. Decluttered your entire desk drawer. Even watched a motivational TED Talk about perseverance.

But here you are, feeling about as motivated as one bar of Wi-Fi.

You tell yourself you should care. This assignment is worth a quarter of your grade and you actually require this course for your programme. You even find the topic somewhat interesting when the professor talks about it. So why does every cell in your body want to do literally anything else?

You scroll through social media and see classmates posting about their productivity wins: 'Just finished my essay three days early! #motivated #studentlife'

You close your laptop and go to bed, promising yourself you'll wake up super early and feel different. (Um, but you *won't*.)

Feel familiar? Welcome to what I call 'the motivation mirage', the false belief that somewhere out there exists a magical state of constant enthusiasm for all our academic tasks, and if we just search hard enough, we'll find it.

Waiting for motivation is like waiting for a bus that doesn't run on your route. What if the problem isn't that you lack motivation, but that you're looking for it in all the wrong places?

The five motivation mistakes

Before we explore a more compassionate approach, let's name the unhelpful (and mistaken, sorry!) stories about motivation that most students carry.

The lightning bolt

You believe motivation should strike suddenly and powerfully, transforming you from couch potato to productivity machine. When it doesn't arrive, you assume something's wrong with you. (There isn't!)

The personality trait

You've decided you're either a 'motivated person' or you're not. This fixed mindset ignores that motivation is a state, not a trait. (Motivation ebbs and flows for everyone.)

The reward repository

You try to bribe yourself with treats and rewards. 'If I finish this chapter, I can watch an episode.' But when the reward stops working, you're left with even less intrinsic connection to the work. (And we often watch the show *anyway* in a state of avoidance!)

The shame spiral

You attempt to motivate yourself through self-criticism. 'I'm so lazy. I'm wasting my opportunities. Everyone else manages fine.' (Shame is motivation's kryptonite!)

The perfect conditions

You wait for ideal circumstances – the right mood, the perfect study spot, complete silence, peak energy. (Life rarely delivers all these conditions simultaneously.)

Most motivation guidance treats your academic life like a Nike commercial:

'Just do it.'

'Find your why.'

'Push through.'

'Visualize success.'

'Hustle harder.'

But wait! You're not a motivation machine that just needs the right fuel!

Standard models and methods of motivation assume you can generate enthusiasm on demand if you just think the right thoughts or follow the right morning routine protocol. They assume that lack of motivation is a character flaw to be conquered through willpower. They assume that caring deeply about every assignment is both possible and necessary.

But the reality for most students? Some classes will always feel like vegetables you have to eat before dessert. Some assignments will never spark joy no matter how many vision boards you create. Some days, your personal life will make caring about eighteenth-century literature feel impossible. You're not flawed; you're human.

What if instead of *chasing* motivation, we focused on *cultivation*?

Motivation cultivation

Building on previous chapters' emphasis on working *with* rather than *against* yourself, Motivation Cultivation asks: how do we create conditions where engagement can grow naturally, even (if not especially) when enthusiasm is absent?

Motivation Cultivation isn't about manufacturing fake excitement or pushing through resistance with sheer will. It's about tending to the soil of your learning life so that genuine engagement has the best chance to sprout – even in required courses, on difficult days or when life feels overwhelming.

Three surprising truths about motivation:

1. Motivation follows action more often than it precedes it. Waiting to feel motivated before starting is like waiting to feel fit before exercising. The feeling often comes after you begin, not before.
2. Resistance contains information. When you don't want to do something, that resistance is data about your needs, not evidence of your inadequacy. Maybe you need a different approach, a clearer purpose or simply more rest.
3. Small seeds grow into big plants. The tiniest genuine connection to your work – even just mild curiosity about one aspect – can develop into real engagement when properly nurtured.

Engagement as ecosystem

I learned about cultivating motivation from watching my husband, a landscape designer, tend our garden. Some plants thrived in full sun, others needed shade. Some required daily attention, others flourished with benign neglect. He never forces anything to grow where it doesn't want to; instead, he has learned over time what each plant needs and provides those conditions.

Just as he knows that 'You can't rush a tomato to ripen by yelling at it', the same is true for motivation. You can't force yourself to care through criticism or comparison. But you can create an ecosystem where caring becomes possible.

An ecosystemic approach to motivation pays attention to several elements that traditional advice ignores:

Environmental factors (what's around you)

Your physical and digital spaces profoundly impact your ability to engage. A cluttered desk or chaotic computer desktop creates unconscious resistance.

Relational nutrients (who's with you)

Who you learn with matters as much as what you learn. Isolation and loneliness deplete motivation; connection replenishes it.

Natural rhythms (what you feel like)

Your capacity for different types of engagement varies throughout the day, week and term. Working with these rhythms multiplies your efforts.

Meaning connections (what does it mean to you)

Even boring content can become engaging when connected to something you genuinely care about.

Recovery cycles (what keeps you going)

Motivation, like muscle strength, needs rest periods to regenerate. Constant pushing leads to burnout, not breakthrough.

When you cultivate mindfully, you're not *demanding* inspiration, incentive and the *desire* to work to appear magically; you're *creating conditions* where it's most likely to visit … and stay a while.

Notice your patterns: uncover your motivation topography

Before we can improve your motivation ecosystem, we need to understand and map your current patterns – the hills and valleys, the landscape and ecotones – of when you feel engaged and all in, and what leads to resistance and checking out.

1. Track your engagement levels for one week.

   Which tasks feel easiest to start and which create the most hesitation or outright avoidance? What repetitions reveal themselves? Does anything make you curious in what you notice?

2 Notice your resistance stories.

When you don't want to do something, what story does your brain tell? ('This is pointless'? 'I'm not smart enough'? 'This will take forever'?) What stories reveal any untended needs, like loneliness's need for friendship or exhaustion's need for sleep and rest?

3 Identify your entry points.

What lifts you out of resistance and moves you towards engagement? What shifted? Did you find a personal connection? Did working with others help? Did breaking it into tiny pieces make it manageable?

4 Map your energy donors and drains.

Which academic activities leave you feeling energized? Which leave you depleted? How might you use energy donors strategically to support you through the drains?

5 Examine your environment.

Where do you feel most naturally focused? What physical conditions support your engagement? What environmental factors create friction?

6 Notice your connection patterns.

When do you feel most isolated in your learning? When do you feel most connected? How does connection (or lack thereof) impact your willingness to engage?

The goal isn't to eliminate all resistance – some challenges are inherent (and important!) to learning. The goal is to understand your patterns so you can work skilfully with them.

Try this today: motivation cultivation

Instead of productivity hacks and tricks, try this approach to fostering your own engagement when you frankly might be feeling as if you just don't care. Motivation Cultivation works with your natural ways of being rather than against them.

Four ways to cultivate motivation

1. **Plant seeds**
   - Open the document, not finish the assignment
   - Write one sentence, not one paragraph
   - Generate one interesting question to pose in a boring lecture, not 100 per cent attention 100 per cent of the time
   - Comprehend one point, principle or concept in a reading, not striving for complete understanding
2. **Tend soil**
   - Clear one small workspace or corner completely
   - Gather materials before you need them, like instructions, rubrics and chargers
   - Remove or silence digital distractions
   - Make or purchase one beautiful thing for your workspace or one feel-good school supply, like paper, a pen or a notebook that's inviting
3. **Add nutrients**
   - Work alongside others, even silently
   - Share struggles with trusted friends
   - Connect topics to personal interests, passions or causes
   - Celebrate small progress with someone
4. **Honour seasons**
   - Notice when different subjects feel most doable
   - Accept that motivation naturally fluctuates
   - Plan challenging work for higher-energy times
   - Include deliberate rest in your schedule

The Growth Spiral

Instead of expecting linear progress, imagine motivation as a spiral:

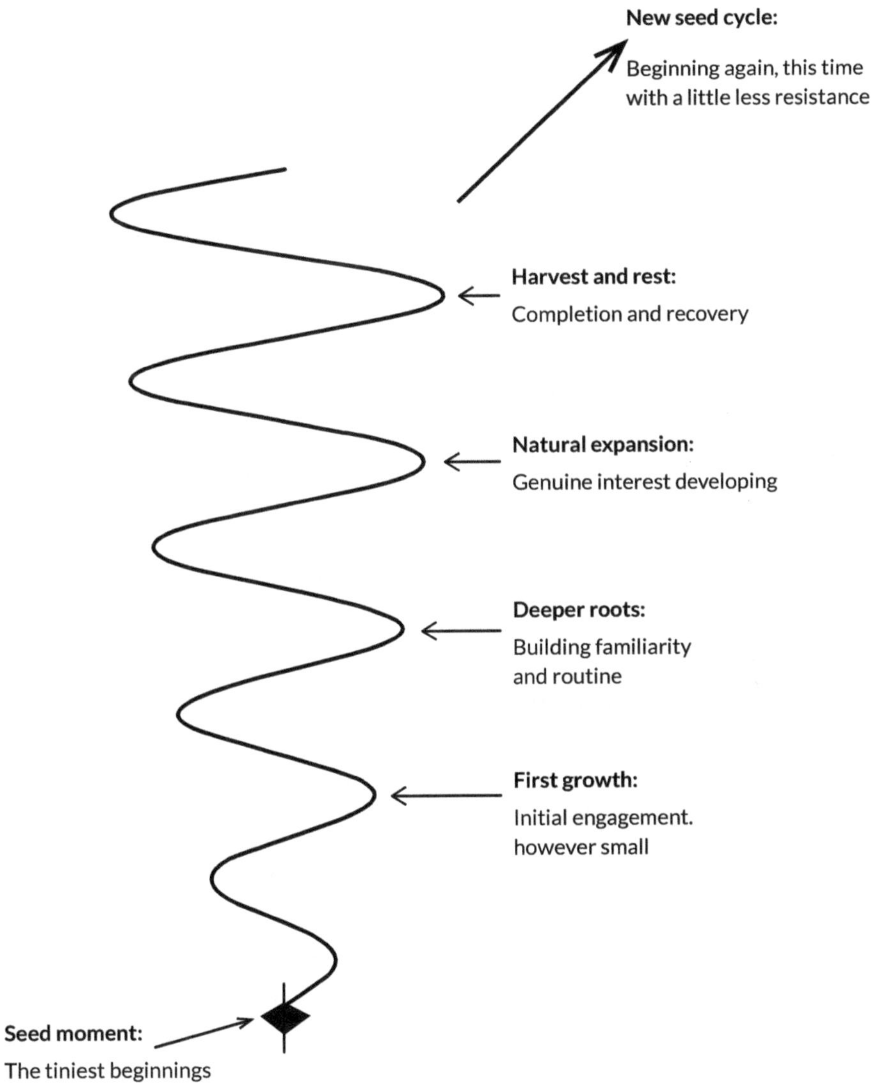

The spiral shape is intentional. While a circle simply repeats and goes in loops, a spiral returns to the same point but rises slightly each time. Each cycle builds on the last in ways that might feel small but accumulate. The resistance you felt at the first seed moment softens over time as familiarity and small wins lower the threshold bit-by-bit for beginning again.

Each stage has its own texture.

Seed moment: Usually the hardest stage to enter. Opening a document, glancing at your notes, or simply letting yourself wonder about a topic can all count. Presence matters here more than enthusiasm.

First growth: A small point of connection forms between you and the material. Even the briefest engagement counts, and this stage is easily undermined by pressure to produce something straight away. Attempt trumps excellence here.

Deeper roots: Familiarity begins to accumulate and the material stops feeling quite so disorienting or off-putting. Routine gradually takes on some of the motivational work, making it easier to return.

Natural expansion: Genuine curiosity begins to emerge without being demanded. Interest grows, as does a sense of curiosity and of accomplishment; learning at this stage starts to have its own pull.

Harvest and rest: You complete something and give it time to settle. Rest at this stage is a functional part of the learning process, not simply a pause between efforts.

New seed cycle: You begin again from a starting point that feels, in some small way, closer than before. The spiral has done its quiet work: returning once has made it slightly easier to return again.

Each spiral builds on the last, creating sustainable patterns of engagement rather than boom-and-bust cycles of cramming and burnout.

See it in action: meet Kwame

Kwame is a second-year international student. When we first met, he was struggling with what he called 'motivation bankruptcy'.

'Back home, I was always the keen student,' Kwame tells me. 'But here, I just couldn't make myself care about anything.'

Kwame was struggling with a particularly technical course – a required class he found painfully boring. He'd wait until the last possible moment to start assignments because of how uninteresting he found the content, then panic write through the night, hating every minute. The cycle was affecting his other courses too.

The breakthrough

When Kwame started tracking his patterns, several things became clear. His resistance was strongest when he felt isolated – living off campus, he often went days without meaningful interaction with classmates. He was trying to study in his bedroom, where his gaming setup provided constant temptation. And he was expecting himself to maintain the same enthusiasm, despite being thousands of miles from family and community.

'I was treating motivation like it was supposed to be automatic,' he reflects. 'When it wasn't there, I figured something was wrong with me.'

Everything shifted when Kwame stopped chasing motivation and started cultivating conditions for engagement.

Kwame's cultivation of motivation

- **Seed moment**

  Instead of avoiding technical writing until the deadline, Kwame committed to opening the assignment document every day and writing just one sentence. 'Sometimes that sentence turned into a paragraph. Sometimes it stayed just one sentence. But I was making contact with the work daily instead of letting it become massive in my mind.'

- **First growth & deeper roots**

  Kwame established a study spot at the campus library ... away from his gaming setup. He'd arrive thirty minutes early to settle in, make tea in the student lounge and chat with whoever was around. 'The library became less about studying and more about being part of something.'

- **Natural expansion**

  Kwame joined a study group for one of his classes and discovered that working alongside others – even on different subjects – made everything feel more manageable. 'We'd take breaks together, complain together, celebrate together. It made the work feel less like punishment.'

- **Harvest and rest & new seed cycle**

  Kwame noticed his focus was sharpest mid-morning and late afternoon. He stopped forcing himself to study during his post-lunch energy dip, using that time for exercise or calling family instead. 'I stopped fighting my rhythms and started surfing them.'

The results

Within a month, Kwame noticed profound changes. The technical writing course never became his favourite, but it stopped feeling like torture. By maintaining daily contact with assignments, he eliminated the panic-writing sessions. His other courses benefited from his more sustainable approach.

'I still don't wake up excited about every assignment,' Kwame laughed when we told me. 'But I don't wake up dreading or resenting them either. I've learned that motivation isn't something you have or don't have – it's something you grow.'

Most surprisingly, Kwame discovered that some of his writing skills were improving his lab reports in other courses. 'When you stop fighting against learning,' he observes, 'sometimes it sneaks in sideways and helps where you didn't expect.'

→ **Key insight:** 'Motivation isn't about feeling pumped up all the time,' Kwame says. 'It's about creating conditions where showing up feels possible, even on the hard days.'

A new way with cultivation

How can I make myself want this? This is the way motivation is usually talked about, but *wanting* isn't always under our control.

When you cultivate motivation, you ask better questions: *What conditions help me engage? What small connection can I make today? How can I lower the barriers between me and beginning?*

This new way recognizes that you don't need to feel passionate about every aspect of your education and you don't have to love a subject area or course in order to get the tasks done. What is needed instead are sustainable ways of engaging with necessary work that doesn't deplete your soul or rely on last-minute adrenaline surges to complete and submit assessments.

Cultivation means accepting that motivation naturally waxes and wanes. It means building systems that support you during the waning times instead of criticizing yourself for not maintaining constant optimism, enthusiasm and keenness.

Most importantly, cultivation means treating yourself like a yard that needs tending, not a machine that needs fixing. You water the garden even when nothing's blooming yet. You trust that seeds planted in good soil will eventually grow.

When you cultivate rather than chase, motivation stops feeling like something you lack and starts feeling like something you tend. Some days the garden flourishes, other days you're just getting the weeding done. Both are part of the process.

Dig deeper: rethinking motivation

Essential reading

Pleasure Activism: The Politics of Feeling Good by Adrienne Maree Brown (2019) revolutionizes how we think about sustainable engagement by centring joy, pleasure and healing in our work – especially vital for marginalized students navigating oppressive systems.

TED Talks

- 'How students of color confront impostor syndrome' by Dena Simmons (2015) addresses how systemic barriers impact motivation and offers strategies for authentic engagement while navigating educational spaces not designed for everyone.
- Sian Leah Beilock's 'Why we choke under pressure – and how to avoid it' (2017) discusses performance anxiety and provides cognitive science informed strategies.

Poem

'The Body Is Not an Apology' is Sonya Renee Taylor's radical self-love poem, book and platform, and centres healing and liberation rather than productivity and performance. Her words can be a helpful reminder on an unmotivated or deflated evening, especially when she reminds us that we're not the tests we take, we're not the answers we flub in class, we're not a failing grade and that no matter our mistakes, *we* are not a mistake.

References

Beilock, S.L. (2017, November) 'Why we choke under pressure – and how to avoid it' [Video]. TED. Available at: https://www.ted.com/talks/sian_leah_beilock_why_we_choke_under_pressure_and_how_to_avoid_it (accessed 1 October 2025).

Brown, A.M. (2019) *Pleasure Activism: The Politics of Feeling Good*. Chico, CA: AK Press.

Simmons, D. (2015, November) 'How students of color confront impostor syndrome' [Video]. TED. Available at: https://www.ted.com/talks/dena_simmons_how_students_of_color_confront_impostor_syndrome (accessed 1 October 2025).

Taylor, S.R. (n.d.). 'The body is not an apology', *Sonya Renee Taylor*. Available at: https://www.sonyareneetaylor.com/the-body-is-not-an-apology

CHAPTER 12

HOW TO FOCUS (WHEN IT FEELS IMPOSSIBLE)

Focus doesn't just feel elusive *a lot* of the time; it feels elusive *most* of the time. Whether you're sitting in a lecture hall with 300 other students, trying to wade through dense academic reading at midnight or staring at a blank document that somehow needs to become a 2,000-word essay by tomorrow, maintaining attention can feel like trying to hold water in your hands.

You're not alone in this.

In fact, if you're struggling with focus right now, you're responding quite naturally to an unnaturally demanding world. We're asked to pay attention through notifications, to global crises unfolding on our phones, to financial pressures that make housing and food costs a daily worry, through the echoes of a pandemic that fundamentally changed how we learn. Is it any wonder that concentration feels fractured?

This chapter isn't about making you feel guilty for struggling to focus. It's about offering genuine, practical ways to work in alignment with your brain, not against it. It's about healing your relationship with attention: focus *can* be healed, even befriended.

The falsehood of perfect focus

Here's a secret: none of your professors have perfect focus – none of your family members and none of your acting, sporting or business idols either.

That researcher who wrote your textbook? They probably checked their email seventeen times whilst writing that chapter.

The student in the row in front of you who seems to take flawless notes? They might be *taking* those notes *to* keep their mind engaged and prevent their constantly wandering mind from *taking* them right out of class.

Uninterrupted, sustained, unwavering attention is a *true* falsehood. And chasing it only makes us feel worse when we inevitably fall short (Sharpe and Tyndall 2025).

What we're after instead is workable focus. Focus that's good enough. Focus that gets us through. Focus that honours our humanity whilst still helping us achieve what we need to achieve.

Creating conditions for concentration

Think of focus less like a switch you flick and more like a musical instrument you tune. It needs the right adjustments to resonate. And just like musicians, different people need different tunings.

The Sensory Sweet Spot

First, we each like a different level of sensory input in our surroundings. Some of us need absolute silence. Others need the café sounds of to-ing and fro-ing all around, like an alive kind of white noise. Many need something in between. This is what I call your personal Sensory Sweet Spot.

What's your Sensory Sweet Spot? Too much stimulation and you're distracted. Too little and your mind goes looking for entertainment. Just right, and suddenly the work flows a bit more easily (Rosen et al. 2013).

The body–mind bridge

We pretend the mind and body are separate, but concentration lives in both.

Some find focus through:

- Sitting on a balance ball instead of a chair
- Using a standing desk converter (even just textbooks stacked on a regular desk)
- Wrapping themselves in a weighted blanket whilst working

Your body's needs aren't a distraction from focus; they're fundamental to it (Tang, Hölzel and Posner 2015).

The pomodoro revolution (with a twist)

You might have heard of the Pomodoro Technique – twenty-five minutes of work, five-minute break. It's popular because, in principle, it works for many learners. But it's not a magic solution and here's the critical twist: you can customize it.

Its usefulness isn't in the specific numbers. It's in:

- Working with your attention span, not overloading it, asking just enough of it and not too much more
- Building in breaks *before* your brain forces them on you
- Making breaks genuinely restorative (scrolling social media doesn't count!)

The art of the return

Weird as it may sound, it's *not* actually about never getting distracted. (Not possible!) It's about noticing when you've drifted and oh-so-gently returning.

When you notice your attention has drifted:

- Acknowledge it without judgement ('Oh, I'm thinking about dinner')
- Take one deep breath
- Return to the task

That's it. No shame spiral. No 'I'm terrible at this'. Just notice and return. Notice and return. Like waves on a beach, this is the natural rhythm of attention (Kabat-Zinn 2013).

Take a moment: reflecting on your focus

Pause here. Take a breath. Let's turn our focus inward.

We're often taught there's one right way to focus. Sitting still, eyes forward, perfect attention. But focus is as unique as fingerprints.

What would it mean to truly accept your own focusing style?

> Maybe you focus best at 5:00am when the world is quiet. Maybe you need to pace whilst thinking, your body's movement unlocking your mind's clarity. Maybe you can only concentrate for seven minutes at a time but in those seven minutes, you're brilliant, sharp and tuned in.

When have you felt most naturally, easefully, successfully focused? What were the conditions? What did you notice about yourself?

> Maybe you need to colour-code everything, turning information into a visual feast. Maybe you whisper concepts aloud – and thus benefit most from regularly booking study rooms in the library – hearing your own voice making sense of ideas. Maybe in spaces like that you speak-as-you-draw, crafting elaborate mind maps on dry-erase boards that look like abstract art but make perfect sense to your brain.

What focusing 'rules' have you been trying to follow that don't actually serve you? What would you do differently if you trusted your own way of paying attention?

> Your focus doesn't need to look like anyone else's. It just needs to work for you (Zimmerman 2002).

What's one aspect of your unique focusing style that you're ready to embrace rather than apologize for?

Try this today: working with your wandering mind

Sometimes, preventing, combating and diffusing distraction, well, that's like trying not to think of pink elephants, or trying to wrangle a wild stallion. The more we resist or constrain, the stronger it becomes.

So, what if we tried out working *with* our wandering mind instead?

The parking lot method

Keep a notebook beside you during studying sessions. When random thoughts, creative project ideas and don't-forget-to-dos pop up – 'Did I pay that bill?' 'I should text my friend back' 'What was that film called?' – jot them in your 'parking lot'. You're not ignoring them. You're just parking them for later.

The thread method

When your mind wanders during lectures, try following the thread. Your 'distractions' during lectures might often be connections, linking what the professor said to a film you've seen, a conversation with your grandmother, a news article (González and Paoloni 2015). Linking personal interest makes lecture material engaging, meaningful and potentially more memorable.

The radical rest method

This might sound contradictory (and like a running theme in *A New Way to Learn*) but sometimes the best thing you can do for your focus is to stop trying to focus and give that beautiful brain some true, restorative downtime. Our brains aren't built for endless concentration.

Student voices

Lola: Lola said it clearly, 'In lectures, I start strong. First five minutes, I'm golden. Then my mind drifts to my part-time job, to my cousin's medical treatments, to whether I remembered to submit that form, to what everyone else seems to understand that I don't.'

Rashida: A mature student returning after a decade in the workforce, Rashida discovered that she concentrated best with brown noise – a deeper, rumbling sound like distant thunder or ocean waves – playing softly. Not music, not white noise, but brown noise specifically. 'It's like giving my anxious brain a blanket,' she said.

Kai: Kai realized they needed visual stimulation but auditory calm. They'd work in busy spaces with noise-cancelling headphones, watching the world go by all the while protected in their bubble of silence.

Owen: A student-athlete, Owen noticed his focus sharpened dramatically when he did ten press-ups before studying. Not a full workout, just enough to wake up his body.

Sanjana: Managing chronic pain, Sanjana found that focus improved when she worked standing at a counter for twenty minutes, then sitting for twenty, then lying on the floor for twenty. 'My body needs variety,' she explained, 'and when my body's happy, my brain cooperates.'

Diego and Aaliyah: Diego found twenty-five-minute Pomodoros too long. He did fifteen-minute sprints with three-minute dance breaks. In turn, Aaliyah found twenty-five minutes too *short* – just as she got into flow, the timer went off. She extended to forty-five-minute focus sessions with fifteen-minute breaks.

Nour: Postgraduate student Nour put it beautifully: 'I used to beat myself up every time my mind wandered. Now I think of it like meditation. The practice isn't perfect focus – it's the practice of coming back.'

Oluwaseun: Oluwaseun told me the parking lot method transformed her reading sessions: 'Before, one random thought would lead to twenty minutes of phone scrolling. Now I write it down and my brain seems satisfied that it won't be forgotten.'

Ethan: Ethan noticed his 'distractions' during lectures were often connections, linking what the professor said to a documentary he'd seen, a conversation with an old friend, a news post on social media. He started jotting these connections in the margins of his notes. 'Turns out my "distracted" brain was actually making meaning,' he said. 'Now my notes are so much richer and easier to remember.'

Skye: Struggling with her dissertation, Skye made a radical choice. Every Sunday: no work at all, like that idea of a tech Shabbat. 'I thought I'd fall behind,' she said. 'Instead, Monday mornings became my most productive time. My brain had actually been processing things whilst I rested.'

→ **Key insight:** There's no universal formula for focus; each person can uncover their own unique combination of sensory, physical and temporal conditions that allow their brain to engage. The breakthrough comes not from forcing 'correct' focus but from experimenting to find one's personal equation. Whether it's brown noise, movement breaks, radical rest or reframing distraction as connection-making, sustainable attention emerges when we honour our individual wiring.

A new way with focus

As we close this chapter, let's re-envision what focus *could* be.

What if focus wasn't about forcing your mind into submission, but about creating a partnership with your attention?

What if wandering thoughts, daydreams, momentary *what-if* meandering minds weren't failures but your brain making connections?

What if needing breaks wasn't weakness but wisdom?

A new way with focus means:

- Accepting that attention ebbs and flows like tides
- Creating personalized conditions that support your unique brain
- Practising self-compassion when concentration wavers
- Trusting that rest and play feed focus as much as effort does
- Celebrating small victories – after all, five minutes of attention is still five minutes
- Knowing that your worth isn't measured by your ability to concentrate

Tomorrow, when you sit down to work or settle into a lecture, remember: you're not trying to become someone else's version of focused. You're discovering your own rhythm of attention. And in that discovery lies freedom.

Dig deeper: finding your own rhythm of attention

Essential reading

Edward Hallowell and John Ratey's *ADHD 2.0: New Science and Essential Strategies for Thriving with Distraction – from Childhood through Adulthood* (2021) sheds light on attention differences, presenting ADHD as a trait that can be harnessed for creativity and innovation rather than simply managed as a disorder, and provides practical strategies for (more) on-task learning.

Mihaly Csikszentmihalyi's *Flow: The Psychology of Optimal Experience* (2008) is now considered an essential read because it shares research-backed insights into how we can create conditions for deep, in-the-zone concentration by aligning challenge level with skill and eliminating distractions.

Podcasts and talks

Brian Christian's (2018) TED-Ed, 'How to manage your time more effectively (according to machines)' applies computer science algorithms to human attention management, offering practical techniques for prioritizing tasks and managing cognitive load when everything feels urgent and important.

The ADHD for Smart Ass Women podcast (Tracy Otsuka) offers a variety of episode themes, including novelty-seeking and rumination. The podcast brilliantly explains the neuroscience behind attention differences and offers doable strategies that work whether you have ADHD or simply struggle with focus in the sea of distraction we all live in.

References

Christian, B. (2018) 'How to manage your time more effectively (according to machines)', TED-Ed, [video]. Available at: https://www.youtube.com/watch?v=iDbdXTMnOmE (accessed 1 October 2025).

Csikszentmihalyi, M. (2008) *Flow: The Psychology of Optimal Experience*. New York: Harper Perennial.

González, A., and Paoloni, P.V. (2015) 'Perceived autonomy-support, expectancy, value, metacognitive strategies and performance in chemistry: A structural equation model in undergraduates', *Chemistry Education Research and Practice*, 16(3), pp. 640–653.

Hallowell, E.M. and Ratey, J.J. (2021) *ADHD 2.0: New Science and Essential Strategies for Thriving with Distraction – From Childhood through Adulthood*. New York: Ballantine Books.

Kabat-Zinn, J. (2013) *Full Catastrophe Living: Using the Wisdom of Your Body and Mind to Face Stress, Pain, and Illness*. New York: Bantam Books.

Otsuka, T. (host) (n.d.) *ADHD for Smart Ass Women* [podcast]. Available at: https://adhdforsmartwomen.com (accessed 1 October 2025).

Rosen, L.D., Carrier, L.M., and Cheever, N.A. (2013) 'Facebook and texting made me do it: Media-induced task-switching while studying', *Computers in Human Behavior*, 29(3), pp. 948–958.

Sharpe, B.T. and Tyndall, I. (2025) 'The sustained attention paradox: A critical commentary on the theoretical impossibility of perfect vigilance', *Cognitive Science*, 49(4), e70061, DOI: 10.1111/cogs.70061.

Tang, Y.Y., Hölzel, B.K. and Posner, M.I. (2015) 'The neuroscience of mindfulness meditation', *Nature Reviews Neuroscience*, 16(4), pp. 213–225, DOI: 10.1038/nrn3916.

Zimmerman, B.J. (2002) 'Becoming a self-regulated learner: An overview', *Theory into Practice*, 41(2), pp. 64–70.

CHAPTER 13

HOW TO DO WORK (WHEN IT ALL SEEMS SO HARD)

It's Thursday afternoon, laptop open, with a to-do list that seems to have developed its own gravitational pull. Every item on it feels impossibly heavy. Not intellectually difficult, necessarily ... just ... heavy.

The essay that needs starting.

The problem set that needs attempting.

The readings that need reading.

The group project meeting that needs scheduling.

Each task sits there like a boulder. No, like ... cement.

You *know* what to do. You even know how to do it. You've read the study guides, you've heard about 'time management' from well-meaning friends and family, you've got a calendar with due dates noted.

But.

Knowing and *doing* have become two entirely different universes and the space between them feels galaxies apart.

So, you sit there. Maybe you open a document and stare at the blank page. Maybe you read the same assignment instructions three times without absorbing a word. Maybe you switch between tabs, hoping one of them will magically contain less daunting work. Maybe you *group* the tabs to feel a little more organized. Or, maybe you just sit, frozen and unable to move, where everything, all of it, all at once, feels urgent and impossible.

Your flatmate breezes past your open door. 'Getting loads done?' they ask cheerfully.

'Yeah, totally,' you respond automatically, minimizing the YouTube tab you don't remember opening.

Getting your work moved along can feel like pushing a car uphill with the handbrake on. You're not lazy. You're not 'just procrastinating' (as if procrastination were simple rather than a complex protective mechanism) (Pychyl 2013). You're experiencing what happens when work becomes tangled up with overwhelm, when tasks become monuments to anxiety, when the very act of working feels like admitting you're already behind.

The hidden physics of stuck

Most productivity advice assumes you're a robot that just needs better programming:

'Set SMART goals!'

'Create those flashcards!'

'Eat that frog!' (Which just feels gross to write).

But you're not a robot; you're a human being trying to function in a system that often feels inhuman.

When work feels impossibly hard, it's rarely about the work itself. It's usually what the work has become entangled with.

- **Emotional weight**

  That essay often feels like so much more than 'just' an essay; instead, it's laden with judgement, proof of whether you belong here, whether you're smart enough, whether choosing this degree was a mistake. No wonder it's hard to start when beginning feels like putting your entire identity on trial.

- **Perfectionism pressure**

  When every piece of work feels like it needs to be brilliant (or at least good enough to justify your presence here), the bar for 'acceptable' becomes so high that not starting feels safer than risking inadequacy.

- **Overwhelm overflow**

  When you're juggling multiple courses, life responsibilities, maybe a job, perhaps family obligations, your brain can hit capacity. It's not that you can't do the work; it's that your system is overloaded and has gone into protective shutdown.

- **Energy depletion**

  University isn't simply intellectually demanding, it's *emotionally* and *socially* demanding too. When you're using energy to navigate new relationships, manage homesickness, figure out who you are becoming, there's less left for academics.

- **Context collapse**

  That statistics assignment might feel impossible not because statistics is hard, but because you're also processing a difficult conversation with family, worrying about finances and trying to figure out if you even want the career this degree leads to.

Understanding this hidden physics helps explain why 'just do it' advice falls flat, and why procrastination doesn't have a simple, singular solution (Steel 2007). You can't bulldoze through complex, interconnected stuckness. You need gentler, cleverer ways through.

Take a moment: mapping your stuckness

Before we explore solutions, it's helpful to understand your idiosyncratic version of stuck. Stuckness – stuckicity? stuckage? – comes in distinct flavours, hues, tones and vibes, and each needs a different approach.

The stuckness inventory

Over the next few days, if you catch yourself in a moment unable to start or continue or complete work, take a breather and ever so kindly inquire:

What kind of stuck is this?

- Fog stuck: You can't quite grasp what you're supposed to do or why
- Freeze stuck: You know what to do but feel frozen
- Flood stuck: Too many things need doing and you can't choose
- Fatigue stuck: You're too depleted to engage
- Fear stuck: Starting feels too risky or exposing

Where do you feel it?

- In your body: Chest tightness? Shoulder tension? Stomach knots? Heavy limbs?
- In your mind: Racing thoughts? Blankness? Harsh inner criticism?
- In your environment: Does your space feel chaotic? Too quiet? Disconnected?

What would 'unstuck' feel like?

- Don't harp on productivity, zero in on sensation
- Would unstuck feel ... lighter? Clearer? More connected? Energized?
- What's the smallest levering, the most minute indication of movement?

What has helped before?

- Think micro: What teensy thing has sometimes made starting easier?
- Think indirect scaffolds: Sometimes a shower, a walk or a conversation unsticks us
- Think contexts: Are there conditions that make beginning more possible?

The compassion check

How would you talk to a close friend experiencing exactly what you're experiencing? Would you tell them they're lazy and should just try harder? Or would you recognize that they're struggling with something genuinely difficult and help them find a way through?

That same compassion you'd offer a friend? You deserve it too. Stuckness isn't a character flaw; it's information about what you need.

Try this today: the gentle momentum method

Moving through work can be extra hard when we try to leap from intention. What we might need most are lifelines, ways in and bridges – small, concrete, achievable steps that nourish possibility even when everything feels impossible. Here's a framework for doing work when it all seems so hard.

Phase 1: Shrink the first step

When work feels impossible, your first step is probably too big. Keep shrinking it until starting feels manageable.

The one-thing start

Open the lab report and write one sentence; read one paragraph; solve one problem; send one email. One leads to two, and in time, momentum can carry you forward (Clear 2018).

The incredibly small goal

Make your first goal so small it would be just about impossible not to be able to do it. Instead of 'write essay introduction', try 'write essay title'. Instead of 'study for exam', try 'find exam study guide'.

The prep-only session

Separate preparation from execution. One session just to gather materials, open documents, write down what needs doing. No pressure to actually *do* the work, just to set it up. Often, this removes enough friction that doing becomes possible.

Phase 2: Create activation energy

When you're stuck, you need help getting unstuck. Build in activation energy – external or internal forces that help you begin.

Body-first activation

Sometimes your mind is stuck because your body is stuck.

- Try: A five-minute walk before attempting work
- Try: Three deep breaths with longer exhales than inhales
- Try: Gentle stretching or shaking out your limbs
- Try: Changing your physical position or location

Social activation

Use connection as catalyst.

- Parallel working: Work alongside someone else, even virtually
- Accountability partnerships: Tell someone your 'incredibly small' goal
- Study dates: Make work a social rather than solitary act
- Voice note victories: Send a friend a quick celebration of tiny progress

Space activation

Design your space to make starting easier.

- Pre-stage your workspace the night before
- Create a beginning ceremony (light a candle, play specific music)
- Change one thing about your environment when stuck
- Use friendly timers or apps as external structure

Emotional activation

Address the feelings that keep you stuck.

- Write a quick 'worry dump' before starting
- Set an intention for how you want to feel, not just what you want to do
- Practice one minute of self-compassion or loving kindness meditation
- Remind yourself this is hard for everyone sometimes

Phase 3: Build bridges with habit stacking

Link difficult work to easier, established routines to reduce the activation energy needed.

The after-comfort stack

Attach work to comfortable routines

- 'After I have my morning chai, I'll review one page of notes'
- 'After I eat lunch, I'll send one project-related email'
- 'After I chat with my flatmate, I'll do five practice problems'

The during-pleasant stack

Combine work with pleasant elements.

- Listen to specific, lyric-free, ambient music while writing (not for focus, but for association)
- Work in a favourite café for reading sessions
- Use nice pens or materials that make the work feel special
- Create comfort through tea, cosy clothes, favourite spots

The before-reward stack

Frame existing activities as rewards.

- 'I'll check messages after writing one paragraph'
- 'I'll have dinner after completing one problem set section'
- 'I'll watch one episode after reviewing one lecture'

The key is making these connections consistent enough that your brain begins to expect work in these contexts, reducing resistance.

Phase 4: Strategic friction for unhelpful patterns

Sometimes we need to make unhelpful behaviours slightly harder while making helpful behaviours easier (Heath and Heath 2010).

Helpful friction for digital escapes

Add in mini-hurdles to help you start or sustain locked-in workflow.

- Log out of social media between uses
- Delete apps during study periods (you can reinstall later)
- Use website blockers with passwords you have to type manually
- Put devices on silent in another room, not just out of sight

Reducing friction for desired behaviours

Make work-entry and next steps as smooth and resistance-free as possible.

- Keep study materials visible and easily accessible
- Bookmark research databases for quick access
- Create templates for common assignment types
- Pre-write email drafts for typical scenarios

The pause practice

If you find yourself avoiding work, insert a tiny pause.

- Count to five before opening social media
- Take three breaths before switching tasks
- Ask 'What do I actually need right now?' before escaping
- Write one sentence about how you're feeling before giving up

These pauses don't prevent escape, but they make it conscious rather than automatic, giving you a chance to choose differently.

Phase 5: Energy management over time management

When everything feels hard, managing your energy becomes more important than managing your time (Schwartz and McCarthy 2007).

Match task to energy

- High energy: New learning, difficult problems, creative work
- Medium energy: Reviewing, planning, familiar practice
- Low energy: Administrative tasks, email, formatting

Protect peak hours

- When is your mental energy at its peak?
- How can you protect at least one peak window a day?
- Notice when you typically have more mental energy and protect that time for important work, even if it's not traditional 'study hours'

Sustainable sessions

- Resist back-to-back work sessions and include transition time between different types of work
- End sessions before complete depletion
- Plan lighter days after intense periods

Weekly recap

- What gave you energy this week?
- What depleted you this week?
- How can you adjust your schedule next week to honour these patterns?

Student voices

Khadija: 'I spent weeks unable to start my literature review. Every time I opened my laptop, I'd feel this wave of dread and end up doing anything else. My breakthrough came when I stopped trying to "start my literature review" and instead made my goal "find one interesting paper". Just one. That felt possible. I found one, then thought "maybe just one more", and suddenly I had five sources and actual drive.'

Jin: 'Group projects were my nightmare. I'd procrastinate on my part because I was anxious about letting others down, which of course made everything worse. I started using what I call "confession sessions". I'd message the group saying "struggling to start, going to work on it for thirty minutes now" and somehow admitting the struggle made it easier to begin. The group was always supportive, which I didn't expect.'

Blessing: 'My problem was that I'd get stuck in planning mode. I'd spend hours making beautiful study schedules and colour-coded notes but never actually studying. I had to create a rule: maximum ten minutes of planning, then straight into doing. I'd set a timer and when it went off, I had to start the actual work, even if the plan wasn't perfect. Turns out, imperfect action beats perfect planning, hands down.'

Ren: 'I discovered that my "procrastination" was my brain telling me I needed different input. When I couldn't write, instead of forcing it, I'd go find someone to explain my ideas to and record the conversation on my phone to transcribe. When I couldn't read, I'd look for videos on the topic. When I couldn't solve problems, I'd try teaching the concept to my potted plants. Finding different ways in helped me get unstuck without the guilt spiral.'

Fatima: 'I used to think being stuck meant I was failing. Now I see it as information. Stuck on starting usually means the task feels too big ... so I shrink it. Stuck *continuing* usually means I need a break or a different approach. Stuck *finishing* usually means I'm being perfectionist. The stuckness tells me what I need.'

→ **Key insight:** Reframing the task changes everything; when students stopped seeing their difficulty as a character flaw and started seeing it as information about what needed adjusting, they found ways forward. Each student worked with their resistance rather than against it by shrinking the task (Khadija), sharing the struggle (Jin), time-boxing action (Blessing), finding alternative entry points (Ren) or treating stuckness as diagnostic data (Fatima). The breakthrough wasn't more discipline; it was strategic adaptation based on self-awareness.

A new way when work feels hard

The old way treats difficulty starting work as a character flaw to be overcome through discipline. 'Just push through!' 'Quit procrastinating!' 'Care More!'

The *new* way recognizes that when work feels impossibly hard, it's usually because work has become tangled up with other things – fear, overwhelm, depletion, uncertainty. You can't bulldoze through these tangles. You need to gently unravel them.

This approach works with your humanity rather than against it. It acknowledges that sometimes a two-minute commitment is a victory. That needing support isn't weakness. That creating easier pathways isn't cheating; it's clever.

Working *with* our stuckness instead of fighting it allows shifts to take place. Work becomes less about heroic efforts and more about sustainable practices. Progress becomes less about giant leaps and more about gentle momentum.

Most importantly, this new way recognizes that everyone – *everyone* – sometimes finds work impossibly hard. It's not just you; it's not a sign that you can't do it, it's a sign you're human, trying to do difficult things under challenging circumstances.

Your work matters. Your voice and views matter. Your contributions matter. And finding ways to do that work that honour your full humanity ... that matters most of all.

The next time everything feels too hard, remember, you don't need to make heroic efforts. You just need to find one point of entry, one gentle way forward. The rest will follow.

Dig deeper: the science of starting (and continuing)

Understanding why starting feels so hard – and what honestly helps – can normalize your experience and guide you in the direction of more effective strategies.

Essential reading

Neil Fiore's *The Now Habit* (2007) sees procrastination not as laziness but as a protective mechanism against fear, overwhelm and perfectionism. His insights into how we make work harder than it needs to be are particularly relevant for students who are feeling numb and stuck.

Key research

- Implementation Intentions

  Research by Peter Gollwitzer (1999) shows that vague intentions ('I'll study tomorrow') are far less likely to result in action than specific implementation intentions ('When I finish lunch tomorrow, I'll go to the library and complete three practice problems'). The specificity acts as a cognitive bridge between intention and action.

- The Progress Principle

  Teresa Amabile's research reveals that the single most motivating factor in work is making progress, even tiny progress (Amabile and Kramer 2011). This suggests that making the first step almost incredibly small can build momentum.

- Temptation Bundling

  Katy Milkman's research on coupling less enjoyable tasks with more enjoyable ones shows how we can make difficult work more approachable (Milkman et al. 2014). This isn't about rewards after work, but about making the work itself more pleasant.

- The Fresh Start Effect

  Research by Dai, Milkman and Riis also shows that people are more likely to tackle goals after temporal landmarks (new week, new month, after birthday) (Dai et al. 2014). This suggests that creating 'fresh starts' can help overcome the burden and baggage of past procrastination.

- Habit Stacking

  Wendy Wood's (2019) research on habit formation shows that successful behaviour change relies on context cues and repetition rather than willpower or motivation. Her work demonstrates that habits form when we repeat behaviours in stable contexts, creating automatic responses that bypass the need for conscious decision-making. Rather than relying on motivation, you leverage environmental triggers and existing routines.

References

Amabile, T. and Kramer, S. (2011) *The Progress Principle: Using Small Wins to Ignite Joy, Engagement, and Creativity at Work*. Boston: Harvard Business Review Press.

Clear, J. (2018) *Atomic Habits: An Easy & Proven Way to Build Good Habits & Break Bad Ones*. New York: Avery.

Dai, H., Milkman, K.L. and Riis, J. (2014) 'The fresh start effect: Temporal landmarks motivate aspirational behavior', *Management Science*, 60(10), pp. 2563–2582.

Fiore, N. (2007) *The Now Habit: A Strategic Program for Overcoming Procrastination and Enjoying Guilt-free Play*. New York: Tarcher.

Gollwitzer, P.M. (1999) 'Implementation intentions: Strong effects of simple plans', *American Psychologist*, 54(7), pp. 493–503.

Heath, C. and Heath, D. (2010) *Switch: How to Change Things When Change Is Hard*. New York: Broadway Books.

Milkman, K.L., Minson, J.A. and Volpp, K.G. (2014) 'Holding the Hunger Games hostage at the gym: An evaluation of temptation bundling', *Management Science*, 60(2), pp. 283–299.

Pychyl, T.A. (2013) *Solving the Procrastination Puzzle: A Concise Guide to Strategies for Change*. New York: Tarcher.

Schwartz, T. and McCarthy, C. (2007) 'Manage your energy, not your time', *Harvard Business Review*, 85(10), pp. 63–73.

Steel, P. (2007) 'The nature of procrastination: A meta-analytic and theoretical review of quintessential self-regulatory failure', *Psychological Bulletin*, 133(1), pp. 65–94.

Wood, W. (2019) *Good Habits, Bad Habits: The Science of Making Positive Changes That Stick*. New York: Farrar, Straus and Giroux.

SECTION FOUR

A NEW WAY TO READ AND WRITE

Does it ever feel to you like university brochures and promotional prospectuses show a version of academic life that doesn't quite line up with your lived experience?

Perhaps you arrived expecting lectures to magically transmit knowledge, readings to make instant sense and essays to flow naturally from understanding. Instead, you've discovered that learning at this level, pace and volume feels *different* – messier, more uncertain, oftentimes overwhelming.

If you're wondering whether you're doing it 'wrong', I have good news: that feeling of confusion isn't a bug in your system. It's a feature of deep learning.

In the pages ahead, we'll explore what nobody explains about university-level learning – not the *what* of your subjects, but the *how* of engaging with them.

Releasing yourself from the discipline dilemma

This isn't about working harder. Straight up. Please don't 'work harder'. It's a phrasing and a framework that assume you're not doing something correctly or effortfully enough. The chapters ahead will:

- Explain why confusion and forgetting are essential to understanding
- Reveal how to read academically without losing yourself
- Lay out ways to write that honour thinking, not just perform it
- Provide memory strategies that go beyond repetition
- Offer critical thinking approaches that welcome your whole self

Stepping sideways

Before we begin, let's gather our thoughts and feelings. *What brought you here?* Not a surface answer like, 'I need better grades' or 'this is a required course text', but the deeper one. *What are you hoping might shift in your relationship with learning?*

Whatever you wrote, hold it close. Your struggles with learning aren't character flaws or intelligence deficits. They're signals that you're ready for a different approach: one that works with how you're built, rather than despite it.

This journey isn't about becoming a 'better' student by someone else's definition. It's about discovering sustainable, meaningful ways of engaging with knowledge that are unique to you.

CHAPTER 14

HOW TO WORK WITH CHALLENGING TEXTS (SO YOU DON'T GIVE UP READING)

Some readings are just ... tough.

Maybe it's that dense philosophy text that feels like it was written in another language. Maybe it's that scientific journal article with seventeen-syllable words in every sentence. Maybe it's that historical document from 1847 that contains a sentence that spans five lines of text. Or maybe it's that required textbook chapter that somehow manages to make even the most fascinating topic feel like watching paint dry in slow motion.

You know the ones I mean.

The readings that make you want to hurl them across the room. The ones where you read the same paragraph four times and still have no idea what happened. The ones that make you question your entire academic path and wonder if maybe you should become a professional dog walker instead (which, honestly, sounds pretty great some days).

This isn't about you not being 'smart enough' or a 'good reader'. This isn't about you not belonging in your programme.

Sometimes texts are genuinely difficult. Sometimes they're written in ways that exclude rather than include. Sometimes they're dense because the author forgot that actual humans need to read them. Sometimes they use deliberately inaccessible language, creating barriers rather than bridges.

And you know what? You can still work with them. You can still extract what you need from them – without losing all hope, without staying up all night, without giving up.

When reading feels like wrestling

First, let's acknowledge what happens in your body when you see that challenging text on your reading list.

Maybe your shoulders tense up. Maybe you get that sinking feeling in your stomach. Maybe you suddenly remember seventeen other things you need to do right now. Maybe you find yourself scrolling through your phone for 'just five more minutes' (that turns into an hour).

This is completely normal. Your brain is trying to protect you from what it perceives as a threat – confusion, frustration or feeling inadequate. But we don't have to stay stuck in this response.

Before diving into that challenging text, take a moment. Literally, just a moment.

Stand up. Shake it out. Do a little stretch. Get yourself some water or tea. Put on music that makes you feel capable (yes, even if it's that one pop song you'd be embarrassed to admit you love).

Tell yourself: 'This text might be challenging, but I have strategies. I'm not going in empty-handed.'

Because you're not. Not anymore.

Take a moment: your reading resistance inventory

Before we explore strategies, pause and consider your particular pattern with difficult texts.

What happens when you encounter a challenging reading?

- Do you avoid it entirely until the last possible moment?
- Do you try to power through and end up exhausted?
- Do you read the same line over and over without absorbing?
- Do you immediately feel inadequate or 'not smart enough'?

Where do you feel the difficulty?

- In your body (tension, fatigue, restlessness)?
- In your emotions (frustration, anxiety, shame)?
- In your thoughts (confusion, blankness, overwhelm)?

What stories do you tell yourself?

- 'Everyone else understands this'
- 'I'm not cut out for this subject'
- 'I should be able to get this by now'
- 'This is a waste of time'

Notice your top ten thinking trends. No need to judge; we're here to make friends. Those mental loops simply shed light on where you might need different strategies or support.

Try this today: the strategic reading toolkit

Before we dive in, let's talk about *AI temptation*. When a text feels frustratingly confusing, it's natural to want to ask ChatGPT or another tool to explain it. And sometimes that's fine – AI *can* be a helpful study companion when you're genuinely standstill stuck, or when you were sick during a key class and need some soundboarding support. But if we hand over too much of the work too soon, we miss out on building the very muscles of understanding that help us grow as learners. We want to rely on our own thinking first – so let's strengthen comprehension, confidence and curiosity before considering outsourcing it.

Strategy 1: The preview power move

Never just dive into a difficult text from word one. That's like jumping into the deep end without checking if there's water.

Instead, try The Preview Power Move:

- **Scan the whole thing.**
  How long is it really? Are there sections? Subheadings? Diagrams? Conclusions? Sometimes just knowing there's an end in sight makes it manageable.
- **Read the introduction and conclusion first.**
  It's not cheating – it's strategic. Most academic texts tell you what they're going to tell you, tell you, then tell you what they told you.
- **Look for the 'pillar sentences'.**
  In many academic texts, seek out the key sentences that carry the weight. Zero in on these.
- **Check for definitions.**
  Is there a glossary? Are key terms defined in the margins? Find these first. It's like getting the secret decoder ring before starting the puzzle.

Strategy 2: The translation technique

You're allowed to translate academic texts into your own words. In fact, you should (Bean, Chappell and Gillam 2013).

Keep a document open beside you as you read. After each paragraph (or even each sentence if it's really dense), write what you think it means in *your* words – the words you'd use to explain it to your best friend.

'This paragraph is basically saying that … '

'I think the author means … '

'In normal human language, this would be … '

This way, you're building understanding, layer by layer.

Strategy 3: The buddy system

You don't have to do this alone.

Find someone else who has to read the same text. Meet up (in person, online, whatever works). Read sections out loud to each other. Pause and discuss. Share your confusion. Celebrate when something clicks.

This isn't cheating. This is collaborative learning. This is how understanding happens – in conversation, in community, in connection.

Strategy 4: The chunk and celebrate method

Under no circumstances should you try to read the entirety of a challenging text in one sitting. That's a recipe for frustration soup.

Instead, chunk it:

- **Set a timer for fifteen to twenty minutes.**
  Read for just that time. When the timer goes off, stop. Even mid-sentence.
- **Take five minutes to move your body (and eyes).**
  Get up. Move around. Look at something that isn't text. Let your brain process.
- **Celebrate what you did read.**
  Two pages? Half a page? Three paragraphs? That's progress.
- **Repeat as needed.**
  Maybe you get through three chunks today. Maybe just one. Both are victories.

Strategy 5: The multiple pass method

Who said you must get everything out of a reading on the first read? Nobody, that's who.

Read the text multiple times with a different aim:

- **First pass:** Lightly peruse the whole of it.
  Don't stop to look things up. Don't take notes. Your only goal is to get from beginning to end with the aim of a broad-strokes understanding.
- **Second pass:** Mark what confuses you.
  Highlight the parts that make no sense. Put question marks or your own personalized symbols in the margins (Simpson and Nist 1990).
- **Third pass:** Look for what you DO understand.
  There will be something. Find it and claim it.
- **Fourth pass (if needed, if available, if required or if interested):** fill in the gaps. Now look up terms. Now check other sources. Now ask for help with specific confusions.

Strategy 6: The context detective

Sometimes a text is hard because you're missing context. It's like walking into a film halfway through.

Be a detective:

- **What's the bigger conversation?**

  What debate is this text part of?
- **When was this written?**

  A text from 1965 uses different language to one from 2020.
- **Who was the audience?**

  Was this written for experts? Students? The general public?
- **What came before?**

  Check your course outline. Sometimes the challenging text builds on something you've already read.

And, if you have multiple texts or agency around sequencing, you may wish to opt for reading the most recently written text first for potentially greater ease of relating to what's been articulated. Or you can intentionally choose to begin your reading session with any grounding texts, like a textbook chapter, to help provide foundational context, before narrowing in on specific topics.

Strategy 7: The good enough principle

You don't need to understand 100 per cent of a text to work with it successfully.

You might understand:

- The main argument (even if you miss supporting details)
- A few key concepts (even if others remain fuzzy)
- How it connects to other course material
- Why it was assigned

And that might be good enough to participate in class, reference in an essay, answer an exam question.

Perfect understanding is not the goal. *Functional* understanding is.

Student voices

Antoine: A second-year philosophy student, Antoine came to me nearly in tears. 'I've been staring at this Heidegger text for three hours,' he said, 'and I honestly think it might be written in code.' What changed everything was when he stopped expecting to understand everything on the first read. 'I started treating difficult texts like puzzles to solve over time, not races to finish.' Now Antoine uses what he calls his 'archaeology method', carefully excavating meaning layer by layer.

Aisha: Aisha, a first-year biology student from Nigeria, was struggling with her chemistry textbook. 'The language was so different from how we learned science back home.' She discovered the buddy system almost by accident when another confused student approached her in the library. They started meeting twice weekly to tackle readings together. 'We'd take turns reading paragraphs out loud and explaining what we thought they meant. Sometimes we were both wrong but figuring it out together made it less scary.'

Chen: An international student from China studying economics, Chen felt like giving up during his first term. 'The academic English was so different from what I had experienced in the past.' His breakthrough came with the multiple pass method. 'First pass, I just read for the feeling. Second pass, I circle words I don't know. Third pass, I look them up. Fourth pass, I try to explain it in Mandarin. Fifth pass, I write a summary in English.' It sounds like a lot, but Chen found it actually saved time.

Meera: A mature student returning after fifteen years, Meera encountered a required reading that seemed deliberately obtuse. She tried every strategy – multiple passes, study groups, office hours. Finally, she went to her professor with documented efforts. The professor admitted, 'You're right. This text is poorly written. I assign it because students need to know the author's ideas, but yes, it's unnecessarily difficult.' They worked out an alternative – Meera read a clearer secondary source and wrote a reflection on why academic writing should prioritize clarity.

→ **Key insight:** Every student discovered that challenging texts aren't meant to be conquered through raw intelligence but navigated through strategic approaches. Whether using archaeology methods (Antoine), buddy systems (Aisha), multiple passes (Chen), or advocating for alternatives (Meera), the breakthrough came from treating difficulty as a problem to solve collaboratively rather than a personal failing to hide.

A new way with reading

Making your way through and getting something out of your academic texts aren't tests of intelligence. It's truly not the case that you either get it or you don't; you're either smart enough or you're not.

Every text, no matter how challenging, was written by a human being trying to communicate something. Your job isn't to worship at the altar of their complexity and superhuman brilliance, or to prove your worth through perfect comprehension. Your job is to engage strategically, to extract what you need, to build understanding bit by bit.

This approach works with you, acknowledges that confusion is temporary, holds that understanding comes in passes and maintains that collaboration enhances comprehension. Sometimes texts *are* genuinely poorly written, and that's not your failure.

Most importantly, this new way gives you the go-ahead to read imperfectly. To use strategies. To ask for help. To say, 'this is good enough for now'. To prioritize your learning over your suffering.

Every challenging text is an invitation to expand – not just your knowledge, but your capacity to sit with frustration, to find patience in the fog and to work with difficulty. But *you* get to decide how you engage with that invitation. You can approach it with curiosity rather than dread, with strategy rather than struggle, with community rather than isolation.

Dig deeper: reading strategically when texts are tough

Essential reading

Scott Young's *Ultralearning: Master Hard Skills, Outsmart the Competition and Accelerate Your Career* (2019) invites us in on his systematic approach to self-directed learning that includes specific tactics for deconstructing complex material, with particular emphasis on directness, drilling and retrieval practice that can be applied to tough academic texts.

Carl Hendrick's 'Ultra-Processed Minds: The End of Deep Reading?' (2024) explores how our consumption of bite-sized, algorithmically curated content parallels ultra-processed food – easily digestible but nutritionally empty – arguing that just as we need whole foods for physical health, we need sustained engagement with challenging texts for cognitive resilience and deep thinking.

Althea Need Kaminske's 'Reading Strategies for College Students' (2021) explores evidence-based approaches for tackling academic texts, emphasizing three key strategies: building background knowledge through lectures and videos before reading, using encoding techniques like outlining and concept mapping to organize understanding and developing reading flexibility to know when to skim versus read critically – skills that help students navigate complex material more effectively.

Video

Ali Abdaal's 'How to Read Academic Papers Efficiently' (2020) demystifies the process of tackling dense scientific literature, sharing his medical training techniques including the three-pass method, strategic skimming and active recall strategies that transform overwhelming research papers into manageable learning opportunities.

References

Abdaal, A. (2020) 'How to read academic papers efficiently', *YouTube*, 31 May. Available at: https://www.youtube.com/watch?v=nH8MF0LLJCI (accessed 1 October 2025).

Bean, J.C., Chappell, V.A. and Gillam, A.M. (2013) *Reading Rhetorically*. 4th edn. Boston: Pearson.

Hendrick, C. (2024) 'Ultra-processed minds: The end of deep reading?', *The Educated Guess*, 14 November. Available at: https://carlhendrick.substack.com/p/ultra-processed-minds-the-end-of (accessed 1 October 2025).

Kaminske, A.N. (2021) 'Reading strategies for college students', *The Learning Scientists*, 19 August. Available at: https://www.learningscientists.org/blog/2021/8/19-1 (accessed 1 October 2025).

Simpson, M.L. and Nist, S.L. (1990) 'Textbook annotation: An effective and efficient study strategy for college students', *Journal of Reading*, 34(2), pp. 122–129.

Young, S. (2019) *Ultralearning: Master Hard Skills, Outsmart the Competition and Accelerate Your Career*. New York: HarperBusiness.

CHAPTER 15

HOW TO THINK CRITICALLY (SO YOU KNOW HOW TO REFLECT, ANALYSE AND READ BETWEEN THE LINES)

You're sitting in your seminar class. The discussion is heating up about a recent policy change and everyone seems to have strong opinions. As voices rise and fall around you, you notice something interesting: some students are quoting headlines, others are questioning sources and a few are sitting quietly, processing.

One student says, 'But the article clearly states ... '

Another interrupts, 'Who funded that study though?'

A third adds, 'Has anyone considered what's not being said here?'

And you?

You're wondering: *How do I know what to believe? How do I form my own opinion when everyone sounds so convincing? How do I participate in this conversation authentically?*

This is critical thinking in action – messy, complex and absolutely essential.

What critical thinking actually is (and isn't)

Let me start by saying what critical thinking isn't, because I've watched too many learners tie themselves in knots trying to be 'critical enough'.

Critical thinking isn't about:

- Being cynical or negative about everything
- Dismissing ideas just to seem smart
- Finding flaws for the sake of it
- Having the 'right' answer
- Sounding academic or using fancy words

Critical thinking *is* about being genuinely curious about how things work, why people believe what they believe and what might be missing from the picture.

It's about holding ideas up to the light and examining them from different angles – not to destroy them, not to tear down the thinker of them but to understand the thought, the person having the thought and the implications of the thought more deeply.

Think of it like this: When you're choosing a new mobile phone, you don't just grab the first one you see. You read reviews from different sources. You compare whether buying it outright or getting a contract makes more sense for your situation. You check which retailers offer the best value. You think about what you actually *need* from a phone versus what the marketing is telling you to want. You're not being negative or overly critical about phones – you're being *thoughtful*. You're genuinely curious about which option works best for you and you're willing to look at the decision from multiple angles before committing.

That's critical thinking.

The four angles of critical thinking

Over the years, I've noticed that critical thinking often involves four key angles. You can picture this like a camera taking different shots. You don't have to do them in order and you certainly don't have to do all of them every time. But knowing these angles – knowing the breadth of shots you can take of a particular 'scene' – gives you options.

Angle 1: Zooming out (context)

This is about stepping back to see the bigger picture (Nosich 2012). When you encounter an idea, argument or piece of information, ask yourself:

- Where is this coming from?
- When was this created?
- Who benefits from this perspective?
- What was happening in the world when this was written?
- What conversations is this part of or connected to?

I had a student, Ameera, who was struggling with a particularly abstract reading. Then she zoomed out – researched when it was written, what was happening geopolitically at that time, what the author was responding to. Suddenly, the abstract became concrete. The philosophy text wasn't floating in space; it was grounded in a specific moment.

Angle 2: Zooming in (details)

This is where you become a detective, examining the fine print:

- What specific evidence is being used?
- What words are chosen and why?
- What assumptions are being made?
- What logic connects point A to point B?
- What's the quality of the sources?

You don't need to be suspicious of everything – noticing what's 'sus', as my girls might say. Sometimes zooming in confirms that something is solid and well-reasoned. Other times, you might notice gaps. Both discoveries are valuable.

Angle 3: Looking sideways (perspectives)

This move invites you to consider other viewpoints:

- Who might disagree and why?
- What would this look like from another perspective?
- How might someone with different life experiences read this?
- What would the 'opposite' argument be?
- Whose voices are missing?

One of my favourite examples comes from a business student analysing a case study about 'successful' urban development. When he started looking sideways – considering the perspectives of long-time residents, small business owners and displaced folks – the definition of 'success' became much more complex.

Angle 4: Looking inward (reflection)

This might be the most overlooked move, but it's crucial (Kahneman 2011) to ask yourself:

- What are my own biases here?
- Why do I want to believe (or not believe) this?
- What experiences am I bringing to this reading?
- How might my patterns of thought, feelings and decision-making be affecting my analysis?
- What don't I know that I need to know?

This isn't about dismissing your perspective; it's about understanding it. Your experiences and insights are valuable data points in your critical thinking process.

Notice your patterns: your critical thinking courage

Take a moment to reflect on how you usually approach new information. Especially when asked –in a class, text or assessment – to 'take a critical view', 'assess critically', or outright, 'approach with critical thinking'.

You might find that you're already *doing* critical thinking without knowing that you're doing it! Or, doing a version of it.

When you come up against something you disagree with, what's your first instinct?

- Do you immediately look for what doesn't fit quite right?
- Do you try to understand why someone might think that way?
- Do you check your own assumptions?
- Do you seek out more information?

When you meet something that confirms what you already believe, what happens?

- Do you wonder why it lands so easily?
- Do you examine its nuances?
- Do you look for exceptions?
- Do you seek to understand its limitations?

There's no judgement here, just curiosity about your current patterns. Knowing your tendencies helps you expand your critical thinking repertoire of strategies.

Try this today: practising criticality in context

Reading critically

The multi-highlighter method

Use different colours for:

- First colour: Main arguments or claims (think green or whatever colour feels like 'yes, this!')

- Second colour: Evidence or support (choose a colour that feels supportive, like a lighter shade of your first colour to signify relatedness)
- Third colour: Questions or things to follow up on (your colour-choice here should be a flag, but not alarming ... no angry red please!)

This visual system helps you discern the structure of an argument and see it at a glance in future referencing.

The 'says/does/suggests' analysis

For each paragraph of a text you're reading, note:

- What it SAYS (the literal content)
- What it DOES (introduces a concept, provides evidence, makes a transition, etc.)
- What it SUGGESTS (what's implied, hinted at or assumed between the lines)

This helps you understand not just what you're reading, but how arguments are constructed.

Let's practise with an actual paragraph from an academic text – one of mine – about *professor* stress and wellbeing:

> That back and forth is happening day in, day out, most often without any of us being fully aware. We can feel evidence of it – times of performance and of calm, times of amplified worry and others of serenity. These are clues of our nervous systems at work. Most have heard that one of those systems, the sympathetic, is activated when we are ready to fight, take flight or freeze on the spot in the face of actual or perceived threat or stress. This may well be where most of us – students? educators? all humans? – exist for much of the time these days – work–life imbalanced and in the context of COVID-19 no less. (Shaffer 2021, p. 75)

SAYS (literal content):

There's a back-and-forth process in our bodies we don't usually notice. We can feel it in our moods – sometimes calm, sometimes worried. This is our nervous system. One system (sympathetic) activates when stressed. Most people stay stuck in this stressed state.

DOES (function):

- Introduces the nervous system concept
- Connects science to feelings you recognize
- Creates a problem (we're stuck in stress mode)
- Includes readers with 'we' and 'us'

SUGGESTS (deeper implications):

- This isn't personal failure – it's how modern life (especially university) works
- Your body has wisdom you're ignoring
- Academic culture creates constant stress with no built-in rest
- There's another mode we're missing (rest) that the text will reveal later

Often, students stop at SAYS; strong critical thinkers, however, reach for SUGGESTS. Try this three-part approach next time you face a challenging paragraph – you might be surprised how much clearer, richer and more purposeful it becomes.

The question generator

As you read, jot questions:

- In the margins, right next to the original text prompt
- At the end of in-class notes to nudge you to follow up for a clarification with a TA, professor or in your next lecture
- Kept in an ongoing course-based document serving as future fodder for assignments

In any configuration, questions generated become excellent discussion points or essay topics.

Listening critically

Thinking critically begins with listening critically; here's how you might go about it:

The both/and approach

- Instead of thinking 'this is right' or 'this is wrong', try 'what's useful here *AND* what might be missing?'

The source check

- When someone makes a claim, mentally note whether it's their opinion, research, experience or something they heard. Each has value, but knowing which is which helps you evaluate appropriately.

The reaction reset

- Before responding in discussion, take a breath and ask yourself, *'Am I reacting or responding, and from what place? What am I assuming? What clarification might I need?'*

Writing critically

Reading critically helps you understand *what others are saying*. Writing critically is how you join the conversation – making your own claims, backing them up and showing why they matter.

Your essay's main argument is the overall claim you're making – your answer to the assignment question. Each paragraph makes a point that supports this main argument. Think of paragraphs as building blocks that construct your larger case.

Here's how to write critically, paragraph by paragraph:

State your claim clearly

Each paragraph needs one clear claim that supports your overall argument. Put it up front, usually in your first or second sentence.

> **Weak**: 'There are many factors that contribute to climate change.'
>
> **Strong**: 'Individual consumer choices, while important, have far less impact on climate change than corporate and governmental policies.'

Back it up with evidence

Once you've made a claim, prove it. Use data, quotes, examples or expert opinions from credible sources.

> **Claim**: 'Individual consumer choices have far less impact than corporate policies.'
>
> **Evidence**: 'Just 100 companies are responsible for 71 per cent of global emissions since 1988' (CDP 2017).

Explain why it matters

Connect the dots. How does your evidence support your claim? Why should readers care?

> **Explanation**: 'This means that even if every individual recycled perfectly and drove an electric car, we'd barely dent emissions without regulatory changes. The focus on individual responsibility, while well-intentioned, distracts from where change would actually be most effective.'

The counter-argument sandwich

Strong critical writing acknowledges complexity. When you're building your argument with supporting claims, consider counter-perspectives:

1. Make your claim (a point supporting your main argument).
2. Acknowledge the strongest counter-argument.
3. Explain why your claim still holds (or how both perspectives might be true).

This shows you've thought deeply about the issue, not just picked a side *un*critically and gone with it.

Let's keep going with our climate change example!

> Claim supporting main argument: 'Systemic change through corporate regulation will create far greater climate impact than individual action.'
>
> Counter-argument acknowledged: 'While individual choices *do* matter and shouldn't be dismissed, they raise awareness and model values.'
>
> Why your claim holds: 'Individual household interventions can't match the scale of emission reductions possible through policy that holds major polluters accountable.'

Putting it together: *'While individual action matters and shouldn't be dismissed entirely, systemic change through corporate regulation will create far greater impact. Personal choices raise awareness and model values, but they can't match the scale of emission reductions possible through policy.'*

The '__what?' test

While you're writing, if you feel like you're retelling, reiterating and restating instead of the critical writing required, consider a '__what?' question.

Understanding:

- So what? (significance/relevance)
- Now what? (action/next steps)
- Then what? (consequences/implications)

Deepening:

- But what? (contradictions/tensions)
- For what? (purpose/intention)
- With what? (resources/tools needed)
- Despite what? (obstacles/barriers)
- Instead of what? (alternatives/trade-offs)

Contextualizing:

- Compared to what? (perspective/relativity)
- According to what? (source/authority)

- Connected to what? (relationships/systems)
- Because of what? (causation/origins)

Analysing:

- If not, then what? (inverse thinking)
- Even if, what? (worst case/resilience)
- Assuming what? (hidden premises)
- Missing what? (gaps/blind spots)

Troubleshooting critical thinking challenges

'I don't know enough to think critically about this.'

You know more than you think. Your life experience, observations and questions are all valid starting points. Critical thinking isn't about having all the answers; it's about asking good questions. Start with 'I wonder ... ' or 'I notice ... ' and build from there.

'Everything seems equally valid/invalid.'

Underneath, this is actually a sign that your critical thinking is developing! You're seeing complexity. The next step is developing criteria for evaluation. *What are your values? What evidence do you find compelling?* You don't need absolute truth, but you can develop informed positions.

'I'm afraid of being wrong.'

Who isn't?! But critical thinking isn't about being right. It's about considering a text, point, opinion or argument. Some of the best critical thinkers regularly say, 'I might be wrong about this, but here's what I'm thinking ... ' Being willing to be wrong means you're open to learning.

'It takes so much time.'

It's completely true: critical thinking *can* slow you down ... initially. It's truly such a challenging, layered endeavour and isn't a straightforward or simplistic skill to teach or learn (Willingham 2007). But like any new skill, it becomes more second nature with practise. Plus, the time invested often saves time later – in writing assignments, studying, analysing and decision-making.

A critical framework for critical thinking

If you need to analyse something critically, try this structured approach:

Comprehension

- What is being said/shown/argued?
- Can I summarize this in my own words?
- What are the key points?

Context

- Who created this and why?
- When and where was it created?
- What conversation is this part of?

Construction

- How is the argument built?
- What evidence is used?
- What assumptions are made?

Critique

- What works well?
- What are the limitations?
- What questions remain?

Connection

- How does this relate to other things I know?
- How might I use this?
- What does this mean for my understanding?

You don't always need to consider every question here. Sometimes one from each category, or all from a few categories, will get you thinking through more deeply, comprehensively, critically.

Critical thinking as self-care

One thing that's rarely discussed is how critical thinking is actually a form of self-care. What? Truly! When you think critically, you're:

- Protecting yourself from misinformation
- Making more informed decisions
- Understanding your own beliefs and values
- Building confidence in your judgement
- Developing intellectual independence

In a world full of competing messages, influencers and information overload, critical thinking helps you find your own ground to stand on. It's not about becoming sceptical of everything – it's about becoming thoughtfully engaged with the world.

See it in action: meet Mariam

Mariam came to see me in her second year, frustrated with her marks. 'I do all the readings,' she said, 'I understand them, but my essays keep coming back with comments like "needs more critical analysis" and "go deeper".'

(I can't tell you how many times I've heard from students, always with a sigh, their frustration with the 'go deeper' comment on a paper, unclear and unsure of how to do this or where to begin.)

The breakthrough

We looked at one of her essays together. She had summarized the theories beautifully, cited everything properly, but something was missing. Her essay read like a very good report, not an analysis.

'What do you actually think about these theories?' I asked.

She paused. 'Well, the theory about social mobility doesn't really account for what I've seen in my community. It assumes everyone starts with the same access to information about opportunities, but that's not true.'

'That's critical thinking!' I said. 'That's your analysis. Your lived experience interrogating the theory.'

The results

We worked on bringing her voice into her academic writing. She learned to write things like:

'While Smith's theory effectively explains X, it overlooks the role of Y ... ' 'This framework is useful for understanding A, but less applicable to B because ... ' 'The assumption that X leads to Y doesn't account for situations where ... '

Her next essay came back with a note from her professor: 'Excellent critical engagement with the material. Your analysis brings an insightful perspective to these established theories.'

Mariam hadn't become a different person. She'd just given herself consent to think critically about what she was learning, to bring her full self to her academic work (hooks 2010).

→ **Key insight:** Students often already possess critical thinking abilities but don't give them credit as being academically valid; they've been taught to hide their own perspectives behind summaries and citations. Mariam's breakthrough came not from learning a new skill but from discovering that her lived experience questioning a theory's assumptions *was* the critical analysis her professors wanted. The transformation happened when she learned to bridge her authentic observations ('this doesn't match what I see in my community') with academic language ('this framework overlooks ... '), revealing that critical thinking isn't about acquiring special knowledge but about inviting yourself to interrogate what you're learning through your own lens.

A new way with critical thinking

Critical thinking is not some kind of elite academic skill; nor is it something you either possess or you don't; nor is it a special talent for picking things apart and finding flaws. Critical thinking is not coldly analytical, emotionally detached or perpetually sceptical.

This new way recognizes that critical thinking is already within you. You questioned that theory because it didn't match your reality. You wondered why certain voices were missing from the discussion. You noticed when evidence didn't quite support the conclusion. That's critical thinking, you just hadn't known you were allowed to trust it.

This approach works with your full humanity. It acknowledges that thinking critically can feel uncomfortable when it challenges beliefs you've held, reveals complexity where you wanted simplicity or shows that institutions you trusted have flaws. This discomfort isn't failure, it's growth.

When critical thinking feels uncomfortable:

- Acknowledge the discomfort without judgement
- Remember that changing your mind shows strength, not weakness
- Take breaks when overwhelm sets in
- Talk through challenges with trusted friends
- Accept that complexity is more honest than false simplicity

Critical thinking doesn't mean you can't enjoy things, believe in things or feel strongly about things. You can analyse your favourite film and still love it. You can examine your spiritual beliefs and still hold them dear. You can question academic theories while respecting their contributions.

Most importantly, critical thinking isn't about becoming removed or wary. It's about becoming more fully engaged with the world, more capable of understanding the layers, more able to make informed choices about what you believe and why. It's about bringing your whole self – including your experiences, perspectives and questions – to your academic work.

Start small. Pick one lecture this week and try one strategy or line of inquiry. Choose one reading and practise active questioning. Engage with one idea that challenges you and lean into the discomfort with curiosity rather than fear.

The world needs thinkers like you – people willing to look closely, question thoughtfully and engage meaningfully with complexity. Not to tear everything down, but to understand more deeply. Not to become sceptics, but to become thoughtfully discerning.

Your critical thinking journey isn't about becoming a perfect thinking machine. It's about becoming a more thoughtful, engaged and empowered learner who trusts their own capacity to engage with ideas, to question what needs questioning and to contribute their unique perspective to academic conversations.

Welcome to thinking critically – where your questions matter, your perspectives count and your intellectual courage grows stronger with every uncomfortable truth you're willing to examine.

Dig deeper: thinking clearly and questioning narratives

Essential reading

Daniel Kahneman's *Thinking, Fast and Slow* (2011) reveals the two systems that drive our thinking – the fast, intuitive and emotional versus the slow, deliberate and logical – offering insights into how cognitive biases shape our decisions and why critical thinking requires conscious effort to engage our slower, more analytical system.

bell hooks' *Teaching to Transgress: Education as the Practice of Freedom* (1994) reimagines critical thinking not as an academic exercise but as a tool for liberation, arguing that true education requires us to question power structures, challenge dominant narratives and think critically about whose knowledge is valued and why.

TED Talk

Chimamanda Ngozi Adichie's 'The Danger of a Single Story' TED Talk (2009) powerfully illustrates how incomplete narratives shape our understanding of others and ourselves, demonstrating why critical thinking requires seeking multiple perspectives and questioning the stories we've been told.

Podcast

You Are Not So Smart podcast by David McRaney explores self-delusion and cognitive biases through engaging interviews with researchers, revealing how our brains deceive us and offering strategies for thinking more clearly about our own thinking.

References

Adichie, C.N. (2009) 'The danger of a single story', *TEDGlobal*, July. Available at: https://www.ted.com/talks/chimamanda_ngozi_adichie_the_danger_of_a_single_story (accessed 1 October 2025).

CDP (2017) *The Carbon Majors Database: CDP Carbon Majors Report 2017*. Available at: https://cdn.cdp.net/cdp-production/cms/reports/documents/000/002/327/original/Carbon-Majors-Report-2017.pdf (accessed 1 October 2025).

hooks, b. (1994) *Teaching to Transgress: Education as the Practice of Freedom*. New York: Routledge.

hooks, b. (2010) *Teaching Critical Thinking: Practical Wisdom*. New York: Routledge.

Kahneman, D. (2011) *Thinking, Fast and Slow*. New York: Farrar, Straus and Giroux.

McRaney, D. (2012–) You Are Not So Smart [podcast]. Available at: https://youarenotsosmart.com (accessed 1 October 2025).

Nosich, G.M. (2012) *Learning to Think Things Through: A Guide to Critical Thinking across the Curriculum*. 4th edn. Boston: Pearson.

Shaffer, D.K. (2021) 'Pendulation: Awakening to rest'. In: Lemon, N. (ed.) *Creating a Place for Self-Care and Wellbeing in Higher Education*. London: Routledge, pp. 71–86. Available at: https://doi.org/10.4324/9781003144397-7 (accessed 1 October 2025).

Willingham, D.T. (2007) 'Critical thinking: Why is it so hard to teach?', *American Educator*, 31(2), pp. 8–19.

CHAPTER 16

WHAT TO DO WITH CITING (SO YOU DON'T PLAGIARIZE)

You're finishing an essay at 2.00 am. You've woven together ideas from lectures, that documentary you watched, three articles, a brilliant TikTok that explained the concept perfectly, and ChatGPT helped you understand one particularly dense paragraph. Now you're staring at your references section, wondering:

'How do I cite a TikTok?'

'Do I mention the AI?'

'What if I can't remember which article mentioned that statistic?'

The whole citing thing feels like a bureaucratic nightmare designed to catch you out. A maze of rules where one wrong formatting choice marks you as academically dishonest.

We're navigating a world where AI can generate text, where social media threads contain scholarly insights, where podcasts break down complex theories and where the line between 'my idea' and 'influenced by' has never been blurrier.

Citing isn't about catching cheaters or memorizing where commas go versus periods. In our current moment – with AI, social, podcasts and traditional texts all shaping how we think – citation has become more important than ever, not as a gatekeeping mechanism but as a way to trace how ideas form in our interconnected world in our interconnected world.

When citation feels like a trap

Let's acknowledge what happens when you face the citing requirements on your syllabus.

Maybe you panic about getting the format exactly right. Maybe you worry you'll accidentally plagiarize. Maybe you feel like your own words aren't good enough compared to the sources. Maybe you're confused about what needs citing and what doesn't.

Most plagiarism doesn't come from malice. It comes from:

Fear

- 'I'm running out of time!'

Confusion

- 'I don't understand the rules!'

Self-doubt

- 'The author said it better.'

Overwhelm

- 'There are way too many sources to track.'

Exhaustion

- 'ChatGPT could get this done in seconds.'

These feelings are real. But citing doesn't have to be scary, burdensome or punitive ... once you understand what it's for.

The real reasons we cite

It's about community, not compliance

Think of citing like being at a dinner party. Someone shares a brilliant insight. Later, when telling others, you'd naturally say, 'My friend had this interesting point about ... ' That's all citing is – acknowledging where ideas come from. It's basic courtesy extended to academic work.

Every citation is you saying: 'This person's work mattered. It helped me think.' You're acknowledging that knowledge isn't created in isolation.

It's your intellectual backup

Citations strengthen your argument. When you write, 'You need sleep after learning to essentially hit the Save button on those new memories so that you don't forget' (Walker 2017), you're not just avoiding plagiarism; you're saying, 'Here's the expert who backs me up.'

It's a gift to your readers

Good citations are breadcrumbs for curious minds. When someone wants to know more, your citations give them a path to follow.

It's about transparency in the AI age

When AI helps you write, citing becomes about being transparent about the origins and veracity of ideas.

The AI element (and elephant): a framework for ethical use

We're all immersed in feeling out the rights, wrongs and edges of generative AI. And it's nearly always there; AI as the ever-present elephant in the room. To help us bring integrity, here are some worthwhile considerations to use as a gauge and guide in your own writing.

- **AI as a thought partner**
  Using ChatGPT to understand a complex concept? That's like having a tutor. Acknowledge it: 'Initial understanding clarified through discussion with Claude AI (2025).'
- **AI as a writing assistant**
  If AI helps restructure a paragraph, think of it like visiting the writing centre. Note: 'Paragraph structure refined with ChatGPT assistance.'
- **AI as a research tool**
  When AI helps find sources, it's like a library assistant. Be clear: 'Sources identified using Perplexity AI.'
- **The golden rule**
  If AI contributed substantively, acknowledge it. Check yourself: If you wouldn't feel comfortable with your professor knowing, reconsider using it.

Notice your patterns: honest questions about citing

Let's take a little time to cultivate a citation inventory to understand where the challenges and conflicts are for you.

What makes citing feel difficult?

- The formatting rules feel arbitrary and confusing?
- You're unsure what counts as 'common knowledge'?
- Tracking sources while researching feels overwhelming?
- You're worried about accidentally plagiarizing?

What stories do you tell yourself about citation?

- 'I'm bad at keeping track of sources'
- 'Citation rules are just bureaucratic nonsense'

- 'My ideas aren't original enough to distinguish from sources'
- 'I'll figure out citations at the end'

Has citing ever felt manageable?

- Has anyone ever taught you how to cite well?
- Have you had a system from the start?
- When have you understood why you were citing?
- When have you considered citations as joining a conversation?

Stay judgement-free. Reflecting on these offers you insight into where you might need different strategies or support.

Try this today: your citation toolkit

The three-column method

When researching, create three columns and continually update:

- Source info (author, date, page)
- Their ideas (quotes, paraphrases)
- Your thoughts (reactions, connections between texts, connections from lived experiences)

This keeps everything organized and distinguishes their ideas from your analysis.

The attribution habit

Practise saying where ideas come from in everyday conversation. 'I read that ... ' or 'My friend mentioned ... ' are good places to start. This makes academic attribution feel natural.

The citation manager

Use Zotero, Mendeley, RefWorks, EndNote, or your own self-styled, well-organized document. Your brain has better things to do than remember publication dates.

Start early, cite as you go

Every time you encounter something useful, immediately note what it was, where it came from, how you used it. Don't leave citations for the end. In truth, though simple, this may well be the wisest citation strategy of all.

Student voices

Zhang Wei: Zhang Wei came to me in tears after receiving a plagiarism warning despite trying to cite everything. 'I didn't think I needed to cite AI, and the YouTube stuff felt like just learning, not sources.' We worked through his assignment, identifying which ideas were original, which came from AI, which emerged from discussions. His revised assignment included transparency about ChatGPT discussions and YouTube learning. His professor responded: 'Thank you for the transparency. This is exactly the intellectual honesty we need in the AI age.'

Mary: Citing informal sources was a persistent struggle for Mary. 'My best insights came from a Reddit thread and my study group. How am I supposed to cite *those*?' We developed a system for acknowledging all intellectual contributions, formal *and* informal. Her next essay included a note about collaborative thinking and unconventional sources. Her professor appreciated the honesty about how learning actually happens.

James: Stuck in the grip of formatting anxiety, James shared this insight with me, 'I spend more time worrying about where periods go than actually writing.' We focused on the underlying principle – giving credit – over perfect formatting. He learned that a good-faith attempt at citation, even imperfectly formatted, is infinitely better than no citation at all.

→ **Key insight:** Students often see citing as a defensive move to avoid punitive action rather than an offensive strategy to strengthen their work. The breakthrough comes when citing is seen as joining a conversation, not simply following arbitrary rules. And in our AI-augmented, multimedia world, intellectual honesty matters more than perfect formatting.

A new way with citation

The old way treats citation as a bureaucratic hoop to jump through, a defensive move to avoid punishment, a set of arbitrary rules to memorize and fear.

The new way recognizes that citation is about intellectual honesty and community. It's about acknowledging that your brilliant essay builds on centuries of human thought, last week's lecture, that clarifying YouTube video, and yes, even that helpful AI conversation.

This approach works with how learning really happens. You're not expected to generate original thoughts in isolation. You're joining an ongoing conversation, and citations are how you acknowledge the other voices at the table.

In our AI-augmented world, citation becomes even more vital – not as gatekeeping but as transparency. It's how we maintain human connection in an increasingly automated landscape, distinguish between human insight and machine generation, and stay honest about the complex ways ideas form.

Your citations tell the story of your learning journey. They map where you've been, who you've learned from, what tools you've used. Whether your sources are ancient texts, cutting-edge articles, TikTok videos or AI conversations, acknowledging them honestly makes you a participant in the grand conversation of human knowledge.

Start with one small step. On your next assignment, try the three-column method. Or practice citing that TED Talk video that helped you strengthen your comprehension. Or acknowledge that AI assistance. Transparency *always* strengthens your work.

Citation isn't about perfection. It's about ... *participation*. It's about saying, 'I'm here, I'm learning and I'm building on what came before while adding my own voice.'

And that conversation? It's waiting for your contribution.

Dig deeper: citing with integrity in the AI age

Essential reading

Diane Pecorari's *Teaching to Avoid Plagiarism* (2013) explores why students struggle with citation, revealing it's rarely about dishonesty and more often about confusion, cultural differences in knowledge ownership and the complex challenge of distinguishing between common knowledge and ideas requiring attribution.

Wendy Sutherland-Smith's *Plagiarism, the Internet, and Student Learning* (2018) examines how digital technologies are reshaping our understanding of authorship and originality, offering frameworks for maintaining academic integrity in an interconnected, digital world.

Videos

Keeta Gladue's 'Indigenous Academic Integrity: Relationships, Stories and Reciprocity' (2020) offers a powerful reframing of citation as relationship-building, honouring where knowledge comes from and maintaining integrity through naming elders, mentors and communities who share wisdom. For students learning to cite in our multimedia world, Gladue demonstrates that acknowledging sources – whether Blue Sky posts, AI conversations or traditional texts – is ultimately about mutuality.

Online resources

Purdue OWL (Online Writing Lab) remains the gold standard for citation guidance, offering clear examples for every citation style and source type imaginable, from old school books to TikTok videos.

The Citation Project (citationproject.net) provides research on how students actually use sources versus how we think they do, revealing the gap between citation rules and real-world practice.

References

Gladue, K. (2020) 'Indigenous academic integrity: Relationships, stories and reciprocity', *Urgent and Emerging Topics for Academic Integrity*, webinar, Taylor Institute for Teaching and Learning, University of Calgary, 24 November. Available at: https://taylorinstitute.ucalgary.ca/resources/indigenous-paradigms-in-practice (accessed 1 October 2025).

Howard, R.M. and Jamieson, S. (2014–) *The Citation Project: Preventing Plagiarism, Teaching Writing*. Available at: http://www.citationproject.net (accessed 1 October 2025).

Pecorari, D. (2013) *Teaching to Avoid Plagiarism: How to Promote Good Source Use*. Maidenhead: Open University Press.

Purdue Online Writing Lab (2024) *Purdue OWL*, Purdue University. Available at: https://owl.purdue.edu/ (accessed 1 October 2025).

Sutherland-Smith, W. (2018) *Plagiarism, the Internet, and Student Learning: Improving Academic Integrity*. New York: Routledge.

Walker, M. (2017) 'The sleep deprivation epidemic', RSA, video, 23 October. Available at: https://www.youtube.com/watch?v=klrxeeFxJv0 (accessed 1 October 2025).

CHAPTER 17

WHAT TO DO WITH A HARD ESSAY (TO GET IT HANDED IN … WELL-CRAFTED … AND ON TIME)

Your essay is due Monday at noon. You've known about it for six weeks. You've thought about it approximately forty-seven times – *usually* in the wee hours when you can't sleep, during other classes or while scrolling your phone with that familiar twist of guilt in your stomach. You've now got three days to pull it off.

Your computer is open. But you decide you need a cuppa first. Then you should probably check the assignment instructions one more time. Actually, you should re-read that article your professor mentioned. Oh, and your desk is untidy – you can't possibly write in this chaos. Maybe check if anyone's posted in the course Discord. Just a quick scroll through social media to 'clear your head'.

Three hours later, you've deep-cleaned your entire room, watched four YouTube videos on 'essay writing tips', messaged three equally panicked classmates and written exactly zero words. The guilt is now a full-body experience. You promise yourself you'll start fresh tomorrow morning. Early. 5.00 am early. This time you mean it.

You don't have a 'bad work ethic'. You're not 'bad at essays'. You are stuck in a procrastination loop that millions of students experience, and it has almost nothing to do with time management and everything to do with how our brains respond to uncertainty, perfectionism and fear.

Procrastination reframe

Putting work off, avoiding starting and struggling to make progress – these are not character flaws. Procrastination is an emotional regulation strategy – a way your brain protects you from uncomfortable feelings like anxiety, fear of failure or overwhelm (Sirois and Pychyl 2013). Procrastination is in-the-moment relief; a momentary mood-uplift. When you don't begin that essay when you've planned to or know you should, you're not being irresponsible; you're trying to avoid present psychological discomfort in a round-about way.

So, viewed differently, that essay due in three days represents multiple threats to your nervous system:

- Fear of judgement ('What if my ideas are stupid?')
- Fear of failure ('What if I get a bad mark?')
- Fear of success ('What if I set expectations too high?')
- Perfectionism ('It has to be brilliant or it's worthless')
- Overwhelm ('I don't even know where to start')
- Impostor syndrome ('I don't belong here anyway')

Your brain, trying to keep you safe, suggests a perfectly logical solution: *don't* write the essay. At least not right now. Maybe later, when you feel more prepared, more inspired, more capable; when you feel like less is at stake.

The problem? That magical moment never comes. Instead, the deadline approaches, anxiety intensifies and eventually, panic becomes your co-author.

The hidden cost of procrastination

Beyond the obvious stress, procrastination extracts other tolls:

The quality tax

- When you do finally write that essay at the last minute, you're writing with a stressed brain that can't access its full creative and analytical capabilities.

The learning loss

- Essays just assessments; they're learning tools. By rushing through writing, you miss the opportunity to deeply engage with ideas, make connections and develop your thinking.

The confidence erosion

- Every time you procrastinate and submit something you're not proud of, you reinforce the narrative: 'I'm not good at this'. This becomes a self-fulfilling prophecy; a loop that diminishes your self-efficacy (Kim and Seo 2015).

The relationship strain

- Last-minute panic affects everyone around you – roommates dealing with your stress, friends you cancel on, family members you snap at, classmates you desperately message for help.

Notice your patterns: your procrastination style

Not all procrastination looks the same. Bringing awareness to why and how you delay, and more deeply understanding *your* particular procrastination pattern, is step one to interrupting it (Klingsieck 2013).

Are you a perfectionist procrastinator?

> You can't start because you're waiting for the perfect opening sentence, the perfect understanding, the perfect conditions. You'd rather submit nothing than something imperfect.
>
> Tell-tale signs: Endless research, multiple false starts, deleting paragraphs, waiting for inspiration.

Are you an overwhelmed procrastinator?

> The essay feels so big, so complex, that you don't know where to begin. Every time you think about it, your brain short-circuits.
>
> Tell-tale signs: Avoiding the assignment, feeling immobilized when trying to start, jumping between tasks without completing any.

Are you a rebel procrastinator?

> You resent being told what to write and when – what to *do* and when. The essay feels like an imposition on your autonomy.
>
> Tell-tale signs: Anger at the assignment, venting about the instructor, doing everything except the essay.

Are you a self-doubter procrastinator?

> You're convinced you don't belong, that everyone else understands better, writes better, thinks better. Starting means risking exposure as a fraud.
>
> Tell-tale signs: Comparing yourself to others, assuming everyone else finds it easy, fear of revealing 'incompetence'.

Are you a busy-bee procrastinator?

> You fill your time with other tasks – all important and urgent – leaving no time for the essay.
>
> Tell-tale signs: Hyper-productivity in other areas, elaborate scheduling that somehow never includes essay time.

Take a moment to identify your pattern. You might embody multiple styles depending on the assignment, the course or what else is happening in your life. No judgement. Ever. Just kind curiosity.

The science of wanting to work

So much of this book is offering loving reassurance that you're not alone, you're not a problem to be solved and you're not going about things all wrong. It's also to share with you that your experiences are actually *so* common that they're the focus of studies, decades of research, publications and whole disciplines. *That's* how common things like procrastination are.

The Zeigarnik effect

Russian psychologist Bluma Zeigarnik discovered that people remember uncompleted tasks better than completed ones (Zeigarnik 1927) – which is why that unwritten essay might be haunting your thoughts. But here's the powerful nugget: once you start, even with just one sentence, your brain begins working on the problem in the background. Not finishing that paragraph, doing the paper in parts – these are actually to your advantage! Which is to say, *don't* do it all ... not all at once ... *on purpose!*

Temporal Motivation Theory

Piers Steel's research reveals that procrastination increases when the reward feels distant (as in, your mark seems far away) (Steel and König 2006); the task's value feels low (you don't see the point); your expectancy of success is low (you don't think you'll do well); and your impulsiveness is high (distractions are everywhere).

Understanding these factors helps you hack your own motivation system.

Try this today: the start-small-build-momentum method

Instead of trying to write an entire essay, make starting so small – a running theme in *A New Way to Learn*, and a truly skillful strategy – that your brain can't resist. Let's use a week's time frame, but it can expand this method proportionally if you have more time, or if the paper you're crafting is particularly challenging or lengthy. And, while these aren't prescriptions or blueprints for 'success', they can be helpful starts when stuckness feels especially stubborn.

Phase 1: the microstart (day 1–2)

The two-minute essay

Set a timer for two minutes. Write anything about your essay topic – questions, complaints, random thoughts, even 'I don't know what to write about this stupid topic but … ' When the timer goes off, stop. You've started. That's the entire goal, nothing more.

The question dump

Instead of answering the essay question, write twenty questions about it. Here are five to get you started.

- What is this really asking?
- What would a good answer include?
- What confuses me?
- What do I already know?
- What do I need to find out?

The messy map

Get a large piece of paper. Write your essay topic in the centre. For ten minutes, add anything that comes to mind. Use arrows, markers, symbols, asterisks. Don't organize. Don't assess. Just dump everything onto paper.

Read a little, rest a little

In tiny intervals, read about your topic; think, a single paragraph, page or article. Then, rest. No need to become a full-time researcher here. Instead, aim to find three relevant quotes from a source, cite, then pause. Repeat.

Phase 2: the expansion (day 3–4)

The Frankenstein draft

Open a new document. Copy and paste anything relevant – question dump answers, quotes from readings (remembering to cite as you go!), snippets of lecture notes. Don't sequence yet. Just collect. It's easier to edit chaos than create from nothing.

The voice note method

Can't write? Talk! Record yourself explaining the essay topic to a friend (real or imaginary). Ramble. Repeat yourself. Then transcribe it. Suddenly, you have pages of material to shape, sculpt and streamline.

The argument with yourself

Write a dialogue between two versions of you. Challenge and provoke. Be cheeky, even. This imagined discussion style of starting bypasses the fear of formal academic writing and gets ideas flowing.

Phase 3: the structure (day 5–6)

The reverse outline

Instead of outlining then writing, write then outline. Take that Frankenstein draft and identify what points you're making, what evidence you have, what's missing, what order makes sense.

The PEER paragraph method

For each body paragraph, check for:

- The central point: What are you arguing?
- The evidence to prove your central point: What supports this?
- The explanation of your evidence: Why does this evidence matter?
- The relevance: How does this connect to your thesis?

The conclusion-first approach

Write your conclusion first. Explain what you've 'argued' in your essay. This becomes your roadmap for getting there.

Phase 4: the polish (day 7)

The read-aloud edit

Read your essay aloud. Your ear catches what your eye misses.

The targeted read-throughs

Read through your paper several times, focusing on one element at a time – argument flow, evidence, clarity, grammar.

The fresh eyes trick

Change your document's font or format. Print it out. This makes familiar text look new, helping you spot issues.

See it in action: meet Jamie and Alex

Jamie saw himself as a perfectionist procrastinator. He came to me teary-eyed during third year. 'I've never submitted an essay on time. Not once.'

Alex, an overwhelmed procrastinator and mature student, felt constantly behind. 'Everyone else seems to just know how to write essays.'

The breakthrough

Jamie started with two-minute essays. 'This is stupid,' Jamie said after the first one. 'I basically just complained about the essay topic.' 'Perfect,' I replied. 'Now you've started.' Jamie learned to embrace the muddled middle: 'Knowing I'm going to rewrite everything makes it easier to start. The pressure's off.'

Alex started with the question dump technique. 'This feels like cheating,' Alex said. 'I'm not actually writing anything.' But those questions became the essay's skeleton. Alex also started using voice notes during commutes: 'I explain the essay to my windshield. When I transcribe it later, I have pages of material.'

The results

By term's end, Jamie submitted every essay on time. 'They're not perfect, but they're done. And honestly? They're better than my old panic essays ever were.'

Alex discovered that essays weren't one impossible task but a series of small, manageable conversations with different questions. Each essay became less overwhelming as the process became familiar.

→ **Key insight:** Both students discovered that perfectionism and overwhelm dissolve when writing becomes a series of small, imperfect attempts rather than one monumental task. Jamie learned that 'done' trumps 'perfect', while Alex found that talking through ideas – even to a windshield – transforms the impossible into the manageable. The breakthrough isn't about finding the perfect writing process; it's about finding any process that gets words on the page.

Troubleshooting: when ChatGPT feels like the only way out

'I'm stuck and ChatGPT could have this done for me in less than a minute.' I understand! It's not that 'we've all been there', it's that we all *are* there; it's where we all live now. There's so much (too much) to do, and AI can feel like quick relief. When you're staring at a blank page and the minutes, or hours, are whizzing by, AI appears to be a lifeline.

Here are some ethical, upskilling ways to use it as a tool rather than a replacement for your thinking. Think of AI as a kind of mentor who asks good questions but doesn't do your homework, who nudges you along but doesn't take over.

Use AI as a brainstorming partner

- 'Help me understand what this essay question is asking.'
- 'What angles could I consider for this topic?'
- 'What questions should I be exploring?'

Use AI as a structure assistant

- 'Help me identify the main points in my messy draft'
- 'What order would make these arguments clearer?'
- 'What feedback might my professor give me about my essay's organization?'

Use AI as a clarity coach

- 'Is this paragraph clear?'
- 'How could I make this transition smoother?'
- 'Where might a reader get confused?'

What's the line you ought not to cross? AI shouldn't write your essay, generate your arguments, create fake citations or replace your thinking. When AI does the thinking for you, you miss the entire point of education – developing your own abilities. Plus, most instructors can spot AI-generated work and the academic consequences aren't worth the temporary relief.

Put differently, using AI to understand is learning. Using AI to avoid thinking is just expensive procrastination.

A new way with hard essays

Essays aren't grand gestures or your magnum opus; they're conversations to have. Every essay is just you explaining something to someone who wants to understand it.

When you feel procrastination rising, remember:

- Starting badly beats not starting
- Messy drafts lead to clear thoughts
- Two minutes of writing counts
- Your first draft's only job is to exist
- Perfection is procrastination in disguise

The essay that gets written – imperfectly, messily, humanly – is infinitely better than the perfect essay that never leaves your head. Your professors don't want perfection; they want to see your thinking, hear your voice and learn from your insights.

Every time you start – even for two minutes, even badly – you're building a new ability and a new identity that shows you, 'I'm someone who starts'. Every long-winded or choppy draft is evidence you can face difficulty and work through it. Every on-time submission is a vote for the kind of student you're becoming.

The hard essay in front of you isn't your enemy. It's an invitation to discover what you think, develop your voice and join academic conversations. Yes, it's hard. Yes, you'll struggle (I will too). But you'll also write sentences that surprise you with clarity or eloquence, make unexpected links, or explain things that suddenly make perfect sense.

That cursor blinking on your blank page? It's not mocking you. It's waiting for you. And you don't need the perfect sentence to begin. You just need any sentence. Even this one: 'I don't know what to write, but here's what I think this essay might be about ... '

Dig deeper: breaking procrastination and finishing well

Essential reading

John Perry's *The Art of Procrastination: a Guide to Effective Dawdling, Lollygagging and Postponing* (2013). A philosopher's counterintuitive approach that transforms procrastination into productivity by strategically choosing which tasks to avoid, showing how to work with rather than against procrastinating tendencies.

Tim Pychyl's *Solving the Procrastination Puzzle: A Concise Guide to Strategies for Change* (2013) distils decades of procrastination research into practical strategies, revealing procrastination as emotional avoidance rather than time management failure and offering concrete techniques for breaking the cycle.

TED Talk

Carol Dweck's 'The power of yet' (2014), *TEDxNorrköping*, video. Available at: https://www.ted.com/talks/carol_dweck_the_power_of_believing_that_you_can_improve introduces growth mindset principles showing how adding 'yet' to self-defeating thoughts transforms fixed beliefs about ability into opportunities for development and learning.

Podcast

iProcrastinate Podcast by Tim Pychyl (2006–present), podcast series. Available at: https://iprocrastinate.libsyn.com. Research-based episodes diving deep into why we procrastinate and what actually works to overcome it, with practical strategies grounded in psychological science rather than willpower myths.

Apps

- *Cold Turkey Writer* locks you into writing mode
- *Focusmate* offers virtual co-working for accountability
- *Hemingway Editor* evaluates your writing

References

Dweck, C.S. (2014) 'The power of yet' [TEDx talk]. TEDxNorrköping, 9 September. Available at: https://www.youtube.com/watch?v=J-swZaKN2Ic (accessed 1 October 2025).

Kim, K.R. and Seo, E.H. (2015) 'The relationship between procrastination and academic performance: A meta-analysis', *Personality and Individual Differences*, 82, pp. 26–33.

Klingsieck, K.B. (2013) 'Procrastination: When good things don't come to those who wait', *European Psychologist*, 18(1), pp. 24–34.

Perry, J. (2013) *The Art of Procrastination: A Guide to Effective Dawdling, Lollygagging and Postponing*. New York: Workman Publishing.

Pychyl, T.A. (2006) *iProcrastinate* [podcast]. Available at: https://podcasts.apple.com/us/podcast/iprocrastinate-podcast/id129144284 (accessed 1 October 2025).

Pychyl, T.A. (2013) *Solving the Procrastination Puzzle: A Concise Guide to Strategies for Change*. New York: TarcherPerigee.

Sirois, F.M. and Pychyl, T.A. (2013) 'Procrastination and the priority of short-term mood regulation: Consequences for future self', *Social and Personality Psychology Compass*, 7(2), pp. 115–127.

Steel, P. (2007) 'The nature of procrastination: A meta-analytic and theoretical review of quintessential self-regulatory failure', *Psychological Bulletin*, 133(1), pp. 65–94.

Steel, P. and König, C.J. (2006) 'Integrating theories of motivation', *Academy of Management Review*, 31(4), pp. 889–913.

Van Eerde, W. and Klingsieck, K.B. (2018) 'Overcoming procrastination? A meta-analysis of intervention studies', *Educational Research Review*, 25, pp. 73–85.

Zeigarnik, B. (1927) 'Das Behalten erledigter und unerledigter Handlungen', *Psychologische Forschung*, 9, pp. 1–85. (Translated from German.) Available at: https://gwern.net/doc/psychology/willpower/1927-zeigarnik.pdf (accessed 1 October 2025).

SECTION FIVE

A NEW WAY TO REACH YOUR GOALS

Goals.

Dreams.

Ambitions.

Intentions.

Whatever you call them, you've probably been asked about them since you were small. 'What do you want to be when you grow up?' evolved into 'Where do you see yourself in five years?' which morphed into 'What's your career plan?' And somewhere along the way, you might have noticed that the more you were asked about your goals, the less clear they became.

Maybe you're the student with seventeen different passions pulling you in seventeen different directions. Maybe you're a learner feeling frozen by the pressure to have it all figured out 'by now' (as if any grown-up does). Or maybe you're somewhere in between – clear on the big picture but lost in the daily steps, or crystal clear on today but unable to see past next week.

The traditional post-secondary approaches – those neat, linear, business-world frameworks – weren't designed for the beautiful messiness of being twenty-something and figuring out your life. They weren't created for people juggling academic demands, part-time work, family expectations, social pressures and the profound question of who you're becoming.

Moving beyond SMART

You've probably encountered SMART goals – Specific, Measurable, Achievable, Realistic, Time-bound – or iterations of the acronym. Borne from corporate boardrooms, this framework assumes you know exactly what you want and just need to break it down into manageable pieces. But what happens when 'achievable' and 'realistic' feel like cages around your biggest dreams? What happens when the specificity required feels impossible because you're still discovering who you are?

In this section, we'll explore a new way. Not goals that shrink your dreams to fit a formula but approaches that honour both your ambitions and your humanity. We'll talk about naming aims when you're full of possibilities, moving toward intentions when life is already overwhelming, removing obstacles that feel immovable, and finding purpose when motivation disappears like morning mist.

Where dreams meet daily life

This isn't about choosing between big desires and practical steps. It's about learning to hold both; to dream audaciously and plan for a future you can't fully see, while also showing up for today's lecture, to work toward long-term visions while navigating short-term pressures.

You'll meet students who've found their own ways through this dance. Students who learned that putting words to your wants doesn't mean having them all figured out. Students who discovered that moving toward intentions requires honouring what's already on your plate. Students who realized that obstacles often carry hidden wisdom. That purpose isn't something you discover once but something you reconnect with, repeatedly.

This section acknowledges the specific challenge of goal-setting in a world that seems to demand you be extraordinary while simultaneously telling you to 'be realistic'. It recognizes the tension between social media's highlight reels and your own tentative or zigzaggy path. It honours the fact that you're trying to build a future while managing a very demanding present.

Most importantly, this section treats your dreams with the respect they deserve – not as naive fantasies to be made 'realistic', but as vital seeds of who you're becoming. Your ambitions matter. Your aspirations are valid. So too are your obstacles real. And your purpose, even when you can't quite materialize it, is already guiding you.

Let's consider how to work with all of this – gently, practically and full of hope.

CHAPTER 18

HOW TO NAME YOUR AIMS (WHEN YOU'RE FULL OF AMBITIONS)

What nobody tells you upon arriving at university is that you're supposed to excel ... while simultaneously making yourself smaller. Stand out ... but not too much. Achieve everything ... but don't talk about it. Be exceptional ... but relatable.

If this feels impossible, that's because it is.

You might recognize this dance. Maybe you've posted about an achievement online, then immediately worried you seemed boastful. Perhaps you've downplayed a mark you worked incredibly hard for, mumbling 'it was nothing' when it was absolutely something. Or you've watched others seemingly glide through this contradiction while you're left wondering which version of yourself to be today.

This tension isn't your imagination. It lives in the space between the dean's list posted prominently in the hallway and the whispered 'try-hard' as someone walks past it. It exists in every 'humble brag' and every deleted draft of a post celebrating your own success. Most importantly, it sits heavy in your chest when you're not sure if wanting something badly makes you ambitious or just ... 'being too much'. (And I have to admit, 'being too much' is hands down one of my least favourite phrases. You are *not* too much, ever!)

Where do these mixed messages come from?

If we trace things back, the pressure to achieve often starts long before university. Some of you carry the hopes of entire families, communities or cultures (Jack 2019). Others rebel against expectations by creating impossibly high standards. Many navigate both simultaneously.

Your ambitions might have roots in:

- Watching family members work multiple jobs to fund your education
- Being labelled the 'smart one' since primary school and feeling like that's your only identity
- Compensating for learning differences by working three times as hard as everyone else

- Representing your community in spaces where you're one of the only ones
- Escaping circumstances through education
- Being a primary caregiver or provider for your family, chosen family or community
- Genuinely loving what you study

And then there's social media (enough said!).

Social media provides a peculiar magnifying glass that makes everyone else's achievements look effortless and yours feel either insignificant or embarrassingly overstated. You scroll through curated success stories while judging your own life as too raw, too real, too all over the place or too ordinary to share.

The geography of ambition

Ambition looks different depending on where you stand. What's celebrated in one culture might be considered inappropriate in another. Some of you come from communities where individual achievement is prized above all else. Others were raised with collectivist values where standing out feels like betrayal (Stephens et al. 2012).

Consider how these cultural maps overlap and conflict:

- Your family's understanding of success versus your university's metrics
- Your home community's values versus your academic community's expectations
- Your cultural background's relationship with visibility versus institutional rewards for self-promotion
- Your generation's redefinition of success versus traditional markers of achievement

There's no universal 'right' way to be ambitious. But universities often operate as if there is, rewarding certain types of visibility while simultaneously maintaining that everyone has equal opportunity to succeed (Yosso 2005). This isn't true and pretending it is only makes the tension harder to bear.

Take a moment: tall poppies and other garden metaphors

The Tall Poppy Syndrome – cutting down those who grow too high – has many cultural versions. Maybe you know it as 'the nail that sticks out gets hammered down' or 'don't get too big for your britches' or simply the look someone gives you when you share good news.

But what's less discussed is how we can sometimes become our *own* zealous gardeners, pruning ourselves before anyone else gets the chance. We shrink our ambitions, quiet our excitement, minimize our hopes. We make ourselves *smaller* (and as someone who's literally six feet tall, I *really* understand this). We tell ourselves we're being 'realistic' when in truth we're scared of judgement – others' and our own – and so take ourselves out of the running, eliminate our chances, and make ourselves less visible (Reay, Crozier and Clayton 2010).

This self-pruning is particularly common among:

- First-generation university students who feel they're betraying their roots by succeeding
- Students from marginalized communities who've been told they're 'lucky' to be here
- Anyone who's been labelled 'too intense' about their interests
- Learners whose ambitions don't fit traditional academic moulds
- Those whose mental health struggles make consistent achievement feel like a lie

If this tracks with your own experience, let's take a moment to trace it back to the root.

Map your influences

- Draw a mind map of where your ambitions come from. Include family, culture, media, peers and personal experiences.
  Which influences feel authentic to you? Which feel imposed?

The contradiction inventory

- List three times you felt pulled between achieving and staying humble.
  What did you choose? How did it feel? What would you do differently now?

Cultural context check

- Get curious about how your cultural background shapes your relationship with ambition.

  Are there specific sayings, stories or values from your heritage that influence how you think about success?

The underground growth

- Take stock of any ambitions you might be nurturing privately that no one knows about yet.

  Why might you be keeping them private? What would need to change for you to share them?

Rewriting the metaphor

- Clear your mind and heart of any imposed images, sayings and models of 'success'.

  If you could create your own metaphor for ambition (instead of tall poppies or hammered nails), what would it be? (Draw or describe it.)

Finding and honouring your heartfelt aims

Beneath the noise of expectations – both to achieve *and* to stay humble at the same time – lies something quieter but more persistent: what you actually want. Not what you *should* want, or what would make *others* proud, or what would look good on LinkedIn. What *you* want.

But I'm aware that this might feel impossible to access. Years of mixed messages may have buried it deep. But it's there. And finding it doesn't require meditation retreats or expensive coaching. Sometimes it's as simple as paying attention to what you think about when you first wake up, what you do when procrastinating (sometimes pointing to a hidden desire), what makes you lose track of time, what you'd pursue if failure was impossible or what you'd do if success was invisible.

If you were to write a list of your ambitions as if no one would ever see it – include the 'ridiculous' ones, the 'impossible' ones, the ones that make you feel guilty for wanting them – what would be on it? This isn't about making a plan yet; it's about acknowledging what lives in you before deciding what to do with it.

Once you've glimpsed these true aims, the challenge becomes holding them with integrity. You don't have to choose between being a go-getter and staying grateful and gracious, driven and collaborative, exceptional and belonging. The imposed either/or is a false choice that serves no one, least of all you. Instead, this means celebrating others' successes genuinely while also honouring your own, asking for help as readily as you offer it, sharing your struggles alongside your achievements and recognizing that your success doesn't take away from anyone else's.

This isn't so much about 'balance' – that persistent myth that suggests everything should be equally weighted. It's about *integration*, allowing all parts of yourself to coexist even when they seem contradictory.

By articulating your aims out loud (or on paper), something shifts. They become real, accountable, possible. But naming them doesn't mean broadcasting them or defending them to sceptics. It means acknowledging them to yourself first. Start with trusted people – those who can hold your ambitions without judgement or jealousy. This might be a study group, student council or entrepreneurial group that celebrates each member's different goals, or a mentor who sees your potential without needing to shape it, or friends who get excited about your excitement. If these people don't exist in your life yet, that's okay. Sometimes we need to be our own first witness, our own cheerleader, our own trusted keeper of aims.

Some days, the weight of your own ambitions will feel crushing. The gap between where you are and where you want to be may seem insurmountable. On these days, please remember ambition isn't a contract. You're allowed to change your mind, take breaks, pursue things privately, have seasons of rest and seasons of sprint, want different things at different times and be ordinary in some areas while extraordinary in others. Your worth isn't determined by your achievements or your ambitions. You're valuable equally in your times of struggle, rest, confusion and clarity. The university might not always reflect this truth back to you, but that doesn't make it less true.

Try this today: minimize minimizing

The ambition audit

Over the next week, notice if you minimize your achievements or ambitions.

Keep a simple tally:

- When did you say 'it was nothing' about something that took effort?
- When did you delete or rewrite something that felt 'too much'?
- When did you compare your ambitions to others and adjust accordingly?

Friendly awareness is the first step to choosing differently.

Connect with others

Form an 'Ambition Circle' with two to three trusted peers.

Meet monthly to:

- Share one ambition you're working toward
- Celebrate one achievement from the past month

- Name one fear about being 'too much'
- Support each other in holding both humility and pride

What's shared in the circle stays in the circle; this creates psychological safety for authentic expression.

Creating your own garden

Instead of accepting the metaphor of tall poppies being cut down, what if you reimagined the garden entirely? What if success wasn't about height but about a whole ecosystem? What if achievement was measured in how you contribute to the soil and seedbed, not just how high you individually grow (Rendón 2009)?

In your garden:

- Different plants thrive at different times
- Biodiversity makes the whole system stronger
- Growth happens underground before it's visible
- Seasons of dormancy are as vital as seasons of bloom
- Every plant has its place and purpose

This isn't about lowering your ambitions. It's about expanding what ambition can look like, who it can include and what it can serve.

See it in action: Jordan's story

Jordan grew up in a small maritime town where their dad worked at the fish plant and their mum cleaned houses. Being accepted to university felt like winning the lottery, exciting and terrifying in equal measure.

'Back home, doing well meant not making a fuss,' Jordan explains. 'But here, professors expect you to speak up in seminars, to promote your research, to network. I feel like I'm betraying my family every time I raise my hand.'

The breaking point came when Jordan won a prestigious scholarship. Instead of celebrating, they spent three days drafting an email to decline it, convinced they didn't deserve it and worried about what people back home would think. A conversation with a faculty mentor shed new light.

The breakthrough

They told me about their own journey, being the first in their family to get a PhD, the guilt they carried, how they reframed it. They said, 'Your success isn't a betrayal of where you come from. It's an extension of it. You're not leaving your community behind; you're carrying them forward.'

The results

Jordan accepted the scholarship but found their own way to honour both worlds. They started a study group specifically for first-generation students, created a blog sharing their university journey with younger students from their hometown and learned to say 'thank you' instead of 'it was nothing' when complimented on achievements.

'I'm still figuring it out,' Jordan admits. 'Some days I feel too big for home and too small for here. But I'm learning that maybe that in-between space is exactly where I need to be. I picture it like building bridges instead of choosing sides.'

→ **Key insight:** Success isn't a betrayal of your roots but an extension of them; Jordan discovered that the tension between 'not making a fuss' at home and 'speaking up' at university could be bridged rather than chosen between. Achievement doesn't have to mean leaving community behind but rather as carrying it forward.

A new way with ambition

As we close this chapter, I'm hoping we can reimagine ambition differently. Not as a ladder where only one person can stand at the top, not as a race with winners and losers, but instead as a constellation – each star bright in its own right, with space to shine, radiance that creates light for others and patterns that none could make alone.

In this new way with ambition:

- Your success brightens and uplifts paths for others rather than casting shadows
- Collaboration and competition can coexist without contradiction
- Rest is crucial to achievement
- Cultural context about 'success', ancestor connection and lived experience enrich rather than confuse
- Your aims can evolve without betraying yourself or your community
- Wanting something deeply is an act of hope, not greed

Your ambitions aren't too much. The framework that makes you feel that way is too small.

Dig deeper: naming your ambitions without shrinking

Essential reading

Brené Brown's *so*-often turned-to *The Gifts of Imperfection* (2010) explores how shame around ambition and success connects to worthiness. Brown's research on vulnerability reveals why we minimize achievements and experience internal barriers to naming what we want.

Daring Greatly (2012), also by Brown, expands on how courage requires both vulnerability and visibility. The section on 'shame resilience' offers practical strategies for standing in your achievements without apology while maintaining authentic connection with others.

TED Talk

Susan David's 'The gift and power of emotional courage' (2017) addresses how we need emotional agility to hold seemingly contradictory truths, like being both proud and humble. Her concept of 'walking your why' helps students connect with authentic ambitions beneath social pressures.

Documentary

First Generation (2015) follows four high-school students as they navigate completing high school and transitioning to post-secondary, highlighting some of the tensions, like family loyalty and academic ambition many learners experience. Available at: https://www.youtube.com/watch?v=pfDx4duheHk

References

Brown, B. (2010) *The Gifts of Imperfection: Let Go of Who You Think You're Supposed to be and Embrace Who You Are*. Center City, MN: Hazelden Publishing.

Brown, B. (2012) *Daring Greatly: How the Courage to Be Vulnerable Transforms the Way We Live, Love, Parent, and Lead*. New York: Gotham Books.

David, S. (2017) 'The gift and power of emotional courage' [TED Talk]. TEDWomen, November. Available at: https://www.ted.com/talks/susan_david_the_gift_and_power_of_emotional_courage (accessed 1 October 2025).

FirstGenFilm (2015) *First Generation* [documentary film]. Available at: https://www.youtube.com/watch?v=pfDx4duheHk (accessed 1 Oct 2025).

Jack, A.A. (2019) *The Privileged Poor: How Elite Colleges Are Failing Disadvantaged Students*. Cambridge, MA: Harvard University Press.

Reay, D., Crozier, G. and Clayton, J. (2010) '"Fitting in" or "standing out": Working-class students in UK higher education', *British Educational Research Journal*, 36(1), pp. 107–124.

Rendón, L.I. (2009) *Sentipensante Pedagogy: Educating for Wholeness, Social Justice and Liberation*. Sterling, VA: Stylus Publishing.

Stephens, N.M., Fryberg, S.A., Markus, H.R., Johnson, C.S. and Covarrubias, R. (2012) 'Unseen disadvantage: How American universities' focus on independence undermines the academic performance of first-generation college students', *Journal of Personality and Social Psychology*, 102(6), pp. 1178–1197.

Yosso, T.J. (2005) 'Whose culture has capital? A critical race theory discussion of community cultural wealth', *Race, Ethnicity and Education*, 8(1), pp. 69–91.

CHAPTER 19

HOW TO MOVE TOWARDS YOUR INTENTIONS (WHEN YOUR LIFE IS FULL OF OTHER OBLIGATIONS)

So you've named your aims. They sit there, shimmering with possibility, maybe written in your journal or whispered to a trusted friend. Now what?

This is where most advice falls short or falls apart entirely. It assumes you have endless time, unlimited energy and a life that bends gracefully around your goals. It forgets about the part-time job that pays your rent, the family responsibilities that call you home, the group project due Thursday, the mental health struggles that make some days about surviving rather than thriving and the very real need to sometimes just … rest.

The question isn't really, 'How do I achieve my goals?'; it's, 'How do I move towards what *matters* to me when my days are already overfull with what's *required* of me?'

You don't need to 'optimize' or 'revolutionize' your life to honour your intentions. Revolution is exhausting (and as a university student, you're no doubt exhausted enough). What might help is something gentler and more sustainable – a practice of alignment that works with your life as it actually is, not as productivity influencers imagine it should be.

The fairy tale of the fresh start

University culture loooooves a fresh start.

New term, new you!

Monday morning, everything changes!

This summer, you'll finally …

But life doesn't work in clean slates. You're always carrying forward – responsibilities, relationships, habits, histories. And that's not a failing. It's human.

Meet Meiying:

> I kept waiting for the "right time" to start learning music production, which was my real passion alongside my engineering degree. I wanted a clear

schedule, all my assignments done, maybe summer break. But that perfect moment never came. Finally, I just downloaded free software during a particularly stressful exam period. Weirdly, spending twenty minutes making beats became my study break. I wasn't "waiting for space" anymore; I was making space inside what was already happening.

The fresh start myth keeps us waiting for conditions that will never exist. Your intentions need to root themselves in the soil of your actual life.

Notice your patterns: owning your obligations

Before you move forward toward your intentions, I recommend mapping what's already claiming your time and energy.

That said, not all obligations are created equal, and it's key to spot the difference.

Consider four types of obligations:

The necessaries

These keep you in school, housed and fed. They include assignments with deadlines, shifts at work that pay for groceries, medications that keep you healthy. These are *foundations* more so than just obligations. I'd also include the weekly family dinner or FaceTime calls with relatives every Sunday.

The expectations

These come from others but aren't strictly required. The study group you feel bad about missing, the extracurricular that looks good on your CV but drains you.

The maintenance

These keep your life functional. Laundry, cooking, sleeping, moving your body, connecting with friends. Often the first things sacrificed, but cutting them usually backfires.

The shoulds

These are the ghosts of other people's ambitions for you. The minor your parents think is practical, the networking events everyone says are essential, the morning routine you saw on TikTok. These take up massive mental real estate for things you never actually chose.

Meet Herleen: 'I realized I was treating everything as equally urgent. My therapist had me list everything I felt obligated to do, then mark which ones had actual consequences if I didn't do them. Turns out about half my stress was from "shoulds" that nobody was actually tracking but me.'

Time isn't the only currency

We talk about time management as if time is the only resource that matters. But you're actually managing *multiple* currencies.

- **Energy**

  Some tasks give energy, others drain it. A two-hour lecture might exhaust you while two hours on your passion project might energize you. Start noticing which is which.

- **Attention**

  You might have time but no focus. This is why 'I'll work on it after all my assignments' rarely works – your attention is already spent.

- **Allowance**

  Sometimes you have time and energy but can't give yourself the 'yes' to use them for your intentions. This internal currency is often the scarcest.

- **Resources**

  Money, equipment, space, knowledge. Sometimes the barrier isn't time but access.

Meet Amrita: 'I had time to write in the evenings, but after my retail shifts, I had zero energy for creativity. So, I started waking up thirty minutes earlier (not *early* early, just earlier). I had less time in the mornings but more energy. Those morning half-hours produced more writing than all those exhausted evenings combined.'

The one small move method

The distance between where you are and where you want to be isn't covered in leaps. It's covered in shifts so small you might not even notice them happening.

Small moves might look like:

- Reading one article related to your interest while eating lunch
- Changing one elective to something aligned with your actual curiosity
- Spending the first ten minutes when you get home on your passion project

- Finding one person who shares your interest and having one conversation
- Replacing one hour of scrolling with one hour of creating – in the words of entrepreneur Marie Forleo, 'create before you consume'!
- Saying no to one thing that's purely a 'should'

The magic isn't in the *size* of the move; it's the directionality. Every choice that points toward your intention, however tiny, is reshaping your trajectory.

The both/and schedule

You've seen this before, I know. I'm just such a big fan! Both/and is so much more helpful, honouring and humane than the either/or we live so many of our days with. Traditional scheduling assumes you do one thing, then another, in neat blocks. But what if your schedule could hold multiple truths simultaneously?

Consider these both/and approaches:

- Study for your exam AND incorporate examples from your area of passion
- Fulfil your work-study requirements AND choose job roles that inch toward your interests
- Complete required courses AND find the thread within them that connects to your intentions
- Maintain family responsibilities AND share your learning experiences with them
- Take care of your mental health AND recognize that pursuing meaningful goals is part of that care

This isn't about multitasking or doing everything at once. It's about finding where your obligations and intentions can overlap, even slightly or indirectly.

Creating containers, not cages

Structure can serve your intentions without strangling them. Think containers, not cages.

Time containers

- 'Tuesday evenings are for my passion project' is a container → 'I must work on my project every day at 7.00 pm or I've failed' is a cage.

Space containers

- A corner of your desk dedicated to your intention. A folder on your laptop. A playlist that signals 'this is my time for this'.

Community containers

- A weekly stroll or hot chocolate with someone who shares your interest. An online forum you check regularly. A group chat dedicated to accountability and encouragement. A monthly meet-up dedicated solely to a non-academic passion.

Progress containers

- A simple document where you note any movement toward your intention, however small. Not a 'tracker' of hours or output, just nudging-you-along evidence that you are indeed moving.

Meet Oli: 'I created what I called "intention appointments", calendar blocks that said things like "meeting with future filmmaker Oli" or "consulting session with my inner artist". Somehow, framing it as a blocked-off session made it feel legitimate. I was more likely to show up for "future me" than for vague "work on film stuff".'

Passion project partners

Your intentions need allies, collaborators, co-conspirators, accomplices. But support can take many shapes.

- **The Accountability Buddy**

  Someone working toward their own intention who checks in regularly. Not to assess, but to witness.

- **The Expertise Sharer**

  Someone further along the path who can offer practical guidance, not inspiration but information.

- **The Resource Connector**

  Someone who knows things, has access, makes introductions. Sponsors are often found in unexpected places.

- **The Cheerleader**

  Someone who believes in your intention even when you don't – especially when you don't. A champion.

- **The Space Holder**

  Someone who creates or shares physical or temporal space for your practice.

You don't need *all* of these. Even one person on your side, in your corner, changes the game entirely.

The practice of integration

Moving toward your intentions while managing obligations isn't about balance – that impossible state where everything gets equal weight. It's about integration – weaving your intentions through your obligations so they become part of the fabric of your life.

This might mean:

- Your economics assignments explore topics related to your passion for social justice
- Your part-time job in hospitality becomes research for your novel about restaurant workers
- Your commute becomes your podcast learning time
- Your required language class connects you to the culture you want to explore
- Your study group becomes your creative accountability circle

Integration doesn't make obligations disappear. But it makes them serve multiple purposes, including purposes you've chosen.

Try this today: intention integration

Instead of trying to carve out new time for your intentions (which you probably don't have), look for places where intentions and obligations can merge.

Step 1: List your current obligations

Write down everything you're required to do this week. Classes, work, assignments, family commitments – all of it.

Step 2: Identify connection points

For each obligation, ask yourself: *How could this connect to my intention, even tangentially?* Could your statistics assignment use data related to your passion? Could your travel time become *learning* time through podcasts?

Step 3: Make one small integration

Choose just one place to start weaving your intention into an existing obligation. Remember, we're looking for *sustainable* integration, not exhausting, eclipsing change.

Step 4: Track the ripples

Notice what happens when you make this small shift. Does the obligation feel different? Does progress on your intention feel more possible? What did you learn?

Troubleshooting: when obligations and intentions clash

Sometimes your have-tos and dream-ofs will directly collide, if not conflict. You'll have to choose between the scholarship-maintaining grades and the project that feeds your soul. Between the family expectations and your authentic path. Between rest and progress.

These moments aren't failures of planning. They're real life. When they arise:

1. Acknowledge the conflict without judgement. It's not a personal failing that you can't do everything.
2. Consider the timescales. What serves you this week versus this year versus this lifetime?
3. Look for the third option. Can you defer, delegate or redesign either obligation or intention?
4. If you must choose, choose consciously. Make the choice that you can live with, knowing you did your best with the information and resources available.
5. Remember that choices are rarely permanent. You can prioritize obligations now and intentions later, or vice versa.

Student voices

Priya: As an international student supporting family back home while pursuing medicine, Priya felt her intention to write poetry was impossible. 'I started by changing how I took notes in lectures. I'd capture key medical concepts in metaphorical language, almost like poetry. Or write a lyrical line in the margins when inspired by a new concept. It kept my creative brain alive during intense study sessions. Some of those metaphors even helped me remember complex processes better.'

Marcus: Working three jobs to pay for university, Marcus thought his dream of learning photography would have to wait until after graduation. 'I started photographing my daily commute with my phone. Same bus route every day, but I challenged myself to see it differently each time. That constraint pushed my creativity. By the time I could afford a real camera, I'd already developed my eye.'

Sofia: With chronic illness affecting her energy, Sofia struggled to pursue her intention of building community. 'I stopped trying to organize big events and started inviting one person for tea each week, sometimes virtually when I couldn't leave bed. Those one-on-one connections grew into the supportive network I'd been craving.'

→ **Key insight:** Your intentions don't need perfect conditions to grow. They need integration with what's already happening in your life.

A new way with taking action

As this chapter closes, let's reconsider what 'taking action' means. It's not about crushing goals or optimizing every minute. It's not about becoming a productivity machine or sacrificing everything for your dreams.

Taking action toward your intentions while honouring obligations is about becoming skillful at living with complexity. It's about making choices that serve multiple purposes. It's about progress that's sustainable rather than spectacular. It's about integration rather than balance, alignment rather than achievement.

Your intentions deserve space in your life, even when that space is small. Your obligations can coexist with your dreams, even when they seem to conflict. You can move toward what matters to you without abandoning what's required of you.

Start where you are. Use what you have. Do what you can. Move toward what calls to you, even if that movement is measured in millimetres. Trust that small moves, consistently made, can carry you to places that giant leaps never could.

Dig deeper: resources for living with complexity

Essential reading

Greg McKeown's *Essentialism: The Disciplined Pursuit of Less* (2014) offers a framework for distinguishing between what's essential and what's merely noise. His approach to selective focus is particularly useful for students learning to navigate between true obligations and perceived expectations.

Jenny Odell's *How to Do Nothing: Resisting the Attention Economy* (2019) challenges productivity culture entirely. She argues for the radical act of refusing to be productive all the time, creating space for reflection and intention that exists outside capitalist frameworks.

adrienne maree brown's *Emergent Strategy* (2017) presents a framework for creating change through small, adaptive actions rather than grand plans. Her work is especially valuable for understanding how individual intentions can connect to collective transformation.

TED Talks

Ruth Chang's 'How to make hard choices' (2013) reframes decision-making when facing competing priorities. Her framework for creating reasons rather than finding them is particularly helpful when obligations and intentions clash.

Laura Dockrill's 'What happened when I learned to live with anxiety' shares how creative practice became both intention and mental health support – a powerful example of integration.

References

brown, a.m. (2017) *Emergent Strategy: Shaping Change, Changing Worlds*. Edinburgh: AK Press.

Clear, J. (2018) *Atomic Habits: An Easy and Proven Way to Build Good Habits and Break Bad Ones*. New York: Random House.

Csikszentmihalyi, M. (1990) *Flow: The Psychology of Optimal Experience*. New York: Harper & Row.

Forleo, M. (2023) *Simple practice, profound results ...*, LinkedIn, 2 May. Available at: https://www.linkedin.com/posts/marieforleo_simple-practice-profound-results-if-activity-7229487464527056897-Oza0/ (accessed 1 October 2025).

Gannon, K.M. (2020) *Radical Hope: A Teaching Manifesto*. Morgantown, WV: West Virginia University Press.

hooks, b. (1994) *Teaching to Transgress: Education as the Practice of Freedom*. New York: Routledge.

Jackson, B. (2021) 'Time confetti and the broken promise of leisure', *Journal of Leisure Research*, 52(3), pp. 315–331.

Kimmerer, R.W. (2013) *Braiding Sweetgrass: Indigenous Wisdom, Scientific Knowledge and the Plant Teachings*. Minneapolis, MN: Milkweed Editions.

Newport, C. (2016) *Deep Work: Rules for Focused Success in a Distracted World*. New York: Grand Central Publishing.

Odell, J. (2019) *How to Do Nothing: Resisting the Attention Economy*. Brooklyn: Melville House.

Palmer, P.J. (2017) *The Courage to Teach: Exploring the Inner Landscape of a Teacher's Life*. 20th anniversary edn. San Francisco: Jossey-Bass.

CHAPTER 20

HOW TO REMOVE OBSTACLES (WHEN YOU WANT TO ACCOMPLISH SOMETHING)

Obstacles aren't character defects.

They don't signify that, somehow, you're less capable than that person in your tutorial who seems to have everything sorted. Obstacles are just ... things that get in the way. And given that we're never *not* going to have them, once we stop judging ourselves *for* having them, we can more skilfully start working *with* them.

Now, sometimes what looks like an obstacle is simply information.

Likewise, sometimes that resistance you're feeling, that thing that keeps stopping you from starting your essay or getting to that reading – it's nudging you to notice something important. Maybe it's saying this approach isn't working for you. Maybe it's saying you need support. Maybe it's saying your body needs rest or your brain needs a different way in.

So before we dive into strategies for removing obstacles, let's recognize that not all obstacles need to be bulldozed through. Some need to be befriended.

The obstacles we're actually talking about

When I work with learners, the obstacles that come up most often might not be what you expect.

- **There's the obstacle of not knowing where to start** – that immobilizing moment when the assignment feels so big, so unwieldy, that even opening the document feels impossible.
- **There's the obstacle of perfectionism** – where nothing you write feels good enough, so you write nothing at all.
- **There's the obstacle of exhaustion** – not just tired, but that bone-deep depletion that makes focusing feel like trying to see through fog.
- **There's the obstacle of competing priorities** – when everything feels urgent and important, and choosing what to tackle first feels like a no-way-out calculation.

- **The obstacle of shame** – from past struggles, from needing more time than others seem to and from having to work in ways distinct from what's expected.
- **The obstacle of environment** – trying to focus in spaces that weren't designed for your brain, your body or your needs.
- And of course, **the obstacle of habits** – both the ones that don't serve us and the absence of ones that could.

Notice your patterns: observing your obstacles

Before we can release or ease obstacles, we need to get crystal clear about what they actually are for you. Not for your flatmate, not for some fake 'flawless', figured-it-all-out student, but for *you*.

Think back to the last time you deeply wanted to accomplish something academic ... but couldn't. What stopped you? And I mean *really* stopped you, not what you think the 'right' answer is.

Was it that:

- The task felt too big or too vague?
- You didn't know how to begin?
- Your environment was working against you?
- Your body was uncomfortable or in pain?
- Your brain felt foggy or overwhelmed?
- You kept getting pulled toward something more immediately rewarding?
- The work itself felt meaningless or disconnected from what matters to you?
- You were afraid of not doing it well enough?
- Something else entirely?

There's no disgrace in any of these answers. They're all possible, all genuine, all well-meaning and *all* have strategies that can help.

The three-part framework for obstacle removal

In these decades of working with learners, I've come to believe that obstacle removal isn't about willpower. Definitely not. It's about *design*. It's about creating conditions where the thing you want to do becomes the easier thing to do.

I'm going to say that again: it's about creating conditions where the thing you want to do becomes the easier thing to do.

This happens in three interconnected ways:

Reduce friction

Friction is anything that makes starting harder than it needs to be. It's the laptop that wasn't charged. It's the notes scattered across seven different documents. It's the reading that requires you to log into three different systems to access.

Here's how we can reduce it:

The two-minute setup

Whatever you're trying to do, can you make the setup take less than two minutes? If your notes are scattered, gather them into one place. If your workspace requires major reorganization every time, create a 'ready state' that you return it to after each session.

The lowered bar

Sometimes the obstacle is that we've set the bar so high that starting feels impossible. 'Write essay' is overwhelming. 'Write one terrible paragraph that I'll probably delete' is doable. 'Study for exam' is paralysing. 'Do five practice questions as best I can' is manageable.

I think of this (and smile as I do) as 'authorization to be awful'. Give yourself authorization to write awkwardly and grammatically incorrectly, to produce work that's just *okay*. You can always improve it later, but at least you'll have something *to* improve.

The conduit

This is about creating a tiny, almost trivial action that serves as a connector from you not working to working. Maybe it's opening your document and typing the date. Maybe it's reading just the first sentence of an article. Maybe it's writing one research question.

This conduit approach should be so small that not doing it would feel senseless. That's the point. It gets you across that inertia threshold from not doing to doing – or doing something else to doing what you need to do.

Create momentum

Starting is one thing. Keeping on going is quite another. This is where habits become crucial – not as moral laws, but as momentum levers.

The task sandwich strategy

Sometimes the obstacle isn't starting, it's sustaining. Your mind might be rebelling against doing the same type of thing for too long. So instead of pushing through until you hate everything about your task, try sandwiching different types of work.

Generative work (creating) → mechanical (formatting) → cognitive (problem-solving)

or

Reading dense theory → organizing your notes → watching a relevant video lecture → back to reading

The key is that each type of task comes with different demands, so you're giving yourself recovery time while still making progress. It's not procrastination if you're still moving forward; you're just moving in a different lane.

The checkpoint system

Create natural stopping points in your work where you can choose to continue or pause. It's not a failure if you decide to stop; those checkpoints are *success* points in disguise. 'I'll read to the end of this section' or 'I'll write until I have three points' or 'I'll solve problems until I get one right.'

Each checkpoint is a small victory. Stack enough small victories, and suddenly you're further along than you realized.

The tomorrow door

One counterintuitive strategy is to stop before you're completely done. (Back to the brilliance of the Zeigarnik effect!) Stop when you know exactly what comes next. Leave yourself a note: 'Next: write about the third argument' or 'Continue with Chapter 4, page 67.'

This does two things: it makes starting tomorrow easier (you know exactly what to do), and it keeps your brain engaged with the material even when you're not actively working on it.

Design for recovery: when things go sideways

Because you're human, you're going to mess up days and miss others altogether. You'll have weeks where none of your beautiful systems work. This isn't failure, it's life.

What matters isn't that you never fall off track; it's how welcoming and easeful you make it to get back on.

The reset ritual

Create a simple ritual for getting back to work after time away. Maybe it's reviewing your last paragraph to remember where you were. Maybe it's spending five minutes reorganizing your workspace to a specific uplifting song that helps move frustration along. Maybe it's writing a brief list of what needs to happen next.

The ritual should be non-judgemental and focused on forward momentum, not punishing yourself for time away.

The gentle redirect protocol

If you notice you've drifted off course – whether it's been one hour or one week – resist the urge to launch into harsh self-criticism or self-correction. Instead, ask yourself three questions:

- What was I trying to protect myself from? (Often it's fear of failure, overwhelming feelings or genuine exhaustion.)
- What did I actually need in that moment? (Rest? Connection? A different approach?)
- What's the smallest possible return step? (Not 'catch up on everything' but 'read one paragraph' or 'email my instructor').

This isn't about excuses. If you can pinpoint *why* you stepped away, you can address the real obstacle, not just the symptom.

The pre-crisis kit

Create a simple document or note when you're feeling capable – not when you're in academic distress, *before* it.

- Three sentences about why this degree/course matters to you (for when motivation disappears)
- The name and contact of one person who gets it (not someone who'll judge, someone who'll genuinely help)
- One tiny task you can always do even on the worst days (maybe it's just re-reading the course outline, maybe it's reading one single page of the most accessible text)

Keep this somewhere easy to find. Think of it as emergency supplies for your academic journey – assembled when you're resourced, available when you're not.

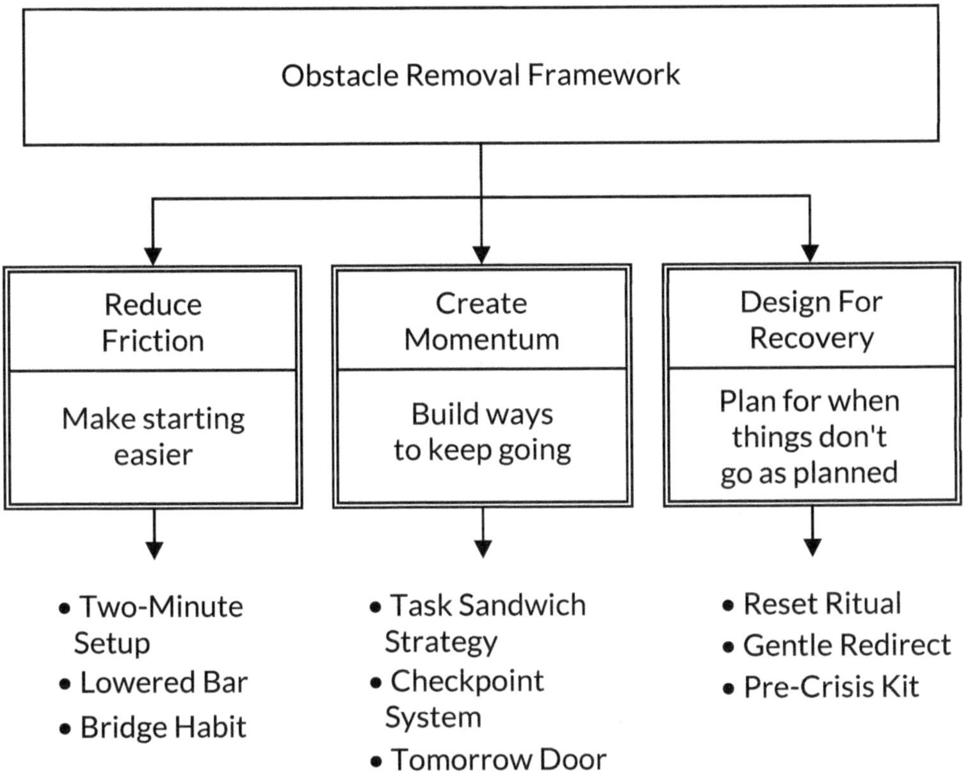

Try this today: the obstacle audit

Instead of trying to intensely power through your obstacles, let's get inquisitive.

For the next three days, whenever you stop working on something you intended to do, make a quick note:

- What were you trying to do?
- What stopped you?
- What did you do instead?
- How did you feel?

After three days, review your notes. What emerges? What do you see? Environmental obstacles (noise, comfort, lighting)?

- Are your obstacles mostly emotional (fear, overwhelm, shame)?
- Are your obstacles mostly cognitive (confusion, not knowing how to start)?
- Are your obstacles mostly physical (hunger, tiredness, discomfort)?

Based on your most common obstacle type, design one small environmental or behavioural change. If it's noise, consider finding earplugs. If it's not knowing how to start, maybe it's going to office hours to ask clarifying questions, or writing 'first terrible draft' at the top of every document (to lower the stakes and up the possibility of joy).

Try your change for a week, then reflect. Does it help? What else (what other strategy, redirect, technique or tool) might you try?

Student voices

Alanna: Alanna came to see me in her second year, referred by her academic adviser who was worried. She was bright, engaged in class discussions, clearly understood the material, but couldn't ... ever ... seem to get assignments in on time.

'I know what I *want* to write,' she told me, tears of frustration in her eyes. 'I can explain it perfectly to my study group. But when I sit down to write, I just ... *can't*.'

We discovered a tangle of interconnected obstacles: perfectionism (her first draft had to be perfect), environment (trying to write in her noisy flat share), and what I call 'format friction' – the formal academic writing style felt so far from how she naturally expressed ideas that it was like translating into a different language.

Here's what we did:

- First, we eased the starting friction – instead of 'write introduction', her task became 'voice-record myself explaining this to a friend for five minutes'.
- Then, we addressed the environment – she booked a study room at the library for her writing sessions. Same time, same room, three times a week.
- For the perfectionism, we introduced 'garbage drafts' – deliberately terrible first attempts where the goal was to be as informal and imperfect as possible.

Three weeks later, she sent me an email: 'Submitted on time. Wasn't perfect. Felt amazing.'

Marcus: Marcus struggled with starting his dissertation because the project felt impossibly large. 'Every time I opened the document, I'd freeze,' he said. 'Six months of work staring back at me.'

We decided to break it down differently. Instead of seeing chapters, he started seeing conversations – each section was just explaining one idea to an interested friend. His daily task became 'have one conversation', whether that was 100 words or 1,000 words. The obstacle wasn't the work itself; it was the overwhelming scope. Once we made it human-sized, he could begin.

Paloma: Paloma found that her biggest obstacle was transition time. 'I'd sit down to study and spend forty-five minutes just getting ready to start,' she explained. 'By then, I'd used up all my motivation.'

We created a 'launch sequence' – a five-minute routine she did every single time: clear desk, get water, write three goals on a sticky note, set a timer for twenty-five minutes, begin. The routine became automatic, eliminating the decision fatigue that was eating up her energy. The obstacle wasn't procrastination; it was the cognitive load of deciding how to begin.

→ **Key insight:** Most obstacles aren't character flaws – they're design challenges waiting for creative solutions.

A new way with obstacles

Obstacles aren't verdicts. They're not pronouncements about your capability or your worth. They're just information about what's not working ... *yet*.

That word 'yet' is doing a looooot of work in that sentence.

It's enabling space for insight and growth; it makes room for you to reflect, try new learning strategies and feel differently.

When we stop seeing obstacles as moral failings and start seeing them as opportunities to rethink our strategies and systems, everything shifts.

It's not, 'Why can't I focus?' → it's, 'What conditions help me focus?'

It's not, 'Why do I always procrastinate?' → it's, 'What makes starting easier for me?'

This isn't toxic positivity (no thank you!). I'm not asking you to be 'grateful' for your obstacles or to see them as beneficial. Some obstacles are straight-up unfair, systemic and shouldn't exist. Those you shouldn't have to navigate.

But while we work toward a more just and accessible world, we also need strategies for the world we're in right now. I don't want you alone and unequipped when you have an essay due the next day. I want your pockets full of strategies that honour your full humanity – your struggles, your strengths and your unique spirit.

So, start where you are. Start with one small friction reducer. Start with five minutes, and be sure to start with compassion.

Dig deeper: understanding obstacles and resistance

Essential Reading

Carol Dweck's *Mindset: The New Psychology of Success* (2006) revolutionized how we think about obstacles by introducing the growth mindset concept. Her research shows that seeing obstacles as opportunities to learn (rather than as threats to our identity) fundamentally changes our ability to overcome them.

Angela Duckworth's *Grit: The Power of Passion and Perseverance* (2016) explores why some people push through obstacles while others give up. Her research on grit – the combination of passion and perseverance – offers practical insights for developing resilience when facing academic challenges.

Gabriele Oettingen's *Rethinking Positive Thinking* (2014) introduces the WOOP method (Wish, Outcome, Obstacle, Plan) for achieving goals. Her research shows that acknowledging obstacles, rather than just positive visualization, dramatically improves success rates.

TED Talks

Carol Dweck's 'The power of believing that you can improve' (2014) demonstrates how changing our beliefs about obstacles and failure can literally change our brain's ability to learn and grow.

Kelly McGonigal's 'How to make stress your friend' (2013) reframes our relationship with stress and obstacles, showing how changing our mindset about challenges can literally change our body's response to them.

References

Duckworth, A. (2016) *Grit: The Power of Passion and Perseverance*. New York: Scribner.

Duckworth, A.L., Gendler, T.S. and Gross, J.J. (2016) 'Situational strategies for self-control', *Perspectives on Psychological Science*, 11(1), pp. 35–55.

Dweck, C. (2006) *Mindset: The New Psychology of Success*. New York: Random House.

Dweck, C. (2014) 'The power of believing that you can improve' [Video]. TED Conferences. Available at: https://www.ted.com/talks/carol_dweck_the_power_of_believing_that_you_can_improve (accessed 1 October 2026).

Gollwitzer, P.M. and Sheeran, P. (2006) 'Implementation intentions and goal achievement: A meta-analysis of effects and processes', *Advances in Experimental Social Psychology*, 38, pp. 69–119.

McGonigal, K. (2013) 'How to make stress your friend' [Video]. TED Conferences. Available at: https://www.ted.com/talks/kelly_mcgonigal_how_to_make_stress_your_friend (accessed 1 October 2025).

Neal, D.T., Wood, W. and Quinn, J.M. (2006) 'Habits: A repeat performance', *Current Directions in Psychological Science*, 15(4), pp. 198–202.

Oettingen, G. (2014) *Rethinking Positive Thinking: Inside the New Science of Motivation*. New York: Current.

CHAPTER 21

HOW TO TAP INTO PURPOSE (WHEN YOU'RE BORED, LOSE MOMENTUM OR GET SIDETRACKED)

Every learner experiences that moment when you're staring at your course outline, or sitting in a lecture or halfway through an essay, and you find yourself thinking: *What am I doing here?*

Not in an existential crisis way (though those happen too, and they're completely normal). But in that bone-deep disconnection way, where the work in front of you feels about as meaningful as organizing paperclips by size. Where you've lost the thread of why any of this matters and motivation has packed up and left the building ... campus? ... entirely.

But can we just call out how fickle motivation can be? It shows up when it wants to, usually at midnight when you have brilliant ideas but need to sleep.

Purpose, though? Purpose is something else entirely.

Purpose is that deeper current that can carry you through when motivation ghosts you.

And the beautiful thing is, purpose isn't something you have to *go* find – it's something you already carry with you, in your values, your strengths and in your particular way of seeing and being in the world.

The distinction between motivation and purpose

Motivation says: 'I should finish this essay because it's due tomorrow.'

Purpose says: 'This essay connects to something that matters to me, even if I can't feel it right now.'

Motivation is often external – grades, deadlines, expectations.

Purpose is internal – it's about alignment between what you're doing and who you are.

And, most impactful of all, you don't need to feel purposeful all the time. It's just not realistic and, honestly, it would be exhausting. But having ways to reconnect with purpose when you've lost the thread? Now *that's* a game-changer.

When everything feels purposeless

Before we dive into strategies, let's give credit where credit's due: sometimes university work *does* feel truly void of any purpose, even tangential. Sometimes you're memorizing information you'll forget next week, writing essays that feel disconnected from anything remotely real, sitting through lectures that seem designed to cure insomnia.

I want to be very clear: Any lagging purpose you feel *isn't* because you're not 'intellectual enough' or 'academic enough'. Sometimes the disconnect is just a disconnect. Sometimes the curriculum wasn't designed with learners like you in mind (and that's on the profs, chairs and deans, not you). Sometimes the way knowledge is packaged and delivered strips it of the very thing that makes it meaningful.

And in fairness, sometimes you wind up in a course being taught by someone who was just hired through a last-minute posting, and they've been given the prior instructor's notes, or sometimes not even that. Other times, there might be a tenured professor digging in their heels to keep teaching the same course in the same way with the same texts and the same resources for twenty – even thirty – years; no wonder you're asking yourself what the point is!

When I talk about tapping into purpose, I'm not suggesting you gaslight yourself into finding meaning where there truly is none. I'm talking about linking the work you have to do and the things that really matter to you. Sometimes those links are obvious. Sometimes you have to get creative. Sometimes you have to make them out of toothpicks and hope.

But those links *can* be found.

Take a moment: unearthing the underpinnings of purpose

Let's back up. Prior to uncovering your purpose, we need to understand what inspires us, what moves us, what ... drives us. This isn't about what you think *should* drive you, but what truly does.

Your strengths: the things you can't help but do

Your character strengths are positive traits that reflect core virtues. Things about you like creativity, perseverance, kindness or fairness (Peterson and Seligman 2004). Research suggests that when you use your top strengths (what VIA, which stands for values-in-action, calls your 'signature strengths'), you often feel more energized, authentic and engaged (Harzer and Ruch 2012). These aren't just things you're good at – they're qualities that feel essential to who you are.

(You can discover your character strengths through the free VIA Survey at viacharacter.org.)

Consider: *What do you naturally bring to group projects? What do friends come to you for? What aspects of learning feel most aligned with who you are?*

- Are you the person who always sees connections between seemingly unrelated ideas?
- Are you the person who always notices when someone's struggling and finds ways to help?
- Are you the person who always asks the questions everyone's thinking but afraid to voice?
- Are you the person who always brings humour when things get too heavy?
- Are you the person who always perseveres when everyone else wants to give up?
- Are you the person who always sees the bigger picture when others are lost in details?
- Are you the person who always finds creative solutions to problems?
- Are you the person who always brings a sense of fairness and justice to discussions?

These aren't just personality quirks. They're your unique and radiant strengths. And when your learning feels disconnected, these strengths can be that link back to purpose (Harzer and Ruch 2012).

Your values: an internal compass

Values are different from goals. Goals are things you want to achieve. Values are the ways you do or want to show up in the world. You can't complete a value, but you can live it every day (Kashdan and McKnight 2009).

Consider: *What are your beliefs, what's important to you, what do you care about and how do you embody these, often without even consciously trying?*

- I feel most frustrated in learning when ...
- I feel most energized in learning when ...
- If I could change one thing about how education works, it would be ...
- The kind of impact I want my education to have is ...
- I lose track of time when I'm learning about ...

Look at your answers. What values are hiding underneath them? If you're frustrated when knowledge feels disconnected from real life, you might value practical application. If you're energized by group discussions, you might value community learning. If you want education to be more inclusive, you might value justice and access. If you lose track of time learning about environmental issues, you might value sustainability.

These values aren't just nice-to-haves. They're essential data about what makes learning meaningful for you.

Try this today: paving your path to purpose

Here's where we get practical. You've got work to do – quite literally. Essays to write, exams to study for, readings that make your eyes glaze over. How do you mind and mend the gap between that work and your sense of purpose (Yeager and Bundick 2009)?

The three ways to connect work with purpose

1: Direct connection

Sometimes you can connect your work directly to your values and bigger purpose. Studying education? Connect it to your value of social justice. Working on environmental science? Link it to your commitment to sustainability.

2: Skills connection

When direct connection isn't possible, connect through skills. That statistics course you're slogging through? It's building skills you'll need to understand research in your field. That theory-heavy reading? It's developing your ability to work with complex ideas.

3: Service connection

When all else fails, connect through service. That group project, how could you help others? That tutorial, how might you explain a tough concept to someone else?

Troubleshooting: your purpose reminder toolkit

Capture it when purpose abounds, then use it when purpose has abandoned you for the time being.

Create your purpose statement

Keep it short and real. Not, 'To change the world', but maybe 'To understand how things work so I can make them work better for more people' or 'To develop skills that let me support my community' or 'To prove to myself that I can do hard things.'

Create your values list

Pinpoint your top three to five non-negotiable values. The things that, when they're violated or ignored, make you feel out of alignment: think humility, perseverance, optimism, justice.

Create your gifts register

Name, proudly, things you bring naturally. Not to brag about, but to remember when you feel disconnected from your capabilities. A 'don't-forget-how-badass-you-are' reminder when your purpose bails and you need a boost.

Your why collection

Gather evidence of your why. Screenshots of messages from people you've helped. Photos of projects you're proud of. Quotes that remind you why education matters to you. Keep them in one place – a digital folder, notebook, whatever works.

Sometimes, despite all of this, purpose feels impossibly distant. You're tired. You're overwhelmed. You're going through life things that make academic purpose feel trivial.

That's okay. Purpose isn't about feeling inspired all the time. Sometimes it's just about remembering, even faintly, that there's a reason you're doing this, even if you can't feel it right now.

On these days, make purpose as minute as subscript:

- This one lecture → demonstrates my value of showing up
- This one paragraph → proves I can and do persist

- This one equation solved → evidence I can do hard things
- This one reading done → signals I kept a commitment to myself

These aren't small, they're about the deeper significance of your academic journey.

See it in action: meet Jamal

Jamal came to see me in January of his first year. He was doing fine academically – decent marks, assignments submitted on time. But he felt ... miserable.

'I feel like a learning robot,' he told me. 'Input information, output essays, receive grade, repeat. None of it *means* anything.'

Jamal had come to university with big dreams about social change but found himself drowning in theoretical courses that felt completely disconnected from the community work he cared about.

We started with his values. Community. Justice. Hope. Impact. Access. Then we looked at his strengths: connecting with people, explaining complex things simply, seeing systems and patterns, building bridges between ideas.

'How can you bring these into your current courses?' I asked.

He looked sceptical. 'You mean my Victorian Literature course?'

'Yup, *especially* that one.'

The breakthrough

What did Jamal do? He started connecting every text to contemporary issues. Jane Eyre became a lens for examining current class inequities. Dickens opened discussions about modern poverty. For his final essay, he created a comparison between Victorian workhouses and modern gig economy exploitation.

But more importantly, he started a study group – not to get better grades, but to make the material meaningful, personal, relational. They'd read the assigned texts, then spend equal time discussing modern parallels, sharing how the themes showed up in their own communities.

The results

'I'm studying the same stuff,' he told me at the end of term, 'but now I remember why I'm here.'

The courses hadn't changed. Jamal had found ways to bring his purpose into them (Damon 2008).

→ **Key insight:** Purpose isn't about finding the 'right' courses or the perfect programme – it's about actively bringing your values and strengths into whatever you're studying. Your courses might stay the same, but how you engage with them might shift. Radically. And those shifts are likelier to happen once we stop waiting for purpose to appear and instead start actively weaving our values into our work.

A new way with purpose

What if purpose isn't something you have to achieve or maintain, but something you practice returning to?

What if losing touch with purpose isn't failure, but just part of the rhythm?

What if your changing sense of purpose is evidence of growth, not confusion?

What if the question isn't 'What's my purpose?' but, 'How can I connect what I'm doing right now to something that matters to me, even in the smallest way?'

Your purpose doesn't have to be grand. It doesn't have to impress anyone. It doesn't have to stay the same year after year.

And on the days when you can't find it – when *everything* feels pointless and you're going through the motions – remember that purposelessness is temporary. Your values, your strengths, your unique gifts – they don't disappear just because you can't feel them.

They're waiting for you, patient and persistent, poised to reconnect you to meaning when you're ready.

Start small. Start where you are. Start with one gossamer thread of connection between what you're doing and what matters to you.

That's enough; *that's* purpose.

Dig deeper: purpose-building resources

Essential reading

William Damon's *The Path to Purpose* (2008) follows young people as they discover their callings, showing that purpose isn't something you find once but something you develop over time through exploration and commitment.

TED Talks

Simon Sinek's 'How great leaders inspire action' (2009) introduces the concept of starting with 'why' – understanding your deeper purpose before focusing on what you do or how you do it. https://www.youtube.com/watch?v=u4ZoJKF_VuA

Emily Esfahani Smith's 'There's more to life than being happy' (2017) distinguishes between happiness and meaning, showing how purpose creates resilience even in difficult times. https://www.youtube.com/watch?v=y9Trdafp83U

References

Damon, W. (2008) *The Path to Purpose: How Young People Find Their Calling in Life*. New York: Free Press.

Deci, E.L. and Ryan, R.M. (2000) 'The "what" and "why" of goal pursuits: Human needs and the self-determination of behavior', *Psychological Inquiry*, 11(4), pp. 227–268.

Harzer, C. and Ruch, W. (2012) 'When the job is a calling: The role of applying one's signature strengths at work', *The Journal of Positive Psychology*, 7(5), pp. 362–371.

Kashdan, T.B. and McKnight, P.E. (2009) 'Origins of purpose in life: Refining our understanding of a life well lived', *Psychological Topics*, 18(2), pp. 303–313.

Peterson, C. and Seligman, M.E. (2004) *Character Strengths and Virtues: A Handbook and Classification*. Oxford: Oxford University Press.

Sinek, S. (2009) 'How great leaders inspire action', [Video]. TED Conferences. Available at: https://www.ted.com/talks/simon_sinek_how_great_leaders_inspire_action (accessed 1 October 2025).

Smith, E.E. (2017) 'There's more to life than being happy', [Video]. TED Conferences. Available at: https://www.ted.com/talks/emily_esfahani_smith_there_s_more_to_life_than_being_happy (accessed 1 October 2025).

Yeager, D.S. and Bundick, M.J. (2009) 'The role of purposeful work goals in promoting meaning in life and in schoolwork during adolescence', *Journal of Adolescent Research*, 24(4), pp. 423–452.

Going Our Own Ways ...

As we come to the end of *A New Way to Learn*, I want to pause here with you – not to tie everything up neatly, but to honour the journey we've taken together, and your next steps.

You're going your own way now.

Not *away* from effort, ambition or depth – but away from the narrow, exhausting stories that once told you there was only one way to succeed. Away from urgency as a measure of worth. Away from the idea that discomfort is undesirable, struggle is unhelpful and that your academic challenges mean something is wrong with *you* (there isn't).

What you're carrying forward isn't a set of tips to memorize or a prescriptive list of academic to-dos. Instead, it's a different relationship – a different *way* with time, with studying, with work, with yourself.

You've begun to relate to time not as something constantly slipping through your fingers, but as something you can work with. You've learned that time 'management' was never really the point. What matters is coherence – how your energy, attention, structure and sense of meaning support one another and support your academic success. You now know how to notice your rhythms, how to create containers for focus and how to let rest work together to restore you. You've learned that time anxiety isn't a personal failure but rather a signal – a longing for creativity, for enoughness, for space. And by starting small with what matters most to you, you've seen that honouring your humanity and interests makes excellence more likely, not less.

Your relationship with studying has shifted too. No more passive re-reading and last-minute panic. Instead, active engagement that lasts! You've learned to work *with* your brain rather than against it – to test yourself, make connections, revisit ideas over time. You understand now that forgetting is part of learning, not evidence that you're 'bad at this' and that difficulty often means growth is under way. Studying no longer has to be punishing or perfect. It can be deliberate, doable and kind.

The same is true of your relationship with reading challenging texts and writing complex assignments. You've begun to loosen the grip of the story that says resistance equals laziness or that focus comes from force. You know how to shrink tasks until they're possible. You know to adjust your environment to work *with* your needs, not against them. You recognize that being stuck is information. You've learned that clarity comes from the messiness, that first drafts are allowed to be awkward and that revision is not a judgement on your ability. Most of all, that your voice matters here and that your ideas deserve space.

These are not one-time insights; they're practices you'll return to whenever pressure builds, whenever old habits resurface, whenever you forget that learning was never meant to hurt this much.

As you move forward, I invite you to keep redefining what it means to be 'doing well'.

Not just grades – but calm before lectures.

Not just output – but ease in your week.

Not just achievement – but moments of genuine joy.

Notice your rhythms. Protect what sustains you. Let feedback become benign data rather than identity. Trust the quiet paradox you've begun to experience: when you prioritize calm, ease and joy, learning follows and so do grades and performance.

Know, too, that this way of learning doesn't end at university. It echoes forward into work, personal projects and even your relationships. The patterns you're practising now are the foundations of a life that can hold both meaning and momentum.

To close *A New Way to Learn* together, dear reader, dear learner, I want you to know this: I believe in you.

Not in a generic, motivational-poster, calendar-in-your-doctor's-office way – but in a specific, attentive, I-held-you-in-mind-every-moment-while-writing-this-book way.

I believe in your capacity to learn deeply without being harsh with yourself. I believe you deserve both excellence and rest, growth and grace. I believe your particular mind, exactly as it is, belongs here.

Wherever you are in your academic pursuits – beginning, restarting, pausing, looping back – you are not behind. Your struggles are not weaknesses. Your small wins count. Learning is non-linear, personal and alive.

Your worth is not your grades. Your value does not rise and fall with productivity. You are already enough, even as you grow. *Especially* because you're growing.

This isn't goodbye. It's *go well.*

Go gently. Go bravely. Go knowing that someone you've never met is quietly cheering you on, hoping your learning life includes real calm, genuine ease and moments of unexpected joy.

You're not just getting through university; you're building a dynamic with learning that will carry you through life.

May you find unexpected mentors and surprising joy in footnotes. May your hardest essays teach you the most about yourself. May you discover you're capable of more than you imagined, not through force, but through finding your own sustainable way. May you experience calm, ease and joy … in abundance.

And may you always remember: you're not just 'getting through' university. You're building a relationship with learning that will carry you through life. Make it a kind one.

With deep respect for your path and genuine excitement for who you're becoming,

Deena.

Index

academic:
- aspirations 9
- burnout 96
- excellence 1, 38, 49, 54, 97
- goals 17, 81, 97
- integrity 186–87
- obligations 36, 48
- performance 2, 48, 85, 96, 197, 209
- responsibilities 11
- success 90
- work 14, 42, 44, 49, 112, 178, 182

academic sequencing 21–2
- cognitive load 22, 70, 144, 227
  - cluster routine tasks 22
  - deep thinking 22, 33, 166
  - mind-clearing 22, 48
  - routines 69, 87, 95, 98, 150, 155
- emotional energy 22
- physical needs 22, 69
  - movement 21–7
- sedentary 22
- social vs. solitary 22
- task type 22

accountability 51
active engagement 54, 238
active recall 166
agitation 61
AI 58, 161, 181–3, 185–6, 195
alignment mapping:
- constraints 23
- energy patterns 22, 26
- momentum-builders 23
- resistance patterns 23
- transition costs 23
- values conflicts 23

ambition 205
analysis habitat 30
analytical work 26
anxiety 22, 38, 43, 64, 136, 189, 218, 238
- spiral 51
- voice 40

apps 1, 10, 117, 150–1, 197
aspirations 9, 36, 49, 200
awareness 15, 39, 56, 153, 174, 205

belonging 85, 159, 204
benchmarks 25, 105
body:
- language 24, 28
- pre-performance warm-up 102
- signals 40–1
- wisdom 88

boredom 47, 128, 132, 134
boundaries 28, 36, 51, 56, 69, 87
brain-dumping 116, 119
brainstorming 24, 27, 30, 33, 195
breakthrough 5, 77, 118, 142, 164, 194, 235
breathing patterns 15

challenges 4–5, 14, 47, 104, 178–9, 228, 238
character flaw 11, 72–3, 149, 188, 227
citations 182
cognitive biases 179–80
cognitive science 100, 136, 144
coherence 11–13, 15–17, 21, 51, 56, 65, 108, 238
coherent breathing 15, 51
collaborative learning 54, 75, 78–83, 162
collaborative work 79, 82
competition 75, 165–6, 207
complex material 25, 83, 166
confidence 24, 53, 61, 104, 161, 189

confusion 76–7, 82, 119, 162, 205, 225, 236
connecting with others 205
consolidation 56, 59, 72, 86, 101, 106–8
constraints 6, 9, 21, 23
co-regulation 116
continuous distraction 31
continuous partial attention 29
the contradiction inventory 203
co-regulating effect 116
cortisol-hippocampus interference 85
the counter-argument sandwich 173
Crawford, Larissa 14
creating containers 213
  community containers 214
  progress containers 214
  space containers 214
  time containers 213
creative abrasion 83
critical framework for critical thinking 175
critical thinking 75, 101, 157, 168, 175, 180
critical writing 187–8

the daily fit-in method 41–2, 47
decision fatigue 16, 30, 227
decision-making 37, 155, 169, 175, 218
deep learning 65, 157
deep work 30–2, 34, 36–7, 219
deeper understanding 54, 62
deficits 32, 158
depleted 15, 25, 28, 77, 117, 130
desirable difficulties 108–9
disconnected 15, 65, 82, 148, 221, 231, 235
distractions 67, 70
downtime 50, 59, 86–7, 141

ecological principles 29
  habitats 29–36
    academic habitats 30, 33
    energy habitats 31
    high-energy habitat 31
    low-energy habitat 31
    moderate-energy habitat 31
  rhythms 27–32, 36
effective learning 4, 62
effort 14, 50, 76, 103, 128, 179, 238
encoding 108, 166
energy 11, 21, 27, 47, 72, 102, 132, 152, 211, 238
essays 196
exams 100–101, 103–9, 111, 233
executive function 85
exhaustion 88, 95–6, 111, 220, 224
expectation 7, 32, 47, 79, 105, 201, 216, 230

family responsibilities 2, 35, 210, 213
feedback 25, 73, 105, 195, 239
flow states 24, 31, 73
Focus 16, 30-2, 34, 36, 67, 69
the four angles of critical thinking 168

gentle movement 25, 95
grief 40, 46
the growth spiral 133
guilt 11

the hidden curriculum 85
humanity 7, 17, 89, 111, 138, 154, 200, 238

idea generation 11
inertia 34, 222
integration 13, 33, 80, 86, 205, 215, 218

journaling 6

lasting memory 54–7, 61–2
learning strategies 5, 62, 89, 108–9, 227
lived experience 88, 157, 177–8, 184, 207
long-term retention 62–3, 101, 106

manageable 16, 48, 107, 129, 161, 194, 222
meaning 12, 17, 41, 49, 64, 142, 231, 239
meeting deadlines 11
memory 53, 59, 72, 85, 101, 119, 182
mini-routines 69
momentum 21, 28, 70, 103, 154, 222, 239
movement breaks 16, 89, 142
the multi-highlighter method 170

natural rhythms 11, 15, 21, 27, 31, 70, 128
neuroinclusion:
  ADHD 2, 5, 16, 32, 47–8, 143–4
  autism 2, 32
  chronic illness 1–2, 8, 217
  dyslexia 2
  learning disability 47

obstacles 6, 46, 72, 94, 174, 200, 220, 225
organisational skills 10
organizing notes 25, 27
overwhelmed 13, 16, 35, 61, 88, 112, 190, 221, 234

panic 2, 50, 55, 61, 134, 181, 194, 238
passive consumption vs. active retrieval 62
PEER paragraph method 193
'perfection' 52, 186, 196
personal memory-forgetting experience 56
personal passions 48
planning 10
pomodoro revolution (with a twist) 139
problem-solving 2, 24, 33, 36, 67, 71, 87, 223
procrastination 82, 115, 154, 189, 223, 227
productivity 5, 7, 10, 14, 23, 39, 88, 147, 218, 239
project management 11
pseudo-productivity 24–25
pseudo-studying 56

rapid task-switching 73
reading:
  complex material 25
  habitat 30
  passive 100, 103
  re-reading 53, 55–7, 60–2, 72, 238
  resistance inventory 160
recall information 57, 61
reliable memory 62
rest 28, 32, 60, 86, 95, 239
restore 28, 32, 70, 87, 92, 96, 238
routines 69, 87, 95, 98, 150, 155

self-care routines 95
skill-building 50, 53, 108
small win 45, 123, 155, 239
SMART goals 147
social connection 68, 72, 90, 95
social media 1, 31, 40, 65, 125, 142, 181, 200
strengths 5, 80, 227, 230, 232, 235
study skills 1, 38, 85, 109
sustainability 17, 233

task management 11
training opportunities 102
troubleshooting 3, 6, 46, 94, 117, 175, 195, 216, 234

unexpected benefits 49, 97
unique neuro-patterns 32

values 7, 21, 174, 202, 230, 232, 234, 236

willingness 5, 131
willpower 10, 16, 27, 64, 72, 127, 155, 197, 221
'work harder' 4, 84, 157
work-alignment 138
workloads 11, 94
worry 1, 10, 38, 47, 71, 109, 138, 150, 181
worthiness 13, 46, 100, 143, 165, 205, 227, 239
writing habitat 30–31